ON
A
ROLL

ON A ROLL

FROM HOT DOG BUNS TO
HIGH-TECH BILLIONS

❖

HOWARD JONAS

VIKING

VIKING
Published by the Penguin Group
Penguin Putnam Inc., 375 Hudson Street,
New York, New York 10014, U.S.A.
Penguin Books Ltd, 27 Wrights Lane,
London W8 5TZ, England
Penguin Books Australia Ltd, Ringwood,
Victoria, Australia
Penguin Books Canada Ltd, 10 Alcorn Avenue,
Toronto, Ontario, Canada M4V 3B2
Penguin Books (N.Z.) Ltd, 182–190 Wairau Road,
Auckland 10, New Zealand

Penguin Books Ltd, Registered Offices:
Harmondsworth, Middlesex, England

First published in 1998 by Viking Penguin,
a member of Penguin Putnam Inc.

1   3   5   7   9   10   8   6   4   2

LIBRARY OF CONGRESS CATALOGING IN PUBLICATION DATA
Jonas, Howard.
On a Roll: From hot dog buns to
high-tech billions / Howard Jonas.
p.   cm.
ISBN 0-670-87902-9
1. Jonas, Howard.   2. International Discount Telecommunications
(Firm)   3. Telecommunication—United States.   4. Businesspeople—
United States—Biography.   5. Entrepreneurship.   I. Title.
HE7797.I58J66   1998
384'.092—dc21   98-9785
[B]

This book is printed on acid-free paper.
∞

Printed in the United States of America
Set in Sabon
Designed by Betty Lew

To my family . . .
at home and at IDT

Contents

Prologue:
Slaying the Meligoth

❖

My wife and I joke that every day, I go out to do battle against an imaginary giant of epic proportions. We call this hydra-headed monster the Meligoth. Some days, the Meligoth only manages to give me a flat tire. Or it may attack in full force as my biggest clients and key employees all threaten to leave the company at once. But on other days, I'm the one who wins, as I successfully regroup, expand, innovate, and outwit this relentless foe. Maybe I make a great telecommunications coup, or just catch only green lights on my way home from work. The main point is, the Meligoth never gives up. And he never goes away. He thrives on our fears and is always ready to slap us down if we rise too far. It is the Meligoth who eventually beats down the overwhelming majority of people, making them give up their dreams and settle for the ordinary.

There is only one way to beat the Meligoth. Be as relentless as he is. Never give up. Keep coming back even when any normal person would quit. You may be going in a direction no one's ever gone in, or trying things that have never been done before. People will tell you you'll lose, but you can not only overcome but completely overpower the Meligoth. That's why, with true respect for this most worthy adversary, and in solidarity with all those who refuse to give up on their dreams in the face of the most overwhelming odds, I go out to do battle, to slay the Meligoth, every day.

ON A ROLL

Chapter One
One Finger for Onions

❖

On March 15, 1996, I made over a hundred million dollars. That was the day my company, IDT, one of the world's largest Internet and alternative telecommunications providers, went public. As IDT's founder, president, and majority shareholder, I was instantly rich beyond my wildest dreams. People ask me if this was the greatest moment in my business life. It wasn't.

Four months later, on July 18, 1996, we released a new technology, a breakthrough that would eventually cut the cost of international calls by a remarkable 95 percent. That day Sara Grosvenor, the great-granddaughter of Alexander Graham Bell, joined us in New York to use our new technology in order to place the first phone call ever over the network to Susan Cheever, the great-granddaughter of Thomas Watson, in London.

Within twenty-four hours of Ms. Grosvenor saying "Come here, Ms. Watson, I need to see you" over our system, CNN, CNBC, and newspapers had spread word of the development to investors and potential users and partners around the world. Combined with a more than fivefold increase in our quarterly revenues for the second year in a row, IDT's stock price started to move upward again. Many people who saw me glowing that morning asked if *this* was the greatest moment of my business life. It wasn't.

The greatest moment actually occurred approximately twenty-seven years earlier on the morning of July 23, 1970. That was the morning I pushed my newly built hot dog stand past Joe and Vinny's butcher shop on Eastchester Road in the Bronx. Only two months before, Joe had driven me from my after-school job in the butcher shop by forcing me to eat five pounds of rice pudding (a task that took me close to two hours) after catching me sampling the pudding while I waited on a customer at the deli counter.

I couldn't resist stopping in front of the butcher shop on my way to the spot I'd picked out three-quarters of a mile away to set up my stand. As Joe, Vinny, and Joe's nephew, Patsy, came out to see the new stand, I was gloating over the fact that I was now just as independent in business as they were. Nobody could make me clean out the rotten chicken tank anymore. Nobody could send me five miles away on the delivery bike in the snow to deliver ribs to a rich finicky lady who would just send them back to be trimmed, and never tipped more than a quarter. Nobody could make me lay in the sawdust and dig ground-up bones, blood, and fat out of the meat band saw. And, most importantly, nobody could do all this while poking fun at what a jerk I was to get all the dirty jobs. I was only fourteen years old, and the wheels would fall off my homemade hot dog stand many times before that summer ended, but that day, in my mind, I was as rich as a Rockefeller.

The idea for a hot dog stand had actually come to me about two months before the rice pudding attack, while sitting at the Crotona Park Lake with my grandmother. She had just fried warm potato latkes (pancakes), and we were taking them out of their wax paper covering and dipping them into an old Maxwell House coffee jar full of cold, sweet homemade apple sauce we had cooked together the night before. Nothing, I thought, could make this moment more perfect than a nice long hot dog with mustard, covered with onions in tomato sauce. There was a cart vendor by the far side of the lake. Unfortunately for me, it was the Jewish holiday of Passover, when leav-

ened bread (buns) and (nonkosher) hot dogs were especially prohibited, and so the lust for hot dogs had to just linger in my mind. Until I
thought, why not run a hot dog stand of my own instead of working
afternoons and weekends in the butcher shop?

I told my grandmother what I had in mind, and she said it was impossible. I was too young. I wouldn't be able to get a license. I would
be robbed. This wasn't an appropriate thing for a nice junior high
school student with middle-class parents to be doing. That settled it. I
was going into the hot dog business.

It wasn't that I had anything against my grandma. Far from it. She
was, in fact, my best friend in the world. It's just that I loved a challenge. Not only that, but in truth, I hated being a kid. I often complained to my parents as I was growing up that I was an adult trapped
in a child's body. I enjoyed adult TV shows, adult books, adult conversation, and spending time in my father's adult insurance office.
Adults were reasoning and tolerant. They enjoyed working, making
conversation, and laughing. Kids, on the other hand, liked wasting
time, ganging up on anyone different or weaker than themselves,
making trouble, and fighting. This was especially true in the increas-
ingly tough part of the South Bronx where I grew up. The rules of kid
society were mean.

I could not have put it into words then, but my basic complaint
against kids was that they were unproductive, takers and users. I still
think one of the highest things a person can aspire to be is productive.
That's why the Bible says, "Six days shall you work and on the Seventh day you shall rest." Everyone seems to know the rule about the
day off, but a lot of people forget the rule about the other six days.
But they're just as important. Man is supposed to imitate G-d's productivity in creating the world in six days by going out and being creative himself. This is the best way to benefit not only yourself, but
humankind as well. I often run into young successful people who tell
me they are retiring to pursue charitable activities. What a crock! I believe in charity. I give away 20 percent of everything I make. I always

have. But I don't kid myself. The good they do is important, but it's also limited. Maimonides, the great Jewish philosopher, said, "Give a man a fish and he'll eat for one day, but teach him how to fish on his own and he'll eat forever."

In that spirit, weigh the work of the good done by all the combined charities in the world against the good done by just one company like General Motors. Thanks to GM, millions of people have productive jobs and can support their families with honor. Hundreds of millions of people are free to travel from place to place to enjoy themselves, and people can use their stock and dividend checks to retire in dignity. What charity can make such claims?

You hear it said a lot that "young people today just aren't as good as they used to be." The usual response to that comment is to point out that people have been saying that for hundreds of years, and this is just a bias that comes with age. But maybe not. I, for one, think that, in general, youth really has gone downhill, and I think there's a perfectly rational explanation for it.

A lot of young people don't work anymore. They mooch off their parents, go to school, hang out, consume indiscriminately, and criticize, or even attack, everyone else. Small wonder. We're all born selfish and it's only having to endure and overcome life's hard knocks that builds character and makes us empathetic to what others are going through. Not only that, but the very process of having to sell our labor or services in the marketplace educates us in how to cooperate and deal with others. Years ago, every young person had to work on the farm, in the family store, or at some other job in order to make a necessary contribution to the family's survival. This work built the character of previous generations. What builds character today? TV? Belonging to a gang? The latest fashion craze? Not much.

Eventually most people, as they get older, work in the productive sphere and develop into pretty well-rounded people. But honestly, do you think this is really the same as learning values young? I don't. I'm sorry to sound like such a pessimistic moralist, but it's just how I feel.

Back to my story. As I sat with my grandmother and dreamed in the park, I had a vision of my own hot dog stand. It was as exciting to me as having my own yacht. I could see it in my mind's eye, all polished, gleaming chrome, with the smell of boiling hot dogs, sauerkraut, and onions wafting out in small puffs from beneath the chrome food doors. And I could see myself in a white apron spearing a frank as a six-person line of eager customers looked on approvingly. Reality, I soon found out, was different.

A new chrome hot dog stand, I found, would cost over one thousand dollars. Even a used one would cost much more than the hundred dollars in tips from the butcher shop that I'd saved in my wooden Macanudo cigar box. I therefore decided, with my father's help, to build my own hot dog stand. Supplies being costly, I tried to use whatever I could find around our garage, to whatever extent possible. I cut down my old crib, nailed paneling all around it to form a three-and-a-half-foot-high square box, and used the wheels from my old carriage to turn it into a rolling box. All that remained was to cut a door in the side for a picnic cooler to hold sodas and supplies. Screw our Coleman camping stove to the top to cook the franks, bore a hole into which I inserted our green picnic table umbrella, and voilà! A hot dog stand! Sort of. All that was needed now was a couple of pots, hot dogs, buns, condiments, sodas, and a vending license. This was graciously supplied by my uncle Freddie, my grandmother's baby brother, who was a World War II veteran and was thus entitled to a special permit. The morning that he got the license, he'd first gone to the dentist and had all of his teeth pulled. I can still see his toothless grin as he handed over the license and shook my hand. With my old jalopy of a stand, patched together with spit and polish and my father's ingenuity, I was ready to go into business.

I wish I could see that old hot dog stand one more time. But after the first year I'd saved enough money for a used regular stand and, not realizing that I was dealing with a potential family heirloom, I junked the old stand so there'd be room in the garage for the new one.

One lesson I learned from this, and would repeat again and again, is that if you have an idea, don't overprepare, just go for it. Sure, I could've spent years saving for the chrome stand, just as later I could've spent years delaying my entry into the publishing business until I could afford good typesetting equipment, or my entry into the phone business till I could afford my first million-dollar switch. But for all I know, I'd still be waiting. If you really want to do something, even if you have to come in on just a wing and a prayer, go for it. Most things will fall into place later.

Another thing I learned in the hot dog business was the importance of quality. I, you see, was a hot dog aficionado, a maven. At eleven, as soon as I got my 50¢-a-week allowance, I would immediately go off on my bike to buy a 25¢ hot dog from a local cart vendor who I determined had the best hot dogs in the world. The other quarter I'd carefully put aside for another hot dog later in the week. There were two things I figured out that made this old man's hot dogs superior to any I'd ever tasted. First, he used all-beef deli hot dogs and cooked them only a few at a time on a low flame so they never got that bland, boiled-out taste. And second, his onions were homemade. This meant they were long and spaghettilike, and the sauce was sweet, thick, and red. In contrast, most carts served commercial chopped onions. Hot dog connoisseurs can spot the difference a mile away.

Since the old man wouldn't give me his recipe, I spent hours with eyes tearing in the kitchen, dicing bag after bag of onions until I got just the right blend of onions, garlic, sauce, paste, and sugar with corn syrup so that the onions were perfect. From April, when I first discussed the idea with my grandma, until July, when I rolled out my cart, it seemed that half my time was spent cooking onions and testing them on my family. But on July 23, 1970, they were perfect. Pepsi couldn't have done a better job imitating Coke!

I wheeled my rickety cart over to the place I'd picked out in front of a nearby hospital. I fired up the flame and waited for the line to form. Business was slow at first. I think the stand scared most people away. The look of it suggested the possibility of stomach poisoning. But once an adventurous few tried the hot dogs, they came back and brought their friends. Soon I had to put a second cooler in the stand, and even then I was selling out. I was earning close to $40 a day, which meant that I was doing almost three times as well as at the butcher shop. Not only that, but I loved every minute of it.

That was probably the best lesson of all. Working hard and running my own business was fun. That was even more important than the money I made. For the first six years I was in the telecommunications business, I didn't take a dime in salary or profits. Many times I didn't know whether I'd still be in business in two months. But I loved what I was doing, just like I loved selling hot dogs.

The thing I really loved best about the hot dog business was dealing with people and learning how to treat them right. Two things come to mind in this, and both were related to where I decided to locate my stand.

The stand stood in front of a hospital and across the street from a bar. The bar was called the Tender Trap and the hospital Van Etten. One of the hospital's main functions was to run a methadone clinic for former heroin addicts. You would think these addicts would be terrible people to be around. Actually, they were great. They were really trying to get their lives together. And in a way, I, with my own hot dog stand, was the most establishment-type person many of them had ever been befriended by. We'd spend hours talking politics, sports, crime, religion—whatever you could think of. I even hired several of them to run the stand for short times while I went to buy supplies. Risky, you say? Well, they never stole a dime from me. A couple of the patients even got jobs driving cabs that summer, and would come back to visit me in their cars, or between shifts. They would proudly insist on now paying for their hot dogs and sodas. I learned from this the great potential (and potential goodness) that's locked inside everyone, if you give it a chance to come out. IDT is known today for hiring people from way-out fields, or promising young people with no background, and quickly giving them big responsibilities. More often than not, our people do their new jobs better than any of our competitors' people.

The story of the bar was perhaps more interesting than the story of the clinic. The bar, you see, served only alcohol (no food), and drinking seemed to build a considerable appetite on the part of many of the patrons. The reverse also seemed to be the case; that is, the more people ate, the longer they were able to keep drinking. As naturally as between man and woman, a partnership formed between me and the bar. At first the bar hostesses would come running across the street to pick up hot dogs for their patrons. Soon they would just yell the order across the two-way, six-lane street and I would prepare the hot dogs and run them over. This was a good deal for me, since I usually got a tip, and sometimes another order as well. Leaving the stand alone for a couple of minutes was no big deal, since one of my friends from the clinic was always happy to run the business while I was away. Eventually the bar and I developed a signaling system similar to that between a major league catcher and pitcher. The hostesses would go to the window and on the right hand hold up fingers to signal the number of hot dogs needed. Then, on the left, they put up one finger for onions, two for sauerkraut, three for mustard only, or four for plain. After receiving the signal, I'd prepare the dogs and, sure as any major league screwball pitcher, deliver them pronto to the bar.

There was one other thing the bar had that interested me besides the hungry drinkers, and that was their ice. (To be honest, there was a third, but I was only fourteen and had never been on a date yet. So though the hostesses were nice to think about, they didn't have as much practical value in my life as hungry hot dog eaters and ice.) Ice was a magical substance that could make my business thrive. You see, I sold twice as many sodas a day as hot dogs. Not only that, but on every 25¢ can of soda I made 15¢, whereas on every 25¢ frank I only made a dime. The hotter the summer day, the more I made. And in

New York City, summer gets pretty hot. Unfortunately, by two or three in the afternoon, my ice was usually all melted, so by four my soda sales were finished—and just before the hospital complex let their hot, tired, and, most importantly, thirsty employees off of work.

The ice machine in the Tender Trap, though, could solve all of my problems. It was huge—the size of a coffin for a hippopotamus. A huge bin opened on the bottom, from which you could literally shovel out ice and new ice would just fall into place. At first I asked if I could just fill up a small paper bag with ice. Eventually, seeing the bartender's nonchalant good humor over my taking ice, I requested more. Soon three times a day I was carrying pails of ice across the street to my stand. Before long, I even stopped bringing any ice from home at all and relied exclusively on the bar. To show my appreciation, I always brought free hot dogs for the bartenders, though they often told me not to bother.

In short, I loved the Tender Trap—everything about it and everyone who worked there. Every morning when I came in to get my ice, their staff and I chewed over details about the day just passed and the day to come. Every day, that is, but Sunday. Sunday, by law, all bars in New York are closed till afternoon. This was probably a good thing for the Tender Trap, since Saturday night was always party night till the wee hours, so on Sunday mornings the place was always in shambles. Cleanup work was not done by the regular staff, but by an elderly, sort of grizzly-looking couple who pulled up each Sunday in an old blue Dodge sedan, unloaded their cleaning supplies, and went to work. This was a problem. I still needed ice, but these people didn't know I was a part of the enterprise, and the first week I asked for the ice, the old lady said she didn't know if she was allowed to give it out. The next week, though, I went in all prepared to tell this tough old lady that Frankie, the bartender, said it was okay, but the old lady said, "Oh, you're that nice young man with the hot dog cart. Well, why didn't you tell me last week? You're so ambitious. Your mother must be so proud. Of course you can have ice; you can have whatever you like." I was stunned. This was no tough old lady. She was like my grandmother. I tried to bring her and her husband free hot dogs, but she said they couldn't eat them because they were on a salt-free diet. No problem. I had another way to say thank you. I had started selling flowers on weekends, on consignment from a local florist. I selected the nicest bouquet of red roses and brought them to the old lady.

"Now, isn't that nice," she said. "But I have so many flowers at home, I have no place to keep them. Plus you need to save your money for college, not waste it on an old lady like me. So you just take these back, but thank you anyway for the lovely thought." No, I insisted. Finally she agreed to take just one rose, which she put in her hair, just above her ear. "Now, aren't I beautiful?" She giggled, spreading her arms—and we both laughed. After that it became a ritual each Sunday morning. After they showed up I'd go across the street to get my ice and bring her the nicest rose I could find in all the buckets.

A word about the flowers. In business if you don't innovate, you're dead. Just opening a hot dog stand on the hospital's corner wasn't nearly enough. If it was, someone else would already have claimed the corner. In fact, the hospital I was in front of was actually the smallest one in a very large medical center. All the larger hospitals already had one or more stands in front of them and the local mob, in cooperation with the police, was paid for these choice spots near the hospital and guaranteed a complete or partial monopoly as the value of the spot warranted. I, a fourteen-year-old boy selling hot dogs during the summer and on weekends, had to take what nobody else wanted. I was forced to ignore the old adage that the three most important things that matter in the retail business are location, location, location. My job, therefore, was to convert my location from a loser to a winner. This I did by asking all my customers what else they'd like me to carry and, if possible, adding it to my repertoire. Thanks to advice from a nursing student, I was one of the first stands to carry diet soda. Thanks to requests from kids, I became an authorized Lay's potato chip dealer. For doctors, I had fruit drinks, and for Hispanics, Coco Lopez soda. Pretty soon my little hot dog stand was like the neighborhood convenience store. In fact, my hot dog distributor let the local powers know that I was selling as many hot dogs as the guys at the busy spots, and I had to fend off payoff requests from the local "protection" agent and even from some cops.

My most profitable innovation, though, was flowers. The section of the hospital center where I stood was the most remote part of the complex, but it was where the visitors' parking was placed. Weekdays this didn't matter much, since most people were busy. But on weekends the lot filled up with visitors. I arranged with a local florist to deliver pails of prewrapped flower bouquets. The deal was I'd get half the money on each bunch sold and he'd take back the unsold inventory to sell at his store during the week. Flowers wound up being so profitable that some weeks just the flower profit for Saturday and Sunday was more than I made on the stand the whole rest of the week. I remember one Mother's Day, which is by more than triple the best flower day of the year, I made over $300! If every day were Mother's Day, I'd advise all entrepreneurs to forget about high tech and go into flowers.

Again and again I proved that by innovating you could take what was essentially a mediocre draw and turn it into a winning hand. Years later IDT would be the first call-back phone company to offer Internet access, E-mail-to-fax service, worldwide direct dialing, real phone calling over the Internet, and our own unlimited on-line service. These innovations raised us from being just another phone company to the most innovative company in the telecom business. Of course, not every new idea we've tried has been as successful as adding flowers. If fact, some haven't worked at all. But the important thing is that whether you're running a hot dog stand or a global telecom company, you've got to keep trying new things if you want to get ahead.

Back to the hot dog stand, the bar, and the old lady, though. One

Sunday morning it seemed my whole business was crashing down around me. That morning another vendor with a huge mechanized stand came with his twenty-four-year-old son to take my spot. This vendor had a great spot in a commercial area during the week, and on Saturday an even better spot in the park where league ball games are played. (I can tell any prospective food vendor from experience that a field with several amateur baseball or football games going on is a gold mine. Even today, when I drive down the highway and see a series of occupied fields with no hot dog stands present, I am mentally tempted to pull over to the side and set up shop.) On Sunday, however, his park wasn't that profitable, and so he came down to cash in on my visitor trade.

That would have been bad enough, as most first-time hospital visitors were unfamiliar with my superior onions and would clearly have preferred his gleaming stand to my homemade wooden one. But at least I'd still have my regulars and the flowers. His son went a step further, though. He came over and told me that this was his spot now, and I had fifteen minutes to clear out or he'd "come over and kick your a—." Then he pulled a switchblade, exposed the blade, and said he'd kill me if I fought back. This was not a good situation, and I definitely did not want to have any part of my anatomy kicked, nor did I want to be stabbed. On the other hand, I wasn't giving up my spot. So I just sat there for about fifteen minutes, and then I went into the Tender Trap and told the old lady that she should keep looking out the window and, if she saw anything happening to me, to call the cops at once. When I went back out to sell my hot dogs, though, the old lady emerged from the bar. I'd never seen her like this. She was hopping mad. She ran over to the father-and-son duo and started screaming at them that this was my spot and nobody was here before and it was wrong to steal a spot from a kid and they'd better leave right now or she was going to do something about it.

The older man started yelling back that I didn't own the street and he'd stay where he wanted and called her a really horrible name. She turned and went back into the bar.

What happened next is so unbelievable that I know you'll think it's the creation of a youthful imagination, but I promise you it's true. Minutes later, three big Cadillacs, the front one pink and the two behind white, came screeching up in front of the stands. Seven enormous men got out slowly while the driver of the lead Caddy came charging out at the two hot dog men, screaming, "Who insulted my mother?" The hot dog seller's son looked plenty scared. "Johnny," he said, "I swear I didn't know she was your mother." The old lady's son started pummeling and kicking the younger man. Two of the other guys tried to hold Johnny back, saying, "Calm down, Johnny. You don't want to kill him." The father, in the meantime, was trying to throw himself in the middle to protect his son, while Johnny was screaming, "You don't teach your son no respect, I will."

Johnny finally calmed down and told my competitors that if they ever brought their stand anywhere near here again, that would be the last day they ever sold hot dogs. He then calmly opened his trunk, took out a baseball bat, and smashed the chromium stand about eight or nine times, terrifying everyone until he told them to leave. They did, and I never had another competitor again.

When it was all over, Johnny and his associates came over to my stand and started laughing and ordering hot dogs like nothing had happened and they hadn't eaten for days. I, of course, just assumed that the hot dogs were on the house for services rendered. Johnny, however, not only insisted on paying, but gave me a twenty-dollar tip as well. When I tried to refuse, he told me it was for the flowers, and anyway, he said, "anyone who is a friend of my mother is a friend of mine, and I don't take no money from friends. You hear? By the way, kid, these are great onions. I might be back." And with that they jumped into their Caddies and roared off.

Why exactly had I originally become friends with the old lady? Part of it surely was I needed the ice, and wanted to ensure my supply. But another part of it was I felt empathy with the old couple. As I sat across the street watching them get out of their old car to clean the bar every Sunday morning I could imagine myself in their shoes. They sure didn't seem rich and their lives didn't seem to be filled with great accomplishment. Clearly, it wasn't easy getting up early in the morning, especially at that age, to clean out a bar. But they weren't depending on anyone else. They were working hard and doing the best they could. That made me admire and respect them. Everyone gets dealt a different hand in life. You have to do the best with the hand you're dealt, and keep yourself in the game creatively.

At fourteen, of course, I had visions of glory dancing in my head. I would go from a hot dog stand to a fast-growing company, and who knew from there—maybe President of the United States! Hot dogs and flowers were just a first step. But even at fourteen I had a sense that things in my life might not always work out the way I expected. Many things can go wrong unexpectedly along the way—illness, business setbacks, bankruptcy, disgrace, war, prison. You just never know.

In life, luck sometimes counts for a lot. Bad luck and good. Take marriage. There's almost nothing worse than being stuck in a bad marriage, and nothing better than having a good one. I've been unbelievably lucky in this regard. Even with eight kids, I'm more in love with my wife than the day we married. But, really, do you honestly think that when we met in high school I was able to rationally divine the future? Of course not. With raging teenage hormones, rational decision making was impossible. I just got lucky; not everyone does. I could just as easily have wound up in divorce court.

I thought of luck and the old couple. They could be me in forty years' time. This double awareness—first, that people should be judged on how much they do with what they're given, and not just how much they accomplish; and second, that in a slightly altered circumstance, you and most other people in the world could easily have your roles reversed—makes me look upon everyone as an equal. This made it easy and natural to want to help them and be their friends, even if I hadn't needed the ice.

Today, I don't sit in a private office but out on the general sales floor. We don't live in a fancy house or neighborhood, but in a relatively modest one. And I don't drive an exotic car or fly first class. (Of course, my inherent parsimony contributes to at least some of this.) I don't have a personal secretary and find it very difficult to ask people to do personal errands for me. I answer my own phone. I also try very hard to include as many people as possible in our company's decision-making process, and I really listen to what everyone who advises me has to say. I never assume I just know better than someone who, at the moment, is much lower in the organization, but who might know more and deserve to be higher.

In our family too we try to be democratic and not arbitrary. It's easy for parents to get power-crazy and impose their wills and preferences on their children, but when children are given responsibility and authority, they develop their true selves. Sometimes this creates chaos. No two kids in my family ever want to do the same thing. No two kids can even agree about what to eat for dinner. Managing this tribe is probably as difficult, and requires as much finesse and creativity, as running IDT. And in the end, it's a lot more important. We listen to everyone, from my sixteen-year-old son who knows it all, to my fourteen-year-old son who only wants to talk about hockey equipment, to my eleven-year-old daydreamer, everybody's best friend, who who would gladly give you the shirt off his back. Then there's my nine-year-old gymnast, smart as a whip and highly opinionated, and her six-year-old brother, who thinks everyone else in the family is out to get him. My four-year-old daughter is that rare gem—a gift from G-d, for whom every glass is neither half empty nor half full, but overflowing. Even the year-old twins are included in our family's decision-making process. In fact, lately it feels like they're running the show.

When it comes to being a father, I think about a pitcher by the name of Jim Abbott, a guy who was born—and made it to the majors—with only one hand. He pitched for the Yankees for a while, then ended his career with the California Angels.

I don't know anything about his family, but in my mind his father is a true hero. Think how easy it would have been to discourage a kid with only one hand. Watch TV, Jim, watch the game. Pitch? Who are you kidding? But they must not have discouraged him at all. My late father-in-law, Irv Yatzkan, used to say that the job of a parent is neither to *en*courage nor *dis*courage your children. Just *courage* them. Help them to have the guts to figure out what they're good at, and pursue it. Help them find their unique way to shine, and then wait and see what happens.

In business, these attitudes wound up benefiting me in the short and long runs in several practical ways. First, many people who in other companies might have been pigeonholed at some lower level, but who have vision, have risen to the top and become crucial to our success.

A second obvious benefit of treating everyone as an equal is that people really put much more of their heart, soul, and creativity into a company when they're given a lot of independence and know their contributions are valued. Even if all this weren't the case, though, treating human beings as equals would be the right thing to do, just because it is the right thing to do. That it happens to work is just one more proof that G-d really did set the world up in the best possible way.

Recently my wife threw a "surprise" fortieth birthday party for me. Now, obviously it's difficult to surprise someone with a party when they reach "the big four-o," unless they turned senile at 39½. What did surprise me, though, is that she had bought me a big, shiny, stainless steel hot dog stand with a customized umbrella (the one I'd always dreamed of but could never afford). It was right there at the party waiting for me to dispense hot dogs from. You can see it on the cover of this book.

I naturally pretended I was really happy. I certainly didn't have to pretend I was surprised. But inside I thought, now she's really lost it. She must have spent thousands of dollars for this stand and, all pessimism aside, I'm not going to give up IDT and go back to selling hot dogs. What am I going to do with this thing?

Little did I know. . . . This year, rather than going to camp, my fourteen- and eleven-year-old sons decided to spend part of their summer going into business in the parking lot of our office selling hot dogs. It wound up being so much fun that several of their friends, and even my younger kids, soon joined them. It turned out to be the best summer they ever had. They're even planning new, innovative items like knishes for next year. Strange thing is, they sold more hot dogs in a day than I ever did. Part of this was no doubt due to their delivery service to our several buildings. A small part, though, was probably due to the fact that many times when someone needed a decision from IDT's chairman, they finally located me hanging out by the cart, and usually heeded my suggestion to buy a hot dog first.

One last thing about my old hot dog stand. I ran it for three years, summers and weekends, and in my whole life I've never enjoyed any business more. In every other thing I've ever done I was only a part of the process, dependent on others to make the whole operation run. Not only that, but in every other business, there have been jobs I truly hated, like facing the rejection that comes from making cold sales calls. I did these jobs because I wanted to succeed and, in general, I liked being in business. But only at the hot dog stand was I constantly happy. Probably this initial, positive experience with entrepreneurship made it inevitable that I would stick with it even when things stunk. Also, during those three years I learned everything I really needed to know about how to run a global company: Treat people right, keep innovating, don't give up your spot no matter who tries to take it from you—either AT&T or the father-son duo from the park—and make the best onions. Follow these rules and you'll be just fine.

Chapter Two
I Want to Live!

❖

At the end of my second summer in the hot dog business, I put away the stand and reluctantly prepared myself for the next great challenge of my life—high school. I temporarily put thoughts of business out of my mind and determined to succeed in a new arena. I was going to join the debate team and become a champion debater. And so it was that a few months later I found myself in the front seat of the beat-up old station wagon of the debate coach, talking to him as we sped down the Interstate.

It was past midnight and the other five members of my high school debate team had already been asleep for over an hour. Only I was still awake, assigned the job of keeping the coach awake at the wheel so we could reach Toledo for the start of a tournament scheduled to begin at nine the next morning. I had already talked him through New Jersey, across the Delaware Water Gap, and halfway through Pennsylvania when the accident occurred.

We were rocketing down the Pennsylvania Turnpike when our rear wheel suddenly flew off the station wagon. The rear of the car hit the ground, causing the car to lose its brakes and veer wildly out of control. In their sleepy stupors, the others in the car were not immediately aware of what was happening. But I knew exactly what was going on. We were going to die. Or, to be more honest in regard to what I was actually thinking, I was going to die! No sound passed my lips as I pressed my knees against the dashboard, waiting for the inevitable impact. I said nothing as I watched the car knocking down dozens of reflector poles, first on one side of the road and then on the other as the car veered wildly back and forth across the turnpike, and the coach struggled to gain control. At any moment I was sure an eighteen-wheeler would come barreling down the highway and crush our Chevy wagon and everyone in it. During those few minutes before the impact, my life flashed before my eyes. This expression is much overused, but that is what actually happened. Suddenly I saw that if I were to die at that moment, it would have been as if I'd never lived. I had never had a girlfriend. I was even afraid to ask someone for a date. I'd never done anything significant. Since my days at the hot dog stand, I'd never taken a risk or done anything out of the ordinary. In truth, I was just a debate nerd and my friends were other nerds who spent all their time having existential conversations about why we were losers and how hopeless it was to try to escape this reality. I realized, at the moment just before the impact, that I was on my way to wasting my life and that I could have done and accomplished so much more, even as a fifteen-year-old high school sophomore, had I only decided to try.

These thoughts, however, couldn't save us from any onrushing tractor-trailer trucks. Perhaps it was late enough at night or early enough in the morning that the tractor-trailers that usually fill the nights were all resting for a few minutes. Perhaps G-d made a miracle and spared our six young lives. Or perhaps, as with Jimmy Stewart in *It's a Wonderful Life*, the moment of my end was so transforming that it actually changed me into a different person who still had a life to live, and out of my former self whose number was up.

Whatever happened, hundreds of perilous yards down the road from where the tire came off, our car came to a halt and lost its other wheel just off the shoulder of the road, literally seconds before three tractor-trailers came hurtling by. Seeing what had occurred, a trucker blocked the road and came running back to see if we were all okay. He radioed on his CB for the police and for a tow truck. The other members of the debate team, now fully roused, were in a panic about how we'd get to Toledo on time. Me, I didn't care. I was in a reverie, one I've never fully come out of, waiting to get back to New York and start my life again.

Previously, I'd run for student body office and, in a class of a thousand, I'd garnered less than one hundred votes. I was considered an unelectable class joke. Now, running again, but with a better self-image, I was narrowly elected to the governing board. And a year later I was elected student body president by a two-thirds majority. I started a new school newspaper. I asked girls out on dates. These dates didn't work out, but I asked.

I remember one particularly memorable disaster. I'd managed to get a date with a girl who most guys considered to be the most attractive girl in the school. I was excited. This time I'd make up for my previous romantic screw-ups. I arrived early at the girl's house to take her to a Sunday afternoon New York Giants football game at Yankee Stadium. Tickets for these games are sold out years in advance. (In retrospect, it finally occurred to me that it was the tickets, rather than my appeal, that proved irresistible in getting me this date.) Through a friend of my father's I was able to get two good seats for the game. I just needed to meet my dad's friend in front of the ticket booth fifteen minutes prior to game time.

Everything would have been fine, but I was so distracted thinking of Suzanne's good looks that I took the wrong bus and we were soon lost in an area where I'd never been before. Suzanne was, to say the least, unamused by my bumbling. By the time we reached the stadium, exactly at game time, any normal person could have seen that whatever slight chance I might have had with her was long gone. While my optimism (or my libido) didn't allow me to recognize this, what even I couldn't deny was that something else that was long gone was my dad's friend. I searched here, and I searched there, but the

S.O.B. clearly hadn't wanted to risk missing the opening kickoff for my sake. Without any regard for my entire romantic future, he had gone into the stadium.

Suzanne suggested that we just forget about it and go home. No way, I thought. I can't give up now. She's really warming up to me. I'll show her how talented I am. I'll just talk my way into Yankee Stadium. Yeah, no problem. I'll just explain to the guard that I was supposed to meet my dad's friend Vinnie, but I took the wrong bus and Vinnie went in without me. And, you know, these things happen. So, you know, I have this date and I don't want it ruined and we're all part of this great brotherhood of man, so why not just let me in?

The guard, however, would have none of this. The brotherhood of man meant nothing to him; my date meant nothing to him. All of morality to him boiled down to one simple aphorism: "No tickee. No laundry." I was outraged. I was desperate. I started to beg. I did have a ticket. I wasn't a crook. I had a ticket and I was entitled to be inside. My ticket was inside. Vinnie had my ticket. If the guard would just let us in, I'd get my ticket and show it to him. He was unmoved. Then I had an idea. He could just let me in and I'd leave Suzanne as security. He could just lock her up in the detention cage and I'd go get the tickets from Vinnie and return. This idea appealed to him. He locked her in the cage and let me in.

Have you ever tried to find one person in a stadium that holds sixty thousand people? It's not easy. It takes more than five minutes. It takes hours. By miracle, just before halftime I found him. Boy, would Suzanne be impressed! She had just spent over an hour, though, on a stool in a cage, listening to catcalls and other endearments from male football fans while waiting for me to return. She let me know I was no hero. She didn't let me know a whole lot more because for the rest of the afternoon she didn't speak to me.

At the conclusion of the date I suggested we go out next week. She was busy. Two weeks then? Busy too. Three weeks? Exams. Next month? Family trip. After that? Real boyfriend in from college.

Unbelievable! It seemed this girl had booked every available hour for the next year, at least as far as being available to me.

I wasn't down, though. I just kept asking girls for dates and they just kept not working out. In the end, though, one went fine. In my senior year of high school I asked out the girl who later became my wife. This time there were no wrong buses, no detention cages, no booked calendars.

Of course, school newspapers, student body politics, and disastrous high school romances were all regular growing-up things. What I wanted to do was something irregular, something unique. And so, at the beginning of my junior year, with thoughts of skyscrapers, worldwide media empires, and tremendous stock exchange valuations dancing in my head, I suggested to my best friend, Alex, that we start our own company. We had no proven abilities or track record, so we chose a business that seemed easy. For a couple of guys as creative and charming as we imagined ourselves to be, it was a no-lose proposition, foolproof, a guaranteed success. We opened our own advertising agency. At first it took some persuading, but then I told Alex I'd even let his name come first. And thus, Demac-Jonas Advertising was born.

True, we were only high school students. True, we had no employees. True, we had no clients. For that matter, if at that moment a large client would miraculously have appeared besieging us for our services, we would not have had the slightest idea what to do for him. None of this mattered to us, though. We were would-be magnates and we would learn.

I was able to secure a single empty room in an office in the Empire State Building that belonged to a friend of the family. It wasn't much bigger than a closet, but they said for the first year it would be rent-free. Alex, my partner, was able to convince the phone company to give us a catchy phone number in spite of the almost total unavailability of such numbers in Manhattan. We were off and running.

Actually, the number Alex secured was 1-212-565-1212. It soon became apparent to us why such a desirable number was still available so many decades after it was first issued. The number, you see, was only one digit off from 1-212-555-1212. This was the number any of the billions of people in the world wanting directory assistance for New York City would call when they needed a number. Apparently, in the era of dial telephones, if people misdialed, the number they most often missed by a digit would be the middle number. And judging by the fact that our new phone began ringing every two minutes, either a lot of people couldn't dial straight or the total number of calls must have exceeded all imagination.

For our first two weeks, while working through the nights marking lists of prospective clients, we answered each of these calls and gave each caller the home number of our debate coach. Within a week, we observed him falling asleep in class, barely able to function. But finally even we couldn't take the incessant ringing anymore, and Demac-Jonas Advertising chose discretion as the better part of valor and opted for a less glamorous number.

Just having a business certificate, an office, and a phone number wasn't enough, though. There was one essential thing you had to have if you were going to run a giant, or at least aspiring-to-be-giant, advertising agency. No, not clients. Stationery. I'm talking high-class stationery on semi-embossed, high-quality bond paper with matching envelopes and, most importantly, matching business cards—I mean, if you had business cards! I'm talking high-quality, raised-print business cards, with a little logo right on them. Then nobody could deny that you were a something. And if the card said you were a managing partner of Demac-Jonas Advertising, then, man, nobody could deny it.

I still remember fondly the day we went to pick up those cards. The printer was a small one on a side street in Midtown Manhattan. He'd gotten our business by offering us the lowest price of all the printers we called, provided we paid in advance, so I dipped into my hot dog savings. (There apparently had been a high failure rate either among new ad agencies or among teenage boys going into business.

These failures, due to catastrophe and unforeseen financial reversal, for some reason most often occurred between the date business cards were ordered and the date they were to be picked up.) In spite of his low price, the printer treated us like adult businessmen and gave us the royal treatment. He took out his big books of stationery samples and we pored over them with at least as much enthusiasm as any bride selecting wedding invitations. He showed us type styles (we chose Helvetica), camera-ready produced logos (we, of course, chose the Empire State Building), paper quality (something midrange—not too showy, but not cheap either), and printing style (we chose standard raised printing for the stationery). For the business card, however, we went whole hog—heat-embossed, raised printing. Sometimes you've got to go all the way!

When I saw those cards, I was transformed. I wasn't a nobody anymore. I was the president of Demac-Jonas Advertising. Soon, if my car crashed, it wouldn't have been as if I'd never lived. Life seemed full of endless possibilities. To this day, I can't walk into a printer's office (and as the owner of a half dozen publications, I walk into plenty) and not be happily transported back to the day of those business cards, just by the smell of ink.

To me it's the smell of youth, of opportunity, of new beginnings.

Many people are similarly transported back to their childhood by the smell of a favorite food, like chocolate pudding being cooked, or my grandmother's potato pancakes. So am I. Many men enjoy the scent of perfume on a well-dressed woman. So do I. But I'll tell you a secret. For my money, forget the Chanel No. 5. Just apply a few smudges of No. 12 black printer's ink behind the earlobes, and I'm game for anything.

The best part of those cards was that they allowed me entrance into an exclusive club, the world of adults and real business. No one had invited me to join. I had bestowed membership and its privileges on myself. I was the president of Demac-Jonas because I said I was. I would succeed because *I* believed I would. A title granted by someone else can always be taken away. Esteem that is dependent on the good-will of others can always be taken away. But status based on your own self-worth and optimism is yours forever, or at least for as long as you choose to believe in yourself.

This is the great thing about America. Here people, no matter what station they are born into, can become anything they want to be, provided their ability and their self-image let them go there. That's why every year hundreds of thousands, if not millions of people go marching into printers to have their dreams heat-embossed onto business cards. Many of them go in knowing no more about what they dream to be than we knew about advertising. But when they leave, the number who succeed is so great that never in the history of man have there been so many jobs created, such wealth produced, and so many dreams realized as in the era in which we live.

Some sneakers companies have sought to exploit this magic, urging people to "just do it" or telling them, "if you dream it, it can happen." This is true, but a bit misplaced. Throwing balls in baskets or running repeatedly around the park doesn't make you great. (I've nothing against running; I do it three times a week, and am, I hope, in much better shape for it.) Going out to achieve your true dreams is what makes you really great, and I think this happens much more often at the print shop than at the shoe store. And while I believe our society uniquely encourages and fosters this self-reliance, these dreams are fulfilled and can be fulfilled nowadays not just in America, but anywhere where the spirit of free enterprise and self-reliance has spread.

We found out, however, that there are a few other things you need when starting an ad agency. Creativity we believed we had, but agency recognition was something we lacked, not to even mention clients.

We thought all you needed for success was a great idea. But, like the framers of the American Constitution—the greatest man-made document ever written—we discovered it takes more than the idea.

You have to establish legitimacy and a track record or no one will take you seriously. Unfortunately, though, this is the ultimate catch-22. You need clients to get clients, and you need to be a legitimate, recognized ad agency in order to make money in the business.

Legitimate agencies place ads for their clients. In exchange, these agencies are rebated 15 percent of the cost of the advertising by the print, TV, or radio media in which the ads appear.

We knew what it took, but no newspaper, magazine, or TV station had ever heard of us, and without the stamp of approval of the media, an ad agency is just an idea. Crest toothpaste or Coca-Cola do not actually pay their agencies to create ads; the agencies make money every time the ad runs. Small publications, which are eager for advertising, will recognize fledgling ad agencies and happily rebate 15 percent, but the *New York Times* or CBS do not automatically acknowledge that you are what you say you are, or what you believe you can be.

In the early 1970s, when the great Alka-Seltzer ads ruled the airwaves, it was easy to see ourselves taking over Madison Avenue. Unknowns went on to become established agencies in what seemed like the blink of an eye. We thought that if our ideas were good enough, business would just flow our way. We could really start to grow like wildfire—gaining widespread agency recognition and building our portfolio and client base—once things got started.

There was only one problem. We had no clients, and even worse, we had no portfolio of previous work with which to convince a new client to choose us. We were confronting the oldest problem in business or wars: how to gain a toehold on someone else's territory.

In business, most people usually don't have to confront this issue because most new ventures are actually spinoffs of existing ventures and thus have their own established client base from the start. Often an account exec and creative director will leave an ad agency, bringing a few of the key accounts with them. Or a group of software engineers will leave a big company and immediately start in business supporting the software of the very company they left.

We, unfortunately, didn't leave any large company to take clients from. We had nothing.

When attempting to establish a beachhead in war, there are two ways to succeed. One is to mass incredibly superior forces and just storm the enemy's strong point, as the Allies did at Normandy.

The business equivalent of this, in our case, would have been to hire away incredibly talented creative people and highly aggressive account execs and start running large ads in *Advertising Age* and the *New York Times* business section announcing that our new Wunderkind agency was looking for business. In World War II, the Normandy assault was a key military victory, but it drained the coffers and arsenal of democracy. And, while launching a first-class agency might be somewhat less expensive, it was far beyond my limited savings from summer hot dog sales.

The second way to succeed is by doing something that seems completely irrelevant to the conflict but that distracts the object of your ambitions so you can infiltrate and attack from within. This is what happened at Troy with the Trojan Horse. Dazzled by the earlier offering from two armies, the citizens of the city took the beautiful horse in, unaware there was an army secreted within it.

Because the Greeks did not have enough strength to launch a frontal assault, they had to come up with a better idea. In business, when starting something fresh, I've found it's essential to have that better idea.

In our case we needed to offer would-be advertisers a reason to do business with us. We had no portfolio, and we couldn't offer them a price advantage, so we came up with a new medium, one that was suited to the small clients we were trying to woo. Actually, our idea was not really new at all, more like a borrowed idea. The fact is, there are very few truly new ideas. Most successful innovators actually wind up taking other people's "new" ideas and adapting them to a new set of circumstances. Did Starbucks invent the coffee bar or McDonald's the hamburger restaurant? Not on your life. They, however, figured out how to adapt the idea in order to have it succeed in new areas and in new ways.

In recent years I have been written up in many articles and been featured as a keynote speaker in many industry conventions as one of the foremost innovators in the communications industry. And yet, I must readily admit that many of my best "innovations" were borrowed from things I've seen in other places or were suggested to me by others. I just knew how to run with them.

Thomas Edison was perhaps the greatest inventor of all time. And one of the things that struck me in a recent biography is that almost all of his inventions, with the possible exception of the phonograph, were borrowed from others. It wasn't so much that Edison was a great inventor, but he was open to new ideas and improved on them.

I also try to be open to new ideas. More than be open to them, I crave them. There's nothing I prefer than to be in the company of creative people. I find they stimulate my own creative juices. I also try not to make snap judgments about which people you can learn from and which you can't. You can learn from everyone, and until you really listen you can never be sure who has something exciting to offer and who doesn't. A former construction worker now manages over two hundred highly trained technicians for me. A nighttime tech support supervisor figured out how to replace a huge multimillion-dollar mainframe on-line system with a few small PCs, saving us millions.

At work, I ask all our senior managers to fill out monthly reports on the departments' operations. I laboriously read through all the pages so I'll know what's going on. Sure it's tedious. The part that makes it all worthwhile, though, is the last question everyone's asked to answer. Suggestions? This is the part my eyes run to. Who knows what someone may come up with? Maybe a new technology, maybe a million-dollar sales idea, maybe a way to cut expenses in half. True, most of the suggestions aren't that dramatic. But you never know!

Back to that book on Edison. Books, I think, are the best places to get ideas. I try to read at least one every two weeks. Sometimes more.

Even when I drive to work, I listen to unabridged books in the car. I tend to prefer history, biography, and business books, with an occasional novel or philosophy book thrown in. It takes a lifetime for a person or a business to accumulate wisdom, and yet in just a few hours of reading someone will tell you most of what it took them a lifetime to learn. What better use of a reader's time? I will have spent forty-one years of living and three summers of writing to finish this book that you're reading. It may not be great, but it contains most of what I've learned over a whole, not altogether uninteresting lifetime. It's sort of hard as an author to come to grips with the fact that the whole thing can be read in a few hours. But what a great deal for the reader!

Demac-Jonas's "new" idea was based on my years of experience camping with my parents all over tourist areas in the Northeast. I'd often seen racks with sightseeing brochures in the hotels and campgrounds where we stayed, but noted that the big hotels in Manhattan never had them. Distributing brochures to tourists in New York hotels seemed a good idea and something that, surprisingly, no one else was yet doing.

Our technique was simple. We put brochure racks in all of Manhattan's hotels. Then we went to retailers, restaurants, theater owners, and anyone else wanting to do business with tourists, and suggested that for twenty dollars per month we'd distribute their brochures through our racks. Eventually, we planned, we'd approach these accounts to handle all of their advertising. Instead, we found, the brochure business was enough. We were satisfied to distribute brochures that someone else's creative efforts had produced, as long as we got paid for it. What I really wanted, it turned out, was just to be in *business,* not necessarily the advertising business.

Sounds crazy, but it was tough work. Because we were both too young to drive, we had to make all our deliveries in large truck bicycles with a big steel delivery box on the front. On hot weekends, after twelve or sixteen hours of delivery, it seemed we drank almost as much in soda as we collected for the service. Brochure pickups were done with taxicabs after school. Only a year later, when I turned seventeen and got a license and an old station wagon, did life get a little easier. But even sweating like a pig on the bike, I was still the president of Demac-Jonas Advertising.

We managed to snag a few real advertising clients besides the brochure accounts. Unfortunately, though, the only clients who seemed to respect me as an advertising man were those who refused to pay their bills. They needed an agency because the newspapers wouldn't give them any credit. Only we were desperate enough to. It was one thing to welch on the *New York Times*, quite another to stiff two sixteen-year-old boys. One client, though, screwed us totally. This was a mail-order seller of computerized horoscopes who, after placing several thousands of dollars of ads with us, just locked his doors and skipped town.

Now we really were in trouble. We owed thousands of dollars and our largest client never answered the phone or came to the door, no matter how many times we called. We couldn't believe it; we didn't know what to do. Finally, in desperation, we broke open the door of his Madison Avenue office, hoping to find his whereabouts or at least something we could hock to help pay the bill.

Instead, we found something unexpected. A totally vacant office with hundreds of pieces of mail from people who had ordered horoscopes strewn across the floor. I added up the contents and came to a new conclusion on my life's calling: We were now in the mail-order horoscope business.

There was only one problem. I didn't know anything about astrology beyond the fact that I was a Gemini and that it was all B.S. I did know a sure moneymaker when I saw it, though. And I also knew where to find the "senior astrologer" of my former client.

We tracked Brother Bob, as he was called. He protested that he knew nothing about the whereabouts of our client, who apparently had taken the money and skipped town without bothering to send out the horoscopes that people had ordered. He, too, had not been paid. Brother Bob had written a complex computer program that would look at how various forces interacted in order to print out a personalized horoscope for each person. He explained that at the particular time each person is born, each of the various planets could be in any one of the dozen quadrants into which the heavens are divided. The quadrant each planet is in influences the characteristics that fall under the domain of that planet. Venus, for instance, "determines" one's love life. Mars, one's material success. The sun sign—what most of us mean when we talk about our astrological sign—determines the general personality. The location of each person's planet at the time of birth can be looked up in an astrology reference manual known as an ephemeris. All that would be needed to replicate my former client's product, he assured me, was to pay him $25,000 for six months of programming and to lease another $50,000 or so worth of time on a mainframe computer. I had neither the time nor the money for this nonsense.

I proposed an alternative to Brother Bob. Why not write up twelve one-page blurbs giving some general mumbo-jumbo about what some important planet says about the aspect of a person's life they influence. We could do this for five different planets. I'd then look up in an ephemeris which of the twelve sheets to pick out for each person for each respective planet, mark it on a cover sheet, attach the five relevant pages, and mail it to the consumer. They'd be happy because they got something personalized, letting them know for instance that Venus was in Sagittarius when they were born. They'd also get valuable advice like to never marry a Capricorn unless they really liked him or her, in which case it would be risky but okay. As to how the various planets interacted within their own personality let them figure it out for themselves. Hey, for a buck, what do you want, Brother Bob?

"A buck?" Brother Bob asked. "Our product costs twenty dollars."

"Well, you had to pay for a computer," I replied.

I'd call the thing compuscope so people would think it came from a computer, but in reality I'd pay high school kids 3¢ apiece to address the envelopes and look up the sign in the ephemeris. I could pay them 2¢ to pick the right sheets from the racks, then staple, fold, and stuff the envelope and apply the postage. Taking into account 4¢ for printing and envelopes and 8¢ for bulk-rate postage, I could make an 83¢ margin on each dollar horoscope I sold; even more if someone ordered an extra for a current or intended loved one, since the postage would stay the same.

"You can't do that," Brother Bob started to argue. "This is real astrology. You're prostituting the art. I'll have nothing to do with it."

"Look," I told him, "this isn't art, it's business. And I'll pay you ten bucks for each sheet you write. Five planets times twelve signs. That's six hundred dollars for two days' work. What do you say?"

"Well," Bob replied, "I guess it really is personalized, and frankly I never really thought the computer got it right anyway. I'll do it."

I had one more idea. I did a little research and determined that all the other horoscope companies advertising in the *National Enquirer* and *Star* were charging $10 to $20 plus $1 for postage and handling. If I was only charging a buck, why not advertise the product as a *free* horoscope to introduce people to our product? The buck would just be the postage and handling charge. I mean, if you could believe in horoscopes to begin with, why not believe they were free? That ought to boost sales, I thought.

It did. Soon, it seemed like half the students at Bronx High School of Science were spending half their school days poring through ephemerides and addressing envelopes while their unsuspecting teachers turned their backs and wrote physics equations on the blackboard.

Nights were even wilder. As the orders from tabloid ads piled in, we started pulling all-nighters at the Empire State Building to keep up with the volume. We ran ads in the *Globe*, *Star*, and *National Enquirer*. Tabloids today may be utterly discredited, but to us that's where the money was. Soon we overflowed our closet, and the fifty-first floor of this prestigious skyscraper began to resemble a long, unending frat party. We played jazz with the night janitor, ate in the twenty-four-hour Belmore Cafeteria, and drank seltzer with the cabbies at three in the morning, and then went back to pack more horoscopes. Craziest of all, the customers loved it and referrals started coming in from what seemed like an endless supply of lunatics who couldn't wait to send their dollar bills to me.

Just handling the money, in fact, became a major problem. My thirteen-year-old sister complained that the stress from stamping so many checks for deposit was ruining her cheerleading abilities. I got self-inking stamps. Then, as the volume grew, my mother refused to open envelopes. I bought a machine to slice them open. Soon, the bank started to complain that they were losing money handling so many one- and two-dollar checks and the branch was overwhelmed and wouldn't accept anymore. Only a threat to go to the press with the story of how Citibank was putting a high school boy out of business caused the higher-ups to relent and instruct the branch to keep accepting my deposits of little checks.

Not that cash was problem-free. A lot of people actually sent dollar bills through the mail. (This was why I needed people I trusted to open the mail.) You could immediately feel the bills through the envelopes. Money has a certain, unique "spongy" quality that no other paper has. Soon I could tell through the envelopes which ones had one dollar and which two. These I'd sort into separate piles and add them up before tallying the checks. Rarely was my cash estimate off by even a dollar. I often wondered why mail handlers and postmen didn't just steal the money. Whether it was their innate honesty, the vigilance of postal inspectors, or just the fear of losing a well-paying government job, I'm not sure. As I struggled to keep track of my cash and keep producing horoscopes, I didn't know that our biggest avalanche of orders had not yet started. In the spring of 1974, my family was going to visit my grandmother for a week at her winter apartment in Florida. I had scheduled our regular free horoscope ad to run in the *National Enquirer* that week. I'd asked my then girl-friend (and now wife) to go to my post office box every day with a shopping bag to bring the mail to my house. She could open it, if time allowed. If not, I'd take care of it on my return. I just didn't want the box to overfill.

Unfortunately, to my consternation, the *Enquirer* had decided to give away their own free horoscope that week as a promotion. They were charging $1 for postage and handling too. All you had to do was send in a self-addressed, stamped envelope. They even advertised the offer in glaring headlines on the front cover. This would surely wipe me out, I was sure. As soon as I saw the paper, I started calling the *Enquirer* and demanding a refund for my wasted ad.

I was not surprised when Debbie called to tell me there was a problem at the post office. What did surprise me was that the problem was not too little mail, but too much. Trays and trays of mail, to be exact. There was no way she could carry it all to my house and open it. She needed a car service just to pick up each day's arrival. By the time I came home, mail had filled the entire family room in my parents' basement and I needed to start using nonfamily members just to open it.

The *Enquirer*, you see, had put their free offer at the back of the paper to encourage people to read all the way through. My free offer appeared toward the front, however, so that the thousands of people who picked up the paper at the supermarket checkout confused my offer with the *Enquirer*'s.

People say you should never underestimate your opponents, or any other person, for that matter. This is very good advice, and I live by it. But there is a corollary piece of advice that I've learned to also keep in mind. Never overestimate people's intelligence either. Most people, at least in some aspect of their lives, never outgrow their childhood. They want reassurance, hand-holding, toys, free gifts, costumes, excitement, surprises. In a word, they want to ignore reality and just be kids. Some are actually short on intelligence; others just choose not to use what they've got.

Fortunes have been made by those smart enough to not overestimate people's intelligence. Look at the movie industry (particularly the action movies). Look at Las Vegas. Look at time-sharing. Look at the mail-order business. Don't just look at those things principally consumed by the poor and uneducated. Look at rich people flying thousands of miles out of their way (and paying more for tickets) in order to rack up frequent-flyer miles, or paying double to buy clothes with a designer label.

Even as I write this, our company is signing up large numbers of phone users by offering them frequent flyer miles and prizes in exchange for slightly higher rates. Actually, the consumers would be better off to take the savings and buy their own tickets or stereo equipment at a discount. To my amazement, however, people are choosing the prizes instead. I'm not fighting it; I'm coming up with better prizes. These are grown-ups. It's their money. They can do with it whatever makes them happy.

Perhaps this is precisely the point. Perhaps people aren't really so stupid after all. Perhaps people just need a little thrill, a little entertainment, a little excitement in their lives. I mean, in reality, no one in America will starve to death or die one day sooner if he or she spends a buck on a horoscope or seven bucks watching Arnold Schwarzenegger battle to save civilization, or a hundred thousand dollars, if you can afford it, to sleep in the White House and have the President pretend he really values your advice. You're just looking to spice up your life. And if people can get a few minutes' or a few hours' excitement reading their horoscope or sharing it with a friend, then I guess they got a really good deal for a buck.

Eventually, as I became more religiously observant, I began to have scruples about whether astrology was entertainment or some kind of phony religion. Concerned that it might be inherently evil, I stopped selling the 'scopes. In retrospect, I think in 99.5 percent of the cases $1 horoscopes were just entertainment, but that half percent just made me uneasy and so I had to quit.

My entrée into the world of mail-order advertising had opened my eyes to a whole new world of possibilities. There were other products that could be sold through the tabloids with even greater potential. I had already learned that there is one thing people are obsessed with more than sex or money or horoscopes. What Americans really want are plants. That's right. Plants. Gardening is America's No. 1 hobby, and I could capitalize on that. I found that plants filled the same void in people's lives as horoscopes did. From the horoscope business I'd learned that people really were most interested in their romantic futures. Would they meet the man or woman of their dreams? That was the most important insight that they hoped a horoscope would reveal. People ordered their horoscopes because they were lonely, the same reason they often adopted pets or doted on their houseplants. Perhaps that is why plants and pets are so important. Putting these thoughts together, I came up with the idea of pet plants—the Venus's-flytrap that consumed insects became the "hungry plant," the plant that curled up its leaves at night became the "praying plant," and the fern that contracts when touched becomes the "feeling plant." You guessed it! These pets could be had for only $1 each, postage and handling, or $2.50 for all three.

I had learned to harness my creative talents to the particular demands of mail order. Okay, so I wasn't responsible for "I can't believe I ate the whole thing," but I could write a coupon that would knock your socks off, and I could make people order pet plants at an incredible clip. I placed quarter-page ads in all the tabloid newspapers, and pretty soon I was sending out so many plants that I had run out of willing classmates and started trying to hire teachers I thought highly of to work for me. This not only kept the orders flowing, but seemed to help my grade-point average as well.

True, we still weren't able to convince any large advertisers to use our agency, but so what? I had developed a better advertising client. Me. And it seemed we couldn't lose.

This was the really great thing about the mail-order business. You could test your ads in small, inexpensive publications, and if they worked, then you rolled them out to the expensive large-circulation journals. As long as you didn't have to invest in a big inventory first, there was virtually no risk involved in trying to sell new things. I didn't have to cozy up to clients and beg for their business, I only had to figure out what the tabloid reading public wanted and then supply it. I have always hated having to be dependent on the opinion of others for my success. This robs you of your self-worth and too often turns people into brown-nosers, always afraid that someday their "benefactor" will turn on them. Think back to the beginning—when Adam was all alone in the Garden of Eden, all G-d gave him was Eve as a companion and helper. He didn't give him a cadre of bosses, kings, or overbearing clients to direct his every move. Even once thrown out of the garden, he was able to farm the land on his own, earning independence and self-respect in his own eyes.

In our much more complex economic society it is no longer possible just to have a nation of yeoman farmers, each looking after his own land. In fact, small self-reliant farmers are having a tough go of it. On the other hand, does this mean you should relinquish all independence and allow your physical as well as mental well-being to be dependent on the goodwill of others rather than your own innate value? I think not. This is probably the reason I've resisted the temptation to run for elective office. It's also the reason I've always made sure that no single client would ever account for more than 5 percent of my business. I've always preferred to make sales based on uniqueness or the superior quality of our offerings rather than on some personal "connection" where friendship gets turned into a commodity and the loss of goodwill adds up to the loss of income.

The mail-order business and the brochure business suited me just fine. I was my own master. Even if you hated a teenage overachiever who went to Bronx Science, if you wanted your brochure in a hotel lobby in New York, you paid us. If you wanted a pet plant, I was your man. In short, things were going great.

In all honesty, though, not *everything* I tried always went right.

Sometimes I got so carried away with how well we were doing that I'd take a foolish risk and lose months of earnings. Two particular cases stick in my mind, even to this day.

At that time, a lot of mail-order marketers seemed to be making big money selling small samples of a large variety of well-known perfumes for one low price. They got samples from the perfume companies who were looking to find new consumers. I realized that the women who were ordering such large varieties of perfumes didn't yet have a strong preference and were searching for the right scent. I also knew from my other products that people wanted something that was created personally for them. I hit upon what I thought was a brilliant idea: perfume personalized for your personality. Women would fill in a whole page of questions about their age, weight, coloring, favorite colors, dreams, pastimes, clothing, education, et cetera . . . and we'd send the perfect perfume for them.

I even invented a fictional Italian perfumer, Guiseppe LaVerde, who was featured in our ads as supervising the blending of your personal fragrances. I was so enthralled with what I thought was the brilliance of these ads that soon I could think of nothing else. Estée Lauder, Charles Revlon, and Nina Ricci would soon be nothing compared to me.

Usually, when testing a new product, I'd first run a sample ad in a small publication before ordering any merchandise or placing a larger advertising buy. This time, though, I was so sure of the brilliance of my concept and so anxious to outflaunt the great cosmetics concerns that I threw all caution to the wind. I actually hired an expert fragrance chemist to formulate dozens of different Guiseppe LaVerde perfumes to be sent to women in accordance with their answers to the questionnaire. I stocked my storeroom with cases and cases of the different varieties. I spent over $10,000 running a full-page ad in the *National Enquirer,* and then I sat back waiting for the orders to pour in as I became rich beyond my wildest imagination.

Even my imagination, however, could not have guessed the number of letters that would pour in to Guiseppe LaVerde. One. That's right. Only one. A thirty-three-year-old, green-eyed badminton devotee from Iowa filled out the survey and ordered the perfume. One! Guiseppe LaVerde had cost me over $25,000. No one was willing to buy his leftover perfume. No one wanted his trademark. No one wanted his formulas. No one wanted anything to do with him.

What Old Guiseppe and young Howard didn't know was that women put on perfume to be Lauren Hutton or Elle Macpherson or Coco Chanel, not to be themselves, a middle-aged, brown-eyed librarian with a degree from a junior college. How could Guiseppe have been so stupid? How could anyone have been so dumb not to even test the idea? What grandiosity. What stupidity. What recklessness. Mea culpa; mea culpa; *mea culpa!*

I never ran an ad campaign without testing ever again. But that didn't mean I avoided making the same mistake in a different way.

Distributing brochures all night to the various Manhattan hotels had made me acutely aware of the millions of tourists who visited New York annually. I had seen firsthand hundreds of them paying for bus excursions at tour desks in all the hotels in the city. Because they had their own desks at the different hotels, these bus tour companies always turned me down for brochure distribution. This was a sore point with me.

Then, one day, our family went to Gettysburg and rented a tape-recorded tour of the battleground. It seemed like hundreds of other tourists were lining up for these recorded tours. Suddenly I had an idea. While the earphone in my ear droned on about the loss of life and the magnitude of the Union victory over the Confederacy on this hallowed ground four score and seven years after the founding of our republic, I could only think of how I was going to vanquish the bus tour companies on the sidewalks of New York, not in eighty-seven years, but next week.

As soon as I returned, I was like a man possessed. I hired the chief guide at the largest bus tour company to write my recorded tour. I persuaded Acoustiguide, which has the tape tour concession in all the country's largest museums, to provide us with several hundred tape recorders for a small cut of our potential revenues. I hired a nationally known broadcaster to record the tour. I persuaded large retailers like FAO Schwarz and large restaurateurs to pay us thousands of dollars a month to be included as stops on the tour; as soon as the tourists started flocking to their stores and mentioning our name, they'd pay up. Then I went to the sightseeing desks at hotels to ask them to rent the tours from me.

They turned me down. It turned out that they were all in partnership with the bus companies and the idea of tape tours was as appealing to them as a methadone clinic would be to a drug dealer. Undeterred, I went to the Empire State Building, the one place all tourists visit, and asked for a storefront in the lobby to rent the tours. Learning that the price was $20,000 a month, I persuaded the Empire State Building to let me have the store for free as a place from which to rent tours if I could persuade the New York Convention and Visitors Bureau to open a branch center in the building. They were anxious to make sure that tourists would continue going there (and paying $3.25 for the elevator tour to the observation deck), and not to the newly opened observation deck at the taller (but less famous and more out-of-the-way) World Trade Center. The Convention and Visitors Bureau, offered free space in the world's most famous building with free staffing of their office (by me, who already supplied them with brochures), readily accepted the offer. The free office was now mine. I only had to spend 80 percent of my life's savings to fix up and furnish the facility in accordance with the demands of the Empire State Building and the Convention and Visitors Bureau.

Not to worry. At $10 per two-hour tour with the two hundred tape players Acoustiguide was providing us, we'd be making $6,000 per day (or $5,000 after salaries and Acoustiguide's cut). This was over $1.5 million profit per year, *before* the advertising revenue. This was *big* money. I was going to get really rich. The bus companies would be sorry they didn't do business with me.

Opening day was a Saturday. I couldn't be there because my father insisted I go to an insurance brokers' training course, which met for thirteen weeks beginning that day. My father, who had never been to college and didn't hold out much hope for my chances as an entrepreneur, reasoned that this would be my "insurance policy" to earn a living, since I could always work in his brokerage if all else failed. Failure, however, was the farthest thing from my mind. All day long as I sat in that class, I looked across at the IBM building and thought: Who knows, soon maybe I'll be as big as them. All day, in my mind's eye, I saw my partners Alex and Eric (later to become Father Eric, an Episcopal priest) taking people's driver's licenses and $10 bills and handing tourists the tape players. In my mind's eye, the tape players were going out not three, but five times. (Saturday was, after all, a busy day.)

I heard not a word the instructor uttered that day. I couldn't wait for the class to end. I drove the ten miles south from White Plains to midtown Manhattan at breakneck speed, blinded part of the way, not by the setting sun, but by the gold in my eyes.

By the time I burst into our office in the Empire State Building half an hour after closing time, Alex and Eric were lying on our expensively carpeted floor, apparently too exhausted from dealing with the hordes of tourists to even stand up. Their giddily jovial mood, however, couldn't hide the magnitude of our success from me. "Tell me," I demanded. "How many tours did we rent today?"

"Guess!" they guffawed back, obviously wanting to milk this triumphant moment for all it was worth.

"Six hundred," I replied, starting with the lowest reasonable answer that could account for this sort of intoxicated mood.

"No, guess again."

I had been too conservative. Of course, three times a day was too low for a full day. We'd actually done four times. "Well, what do you know, eight hundred!" I shot back.

"Guess again, you're not even close."

Now I saw the reason for their exuberance. They began to cackle wildly. I couldn't believe it, five times a day! The tape players must barely have had time to recharge. Five times a day—this was better than $2.5 million profit a year. Even before we increased our inadequate supply of players and tapes. Five times a day! We were rich beyond belief. I was going to cut Eric in on the windfall. I wasn't greedy, plus, at this moment, I loved everyone. "A thousand," I finally cried, beaming. "I can't believe you actually did a thousand! We're rich."

"Not a thousand," they replied. "Let us tell you how many we did." Then they rose from the floor and these two large, macho guys started to hula dance ecstatically around the information center, bumping and grinding into each other. "You want to know how many we sold?" they sang out wildly. "This is how many." Then they both turned to me and, still dancing, gave me the "A-okay" symbol with each of their four hands.

"Zero?" I blurted out in disbelief. It couldn't be. Yes, they shook their heads, wordlessly nodding. Then they collapsed back on the ground, back to their intoxicated guffawing. "Zero?" I asked once more, falling to the floor of the elegantly (and expensively) appointed information center next to them.

"Yes," they said. "Zero, zero, zero. Not a one. Tourists were way too scared to walk around New York City all by themselves. We couldn't *give* the damn tours away. We dropped the price to five dollars, then one, then free just to get the ad revenue, and still nobody would take them. This is the biggest boner of all time." After several beers, taken from a case Alex and Eric had already almost finished, I was lying on the floor guffawing too. Zero—I couldn't believe it, zero. I laughed and I cried. Boy, was I a jerk.

Though I had lost most of the money I'd ever made up to that point, I did learn—again—a valuable lesson. Test before you spend. Test before you commit. Test. Test. Test. Test. I could have saved $40,000 by just putting a folding table in front of the information center and seeing how many people would have rented tape tours for a few hours. I could have saved all the fix-up costs of the center. In fact, I even could have avoided the expense of producing the tours by just putting up a sign for tape tours. Every time somebody gave me $10, I could just take out a machine and say, "Oh, damn, the battery's dead. Sorry. Here's your money back." Sure, for a couple of hours a few people might be mildly annoyed, but literally six months of wasted time and money on my part would have been saved.

This rule of testing holds true not just for tape tours, but for every business venture. Over the years it's saved me literally millions in mail order, publishing, software, and telecommunications. In each of these businesses, I've many times found that things I was sure of weren't such sure bets at all. When people think they're right or they're on a winning streak, they seem to have an almost religious need to "put their money where their mouth is," to justify or affirm their faith in their idea. You see this every time somebody lets it all ride on the gambling tables in Vegas or when some quiet employee loses thirty years of savings in an instant on some risky investment or new business. Sure, there's a temporary mental rush that goes with "taking the risk," "letting it all ride," "having the strength of your convictions," but it's B.S. There's no reason to take a risk. There's always a way to test first, a way to gather information, to scope out the competition, and generally hedge your bet. The most successful people who seem to be the biggest risk-takers actually never make any bets that aren't hedged.

Do you honestly think any of history's great generals, like Robert E. Lee, Alexander the Great, or Hannibal, ever went into battle and just "let it all ride" without sending out spies and doing thorough intelligence work to gauge the enemy's capabilities first? Don't bet on it!

Recently, Sun-tzu's *The Art of War* has become popular reading (or at least popular to display on the bookshelves) among top corporate executives. These latter-day commanders, as they envision themselves, are brave, fearless risk-takers taking on a bunch of lily-livered corporate types. Or so they'd have you believe. That's the message having the book up on the shelf is supposed to convey: "Watch your back around me. I'm a wild man."

If they actually read the book, they'd find the main thing Sun-tzu advocates is sending out spies and doing your reconnaissance work. For a general, this involves military reconnaissance, the kind of secret spying that's won more than one or two wars for the clever and patient commander. In business it means keeping your nose to the ground, keeping abreast of the competition, and yet testing even the surest of sure things, even if it seems that you may compromise the element of surprise that a military general relies on. Never get into a battle you're not sure to win. Test first. They say in real estate the three most important things are location, location, location. In my opinion, business has three similar rules: test, test, test.

To get back to my story, though, these perfumes and tape tour fiascos were just small bumps on the road. No more than getting tackled in a football game and failing to make a first down. As far as I was concerned, life was a game and I was still headed for the Super Bowl. Youth is that way. Resilient.

The mail-order business continued to churn out profit. The brochure route kept growing and soon we found ourselves in other exciting endeavors as well. Sure, it's impossible to succeed in business if you don't concentrate on one thing. Sure, if you spread yourself too thin you'll risk losing everything. But we were too young to know these rules and our youthful exuberance (and extraordinary good luck) seemed to overcome everything.

Things were going well and just seemed to be getting better. I was president of the student body, had a great girlfriend, had a successful and expanding set of businesses, and was even doing pretty well in school (especially since many of my teachers worked for me). Life seemed like a smorgasbord where I could just have more and more of whatever I wanted. There was just one ominous storm cloud on the horizon: college.

To say I was schizophrenic about the topic of college was an understatement. All of my upbringing pointed toward it, yet many of my inclinations pointed against it.

On the one hand, I was a Jewish son, a descendant of the People of the Book. You know, the parents who left Egypt so their kids could get into good colleges and medical schools (or law schools if they were dumb). I had always done what was expected of me. I read high school books by third grade, was always in advanced classes, attended the city's top gifted high school, had won first prize in the National Science and Inventors' Competitions (I developed a rudimentary artificial spinal cord and subsequently sold development rights for it to a medical research facility). I was a nationally ranked debater, had high SAT scores and a decent scholastic average. Not only that, but all of my friends' top goal at that time was to get into a good college. On top of this, I enjoyed learning things. My mother (one of the truly great people in the world, but a Jewish mother nonetheless), whose parents left Europe for economic reasons, never went to college. She strongly shared the values of my schoolmates (and their parents) regarding university education, and wanted only the best for me. And what Jewish boy wants to disappoint his mother?

On the other hand, right now I was free. I was already doing better economically than most college graduates. I was an independent thinker, and I couldn't stand the rigid structure and rules of school. By senior year school was already feeling like a time-wasting prison. I was unimpressed by the intellectual ability of most teachers (and Bronx Science attracted the best in the city) and doubted college professors would know much more. I also had strong conservative leanings and was turned off by the drugs, draft card burnings, and left-wing ideology that in the early 1970s seemed to characterize academia. My father, who without any formal education had worked his way up from repairing broken radios to running a commercial insurance brokerage, was also against college. This also affected me, though, as everyone knows, Jewish boys have to live up to their mother's, not their father's, aspirations. My dad, probably sensing this, mostly kept quiet on the subject.

Most importantly, I didn't want to give up Debbie—who was still a high school junior—by leaving town, no matter how prestigious the school. I didn't know what to do.

Obligatorily, I applied to Harvard, although I hoped to go to Columbia. It might be less prestigious, but it was Ivy League and it was in New York. If I went there, I could have everything. My relationship with Debbie could continue just as before, and by taking a jock schedule, I could skip most classes and keep building my business, while still getting a degree and paying lip service to a well-rounded education.

Unfortunately, the day I visited Columbia to accept the offer of admission was the day Cambodia fell to the communist Khmer Rouge. All over the campus this event was being celebrated with bonfires, dancing, and hot dog roasts. This was just too much for me.

Even at that time, it was abundantly clear to me that the Khmer Rouge were very bad guys. Yet the students at Columbia clearly thought that, by comparison to any regime linked to America, the Khmer Rouge were great heroes. Worth calling off classes and having a weenie roast for. That was enough for me. If Jane Fonda wanted, she could go to Columbia. For me, I was forgetting about elite colleges and going to the local community college. I might not get a great education, but I'd still be in business and I'd still have Saturday nights with Debbie to look forward to.

The next day Harvard accepted me. Harvard. The best. Crimson. Ivy. Tradition. So much for all those teachers who thought I wasn't brilliant. Not only that, but they were offering all new freshmen the chance to take a year off before attending, to become worldly, to travel, to sow their wild oats. This solved everything. It would make my mother happy; it would make me more attractive to Debbie's parents, who always felt I was from the wrong side of the tracks and not quite good enough for their daughter; it would let me stay with Debbie. Best of all, it would let me work full-time. Now I was really going to have fun!

What would happen when the year ended? you ask. Good question! But you know youth: Live for today. Tomorrow will take care of itself. And I really believed it. After all, up to that time everything had always fallen into place.

Maybe by the end of the year I'd be so rich and famous everyone would agree I didn't need my degree. Maybe Harvard would give me an honorary degree, or count my business activities as independent studies, or give me another year off. Like a person facing long prison time who just keeps appealing to stay out on bond till his pardon or new evidence shows up or the judge forgets about him, I didn't worry about tomorrow. I just wanted to keep enjoying today.

Chapter Three
Rejecting Harvard

❖

The year I took off between high school and college was like a little oasis in time, a sweet bridge between adolescence and adulthood. I had two goals for that year. The first was to spend as much time with Debbie as I possibly could, and the second was to earn enough money to pay for my college education. No loans for me, no handouts from Daddy or Uncle Sam. If I was going to get a Harvard diploma, I was going to get it the old-fashioned way. Earn it. If I'd known how little it was worth, I wouldn't have worked so hard.

My partner, Alex, went off to Columbia (he eventually became a doctor, so at least someone wound up with a proud mother), so I was on my own in the mail-order business. Since I'd also passed the insurance broker's licensing exam that I'd been studying for on the day of the tape tour fiasco, I had another angle to pursue as well. So I spent part of my time hawking plants in the tabloids, and part of the time working in my father's commercial insurance business. In April, Debbie got into Harvard, which meant we could stay together. We'd go from being high school sweethearts to college sweethearts. Everything was coming up roses.

This, as it turned out, was my undoing. Her educated, liberal parents had their every dream fulfilled with her acceptance. Although I'd had second thoughts about dropping everything and moving to Cambridge, she was going there and that was that. Either I could follow or she'd probably find a better-looking, nicer guy from a better family up there. They suggested that maybe I should stay in New York. Oh, no, not me. I wasn't going to lose her. I was going to Harvard. I could leave my business in New York and run it and still have Crimson, Ivy, tradition, great education. After all, I'd always been able to have it all up to now. During the year off I'd taken and passed advanced placement exams that gave me full credit for my freshman year, so I only had three years to go. It would go by in the blink of an eye. Harvard wasn't Columbia. I ignored my misgivings and told Harvard to expect me in September. Big mistake.

From the start, it was a disaster. Debbie wanted to live "the college life," felt I was suffocating her, and started to cool down the relationship. This began a turbulent time for us that, though finally and happily culminating in our marriage five years later, was a period that could be described as stormy at best, and hell at worst.

The political orientation of the school was just as left-wing as Columbia. The only difference was that the administration was just as left-wing as the students and faculty, making for less visible intercampus turbulence.

I and, it seemed, the entire rest of the university were always at loggerheads, ideologically. I cite three examples. During my first year I was taking a course in the ideology of the American Revolution. The professor invited me into his graduate section, where I noted that many of my fellow students seemed to be Marxists, ascribing to Charles Beard's theory of the Revolution (that is, Washington, Adams, and Jefferson did the whole thing because they were rich capitalists whose ascendancy was being thwarted by the British. Also, they needed a diversion to distract the lower classes from the growing concentration of common wealth).

When the time came for the final, a friend came to me and told me that he had not attended classes or read anything all year. Now he would surely fail. Not to worry, I said. I spent all night drilling him on the seven essay questions I felt the professor was most likely to ask. Sure enough, six of the seven questions actually appeared. My friend chose three to write on and got an A- for the class. I took the same exam, but my paper was graded by one of the Marxists. He disagreed with my point of view and gave me a C. Outraged, I took my test to the professor and asked him to regrade it. He gave it an A but refused to change the grade, saying that to do so would be unfair to all the other students who didn't get the opportunity to have their exam reviewed. What about absolute justice? I asked. What if my admission to Law or Business School would be denied because of this mark? How could you give a course on ideology and then disregard it in your own class? I never took another class from this professor or even spoke to him again. And he was one of the best.

In my sophomore year the student body organized a huge protest in favor of affirmative action. What a joke. These students, supposedly the cream of the nation's intellectual elite, all chosen for their superior intelligence and all choosing to go to Harvard in order to be surrounded by others choosing academic superiority, were now holding a rally demanding that in the future students not be admitted on the merit system. Such a policy would discredit every minority student accepted as merely a quota filler, destroying incentive to really upgrade primary education for the poor.

I resolved to oppose this demonstration with a demonstration of my own. Unfortunately, the small cadre of libertarians and conservatives who had originally agreed to a counterdemonstration all backed out as the hour neared. Thus, following a mass of placard-waving students marching down Massachusetts Avenue chanting for affirmative action, was me, universally booed, taunted, and jeered at, carrying a sign that read ADMIT ON MERIT.

At this demonstration, however, one of the leaders made a point that really struck me. In the jungle, he said, there were two animals out to get you: the hyena and the snake. The hyena, he said, pointing to me, isn't really dangerous. He's just a big fool, with no power, who makes a lot of noise, and this can easily be dealt with. The snake, on the other hand, he said, pointing to the administration building, is far more dangerous. They never speak in opposition to you. They yes you to death. They set up committees to study your grievance, and then, when you least expect it, they quietly bite you on the heel and ignore your demands and do you in.

This, I thought, was a really good point. What was I changing out there? In the future, I resolved to be more of a snake, letting the other side blow steam while I just kept quiet and did in their smug world of entitlement, regulation, and the like.

Not that I was able to keep my mouth shut for long. In my senior year, some of the student leaders organized OXFAM Day. This was to be a day where students fasted, skipping dinner in the dining hall so Harvard Food Service could donate $2.37 per faster to OXFAM's programs for the world's hungry. I thought this was a crock. I was happy to give $2.37 to OXFAM so I could have supper. In fact, I was donating thousands of dollars a year to the world's poor. I went out alone one night a week to give sandwiches and drinks to the homeless.

But I thought conformity was garbage. Like Gandhi, I was going to protest. Only I wasn't going on a hunger strike. I was having supper, the only student to have supper in North House on OXFAM day. I ruined North House's 100 percent fasting record. Nobody talked to me or would sit with me in the dining hall for weeks. This was okay by me. Usually I had supper at the neighborhood pizza place, anyway. If students had only protested against the grub that Harvard Food Service tried to pass off as food, rather than in solidarity with the third world totalitarian regimes. I gladly would have led it.

My disenchantment with Harvard, though, like most disenchantments, got worse over time. In the beginning, it seemed like the most exciting place in the world, the ideal place in which to get educated *and* build a world-class mail-order business.

And so, from the moment I moved into my Harvard dorm, my double life began. By day, I led the life of an eager young intellectual,

working my way into the best classes, talking with the professors after class, joining the pistol team, even starting an alternative student
newspaper with a group of like-minded libertarian students who
came together for a course on the philosophy of free market economics. (Many of these guys now run Washington.)

By night, though, I was "Mr. Mail Order," coming up with more
and more ideas to sell cheap merchandise in low-class publications.
While in the late afternoon, after classes, my fellow students went to
their mailboxes to pick up their copies of *Foreign Affairs, Scientific
American*, and an occasional letter from home, I would show up daily
at the mail room and bring back armfuls of the trashy publications to
which I subscribed in order to stay abreast of the latest mail-order
fads. Most of my fellow students had never even heard of magazines
like the *National Enquirer, Midnight, Globe, Photoplay, True Con-
fessions*, and the dozens of others that were piled all over my room,
and which I spent my nights reading. Undoubtedly, students working
in the mail room must have assumed I was taking a comparative so-
ciology course on the effect of the media on middle-class consumption
patterns. (And, in a way, they would have been right.)

Nights when other housemates were attending cheese and sherry
seminars or going to the common rooms to hear classical music per-
formances by student prodigies like Yo-Yo Ma, I was in the TV room
spending the whole night watching *All in the Family, Maude*, and *The
Tonight Show* so I'd be in touch with what "middle-class America"
was thinking.

Not that I enjoyed the magazines or the TV shows, but watching
them was my "job." In fact, I have come to hate television and blame
it for many of the ills in our society. As a parent of eight children, I
have found that TV is the worst thing in our house. When it's on, the
kids just sit there, watching it like zombies. They don't interact, except to fight over the channel. They don't read, they don't play, they
don't talk to each other. Do their homework? You've got to be kidding! They don't do anything. They sneak downstairs, stay up late
watching, and wind up depressed and unable to function.

I have solved this problem by replacing our old larger-screen set with one very small portable, the kind you can easily pick up and throw in the car. And this is precisely what I do now, every Monday morning. I take the TV to work and don't bring it home till the weekend.

My kids have now discovered computers, Little League, basketball, pottery classes. They play board games with each other; they talk; they read. It's amazing. The other night I came home and the whole family was gathered around while my wife was reading to them. I'm serious. I thought I was in the wrong house. It was like *Little House on the Prairie*.

The negative effects of TV go beyond zombieism. They even go beyond the violence, irresponsible sexual partnering, and general immorality that characterizes most shows. TV is actually destroying people's ability to think, to concentrate, to have the patience that is necessary to complete a long-term project.

The problem is in the nature of the medium itself. In order to accommodate commercials, all actions much reach a conclusion in, at most, a five-minute segment. Most total shows must be completed in a half hour. From years and years of being exposed to this medium for hours a day, people's minds have come to function in these same short clips. No one can concentrate on an idea for more than five minutes. Articles in *People* magazine and even in *Newsweek* have become snippets rather than the in-depth reporting of times past. Print advertisements, instead of describing product benefits, have become just logos with feeling. Politicians speak in sound bites rather than putting out detailed position statements.

Whereas once we were a nation with the patience to read through an entire book or sit through a movie drama like *Gone With the Wind* as it unfolds, now we can just make it through enough of *Seinfeld* to visit the fridge during commercials.

Our short attention spans are reflected in our changing sports preferences, as well. Once the American pastime was baseball. Sure, sometimes you'd have to wait through three innings till your favorite player came up to bat. Meanwhile, each player, as an individual, would have his own moment of drama facing the pitcher, and the whole team would be dependent just on him, just as in real life, where success is not just a function of our group identity, but of our own individual achievements. Sure, nothing might happen for an hour, till some great play would bring you to your feet. But this was a true reflection of life. Not every minute is your wedding or D-Day. Good things require patience to develop.

No longer. Now the great American sport is basketball, a game where five pituitary cases endlessly run back and forth across the court, throwing the ball first at this basket and then at that. Each minute is packed with action. Each minute is not that much different than the last. The beginning of the game is not that much different from the end. Basketball is a lot like TV, not much like baseball.

This lack of patience manifests itself even more ominously in our political and economic lives. Let IBM have just one bad quarter, one quarter in which they decide to reinvest and change direction rather than exploit the present for all it's worth, and their stock value will fall by billions or tens of billions. Across the world, corporate chieftains are making decisions based solely on the quarterly numbers rather than on the long-term prognosis, trying to satisfy investors and mutual fund managers brought up in a TV culture. Investors are barely able to wait till the next quarter or commercial break to hit the remote control and change channels or trade stock.

Divorce has become the quick fix solution to normal marital turbulence. Politicians watching every new poll switch long-held positions overnight. They change laws, and the very foundations on which society has come to depend and function, as quickly and easily as the voters change their positions or their channels or their spouses. Are we all nuts? Don't we realize that good things come only with time and patience? Don't we realize that businesses, societies, and relationships need long-term goals and plans to succeed?

I must confess that for this reason I generally keep off the Internet (in spite of my company IDT's role as the country's second largest independent provider of Internet services). The medium is simply too surfacy. People jump from Web site to Web site without actually ever getting into the heart of any topic. They grab just one little fact and— zap!—they hit a hot link to jet to another site in even less time than it takes till the next commercial. Sure, it's better than the pure garbage you get from TV, but even if people are picking up random facts, is anybody really learning anything? Would someone left in front of the Internet for ten years come out as worldly as the same person left in a library? No way! Computer aficionados may hate me for saying this (and some might even cancel service with me), but I repeat: No damn way!

I can't change everything, but three things are for sure. I'm going to keep reading, keep being a baseball fan—and pretty much ignore TV. I will keep throwing the set in the back of the car every Monday morning. And Wall Street can go to hell. I'm going to ignore the quarterly numbers and run my business for the long run. In the end, this will make them switch to me, anyway.

But back on campus, reading garbage magazines and watching mind-numbing TV programs five hours a day could not completely offset the effect of living in the Harvard environment the whole rest of the time. Slowly, inexorably, as my mannerisms and tastes were becoming slightly more upscale, so, too, were my mail-order ads. Whereas before my ads were designed only to appeal to the lowest classes ($1 horoscopes, for instance), suddenly the bent of these ads started appealing to those who, like myself, were searching to raise their status. In other words, the great middle class.

My dorm became full of endless parades of graphic artists and photographers whom I was hiring to class up my ads. Now I was selling gourmet "coffee of the month." Years before the advent of Starbucks and Martha Stewart, we were photographing a large array of expensive coffees arranged Ralph Lauren–like on oak steps in burlap bags.

Fresh from a course in Asian history, rather than trying to move out a load of teak chopsticks I had acquired cheap, I billed them as "authentic imperial chopsticks" in celebration of the two thousandth anniversary of the Hang Dynasty, complete with a booklet of authentic recipes from that era.

Plants, however, remained my first love. I had been content to sell Venus's-flytraps masquerading as pet plants, but now I wanted something better. I needed a plant with real class, a plant that said you'd arrived just as certainly as a Mercedes or Jaguar in the driveway. I needed the Beverly Hills plant.

Unfortunately for me, G-d is very democratic when it comes to farmers. More or less, you get what you plant. Plant a radish, get a radish. Plant a watermelon, get a watermelon. Plant a rose, get a rose. Radishes, watermelons, and roses, therefore, are as available to the poor as to the affluent—all you need is a seed and a pot. Sure, a kumquat or a kiwi out of season is somewhat of a luxury item, but really, how many people are going to buy a kiwi tree for their living room so their friends and neighbors will think they've arrived?

Then I heard about a plant that only the very rich had. A plant that could cost over a thousand dollars each. A plant with real status. The bonsai tree. These dwarf Japanese trees were carefully bred over years, and sometimes generations, to completely resemble their full-sized counterparts. The only difference was that where the natural tree might grow from a seed to be a hundred feet tall or more, the bonsai, subject to continuous pruning and constraint, was allowed to grow to only eighteen inches or less. A full-sized ancient tree you could put on a coffee table. Now, that was class!

There was only one problem. Even in my upscale mode, I specialized in mail-order items that sold for $10 or less. How many lunatics were going to send me $1,000 through the mail for a bonsai tree? I needed a way to reduce costs by better than $990 per item if this idea was going to work. Even volume purchasing wasn't going to help me here. I needed a better idea. And I got one.

True, there is a big difference between *full-grown* regular trees and *full-grown* bonsai trees, due to the special care with which bonsais are raised. But there is absolutely no difference between a regular, newly grown seedling and one that is to become a bonsai tree. All seedlings could be bonsai trees if they were raised that way. It's just a state of mind. In fact, if you just gave people a little booklet telling them how to raise their seedlings into bonsai trees, anyone could do it (providing they have a few thousand hours to spare, but why bother with details?). Why, with a little booklet, a $2 nursery seedling (wholesale cost 27¢; cost after packaging and mailing, 65¢) was a bonsai tree. You could even tell people what they were getting, but show them a picture of a full-sized bonsai tree in the ad just so they got the idea.

And thus "Baby Bonsai Trees" ($1.99 plus postage and handling), one of the most popular ads in the history of the mail-order business, was born. It's easy to read those words; it's difficult to imagine what it meant in reality. Suddenly I was placing ads everywhere, not just in the *National Enquirer* and *Star*, but in *TV Guide*, in Dow Jones publications, in daily newspapers, in Sunday supplements. The country was going bonsai crazy. For just $1.99 and postage and handling ($7.50 for all four varieties offered in the ad; few people took just one), you could have class. Now, that was a bargain!

The real challenge, though, was shipping the thousands of orders for bonsai trees that arrived at our offices by the sackful daily. The problem had to do with a misunderstanding between Mother Nature and the U.S. Postal Service. The U.S. Postal Service, you see, says all orders must be shipped within thirty days of being received. Mother Nature, however, says it takes at least ninety days for a seed to grow into a seedling.

For the first few thousand trees this was no problem. The large commercial nursery we were dealing with had thousands of extra seedlings on hand that they were more than happy to ship to us by air. I would drive down from college, load my old station wagon with cardboard crates of young trees, and drive them to my packing storefront in the Bronx. A few sprays of water, a plastic bag around the base, pop them into mailing boxes, put on an address label, and just count the profits.

Then the orders really began.

Soon the crates could no longer fit into my station wagon, but had to be piled five and six high on the roof and securely tied down for the trips from the airport. The bumper of the car would drag on the ground from too much overload. The tower of boxes atop the car would sway back and forth. Debbie, in a panic, would be hanging out the window checking if the ropes were still holding while I, unable to see her through the trees piled between us and barely able to see the road with trees on the dashboard, would slowly drive the car over the Whitestone Bridge, hoping not to be stopped by the police.

That we or some poor soul behind us weren't killed or injured on one of these tree runs from the airport was a miracle. On arrival, workers would fall over the car unloading trees. No longer was there time for water spritzing. Plastic bags were attached, and off they went.

Those ordering redwoods got juniper, those ordering junipers got cherry. Whatever came out of the box first, that was what you got. We had lost all control. In the days before computerized inventory control and tracking, we were just in a crazed frenzy to get out trees. Some people's orders were filled two or three times, some not at all. No matter. Just complain and we'd send you another tree. Complain twice, and we'd send you two trees. If not for an almost 90 percent profit margin, we would have gone broke for sure. Still, the orders kept coming.

Back at Harvard I kept ordering more and more ads, unaware that with my departure the "troops" in New York had lost their fighting spirit and were now in a malaise, mechanically continuing to send out trees, but not at a frenzied pace. The backlogged cartons of trees were growing by the day, unwatered and dying. The complaints were be-ginning to pour in, draining the profitability from the business. My father was in a panic phoning me at school, calling my staff "lazy, rotten tree-killers." No matter, because soon the nursery was out of trees. Soon all nurseries in Florida were out of trees. Soon we exhausted all the nurseries in California and were starting to scour other states—and still the orders kept coming.

Soon, the U.S. attorney general's office was calling me too, a small matter of mail-order fraud. Not knowing what to do, with exams coming up and making it impossible to go to New York to supervise shipping, I finally did the only thing I could. I cut the advertising, giving up most of the potential profit on my most successful mail-order promotion, and slowly we caught up with the backlog.

The whole experience taught me a lesson about absentee management (though it would take a few more disasters to drive it into my consciousness). Absentee management is an oxymoron. It doesn't exist. When the cat's away, the mice will play. It's that simple. Uninspired phone-holding managers who are only interested in drawing a paycheck will do their job lackadaisically at best, and steal you blind at worst. If you want a superhuman effort (and in today's competitive environment nothing less will suffice), you'd better do it yourself.

But as businesses get larger, do-it-yourself is often impossible. That's why, to grow, you'll need to surround yourself with a cadre of highly competent, highly trusted, highly motivated managers with an equity position to whom the business's success matters as much as it does to you. Only those parts of your organization that are directly supervised by one of these individuals, or supervised by a like-minded assistant manager reporting to one of these individuals, will function to the highest quality level. One weak link and the chain of competence and caring is destroyed.

It's fine to mouth platitudes about the importance of the little people in an organization, and, for sure, they matter. But what really matters is the top people. If they're good, they'll see that everyone under them is good (or becomes good, or leaves). I'd gladly trade a million dollars in sales for one top manager, because you can do many times that much with a good manager.

One more word about absentee management. Beware of distance. Out of sight is out of mind. Every caution regarding running businesses or parts of businesses with strange hands goes double or triple when the operation is in a foreign country or different city. Believe me, I know. Unless you're prepared to sacrifice and deploy your very best people to manage your field operations, you're best advised not to undertake them at all.

I know this isn't the common wisdom in the era of decentralization, but remember, autonomy is only as good as the people autonomy is given to, and the rewards system under which they're allowed to operate. By this I mean that capitalism functions well because the different players (businesses or businessmen) in the game profit or lose depending on how well they satisfy the demands of the marketplace and of profitability. You can't set up an autonomous operation without letting the managers function in this same manner, judging and rewarding them and their division based on their profitability and productivity, not on arbitrary criteria like the amount of time they're in the office. You can't control everything, from near or from far, so let this be your simple rule: Everyone needs a guiding hand. If it's not your hand, then it better be the invisible hand.

I've learned over the years that one of people's most fundamental needs is to better themselves. The wise can harness this phenomenon for monetary benefits as well. All the products and services you offer will sell much better, or for a much bigger markup, if the idea of self-improvement or upward mobility (not necessarily in the economic sense) is packaged with it. People are thus more inclined to buy products that confirm they are more on the cutting edge (sexier or smarter, richer, younger . . .) or soon will be, than a similar product that just does its job. Perhaps even more importantly, people only *want* to be involved in activities that confirm them in their dreams. Fat people want to be thin, poor people rich, rich people respected. Weight Watchers, Amway, adult education programs, sports cars—they're all reflections of people's dreams and ongoing desires to be more than they currently are. This is good. When people stop dreaming and aspiring, they may as well die. There's nothing left for them.

This is as true of taking a job as it is of buying deodorant. Sure, if they're desperate, anyone will take any job. But top people really dream of running their own giant companies, or making their own decisions, of having their own autonomy. If you can make this possible for people within a corporate environment, you can get people who might otherwise leave to risk starting their own businesses. These, I believe, are the very best people to have. When looking for top managers, what I'm really looking for are people who are just as good as me and would make formidable competitors. The challenge, then, is to give them enough autonomy and opportunity that they feel like they are in business for themselves, or at least partners with you.

Obviously, this can't go on forever. Not all new hires will have the same closeness to the boss or opportunity to have their talents recognized as the original ones. While everything should be done to allow employees to show their talents—and while the difference between a great organization and a mediocre one lies in the ability to recognize and give autonomy and responsibility to this young talent—the fact remains that when employees number in the thousands, this becomes more and more difficult and eventually impossible. This fact is not to be mourned, however. If things didn't work this way, the larger companies' business would just keep growing until eventually one or two companies would dominate the world, leaving no room for anyone else.

Recently, I was on a panel with IBM's most famous inventor, who was also the head of one of their research labs in California. He was lamenting the fact that excellence in research wasn't really recognized or compensated for properly. Because of this, he'd already lost some of his best people and might lose many more in the years to come. But that is a necessary problem that he can't avoid. Surely, I told him, you wouldn't want IBM or Microsoft to dominate the world without room for mobility.

You see, these sorts of self-correcting mechanisms, which ensure no single family or company gets too powerful, all protect the economy. The children of rich industrialists, for instance, generally don't work as hard to get ahead as the children of less wealthy immigrants. Believe me, I know. At Bronx Science and Harvard I went to school with both groups. Every day, the sons of alumni fill the tennis and squash courts. The scholarship children of grocery store owners are filling the libraries and labs. This virtually ensures a massive wealth shift over the next generation. And that's good.

Back to the mail-order business, though. Even having cut back my advertising schedule, I was one of the largest mail-order advertisers in the country. Even more important, I was one of the few whose ads were wholesome enough and broad-based enough in their appeal that they could run successfully in virtually any publication in the country. This brought me to the attention of some shady "businessmen" anxious to establish a relationship with me.

It is a much-glossed-over fact that there is a strong historical connection between the mob and many of the country's leading newspaper and magazine publishers. Moses Annenberg, whose family was until recently owners of *TV Guide*, the country's largest-circulation magazine, had his start running a racing wire in the twenties.

Many other publications had similar original backing. Perhaps more importantly, newsstand (and later supermarket) distribution of periodicals and papers around the country has long been controlled by mob-backed unions. It is a well-known fact that new publications wanting premium placement need only pay the right-connected someone, and presto, the magazine is suddenly on newsstands. Cross the wrong people, and even an established magazine suddenly has circulation problems. Finally, the porn industry is a Mafia-connected business, and the biggest money market for newsstands are the "skin" magazines.

These skin magazines are not exactly the place where Procter & Gamble wants to advertise Pampers. In fact, no legitimate advertiser wants to risk being associated with the skin rags. They are, therefore, dependent for ad revenue on mail-order ads. Guess who sells these ads? You got it. You want to advertise in the magazine at a good rate? You go to them.

Once the mechanism was set up to sell mail-order advertising, they didn't want to stop with skin magazines, though. How about all those other magazines the union drivers were distributing? Surely the publishers would allow a special, discounted mail-order rate if you came through the "right agency." You wouldn't, after all, want to risk the "efficiency" of your newsstand distribution, plus its good business. Mail-order firms can't afford to pay fifty grand a page like Budweiser, Nike, or General Foods. They need a discounted rate. It's sort of hard, though, for the magazine's advertising sales staff to be selling ads for full price to one guy and at more than half off to another. Why not just farm out the job to someone else and let them keep part of the revenue for themselves? Mail order's not that big a deal anyway. And why get the wrong people upset? Guess who you have to buy the ads through? You got it again! Incredible!

It's my experience that you deal with these guys with caution and you always pay your bills.

But usually you don't even have to pay your bill when you work with these guys. They pay them for you and become your partner. Isn't that a great deal? Well, maybe not, but given the fortune it costs to advertise nationally, it's a deal few small-time mail-order promoters can resist. Here's how it goes.

You run a mail-order ad once or twice in a publication, and you pay for it. If the ad is highly successful, meaning that it pulls in more than double what it costs, leaving ample margin to pay for the merchandise and still turn a profit, then they run the ad once or twice at their own expense with the response going to them to make sure it really works. You ship out the merchandise at your own expense for the privilege of being considered for this partnership relationship. If the ad is successful, a deal is struck. The deal typically goes like this.

They'll spend half a million on advertising, the first half million of which comes back to them. After that, you get the money you need to ship the merchandise. After you both cover (this assumes at least $750,000 in sales) the money is split as follows: One-third of each dollar goes to you to pay for the actual cost (and you better not cheat) of the merchandise. The balance is divided 75 percent for them, 25 percent for you. You put up no money. You have no risk (unless your ad does less than $750,000 in sales, in which case you could be out $100,000 or so to pay for the merchandise) and you get 25 percent of the profit. If the ad really does well, they'll even put up another million or more.

The market for bonsai trees, pet plants, chopsticks, and the like seemed almost unlimited, however. Not only that, but running these kinds of ads could legitimatize their "agency," allowing them to keep ads going in all the legitimate publications they had "arrangements" with, but for which they had no wholesome advertising to place.

There was only one problem. I didn't want to deal with them. I knew enough about "connected" people from my hot dog days to know when to be careful. I didn't want any partners. And I didn't like any deals where I took the risk of paying for merchandise while getting only 25 percent of the profit. I did want to avail myself of their big publication discounts, however, and so I started to buy from them. (Who else could you buy from?)

When they saw the volumes I was doing, they kept pushing for a partnership, withholding valuable discount and remnant deals (bargain basement price on last-minute, unsold ad space) until I relented. Finally we made a deal. I'd let them run some advertising, but on every order I got the cost of merchandise before the money went into the ad kitty. Then once the ad was paid we'd split fifty-fifty.

The arrangement worked fine until I had to cut back on advertising because of my shipping problems. If I could only run a limited schedule, why not pay for everything myself and keep 100 percent? Sure, there'd be some risk, but I'd be making double the profit. The "agency" didn't like my idea. I was jeopardizing their relationship with big periodicals. Pulling out now was just unacceptable, they said. "Fine," I countered, "then pay me ninety percent of the profit and you can keep running the ads."

"No way," they said, "no one gets ninety percent."

"Fine, then I'll just place my own schedule."

"We need to talk," they said.

"Well, I've got exams," I replied.

"Fine," they replied. "We'll come up and visit you, Perfessor."

"You're gonna visit me? At Harvard? You gotta be kidding!"

"Nah, business is business. The top guy and the boss's son will be there next Wednesday."

I should've been scared. Instead, I was excited. Wow! I was going to have visitors. Real visitors, not just local graphic artists or photographers. Important visitors. From New York. Guys with suits and ties who were going to take a plane and a limousine and come to visit me right in my dorm room. Now, this was exciting. I had to prepare. I had to clean up. I had to decorate. I needed hors d'oeuvres. I needed help. I called Debbie.

We had no coffee table, but the trunk in my closet when covered with a doily sufficed. The bed covered over with a bedspread borrowed from one of Deb's roommates doubled as a couch. Real men, I knew, drank liquor at business meetings, but which kind I didn't know. An assortment of a dozen airline-sized miniatures purchased from the local liquor store and lined up on my dresser, along with sodas and ice cubes, looked good and should be enough to quench any thirst. Why, all I needed to do was drag in an armchair and everything was ready.

I already knew the big guy from New York. I liked him. The feeling was mutual. It was sort of nice, just the feeling of having him visit me here. The boss liked the finer things, though. Soft Gucci loafers, silk shirts, diamond initialed cuff links. That's probably one of the reasons he came to Harvard. Boston. Cambridge. Ivy. Tennis. Class. The good things.

My seven-by-twelve single garret room on the Radcliff quadrangle wasn't what he was expecting. You could see the disappointment on his face as he wondered whether he was really going to sit on this bed or not.

Then Debbie came in with stuffed mushrooms, and suddenly the big guy (and the boss's son) were in a good mood. Like Amelia Bedelia's lemon meringue pie, the mushrooms turned everything around. Now it was like family and Uncle Big Guy was just coming up to the dorms to visit. After picking out and drinking the little bottles of Chivas (now I remember—scotch, of course!) on my dresser, we sat down to talk.

When they got into their waiting car two hours later, I was the first person the "agency" had ever given an eighty-twenty deal to. They lovingly called me a "son of a bitch," while cuffing me on the neck. Frankly, I think I could have held out for ninety-ten if I really wanted. But they were, after all, putting up all the money and taking all the risk and they'd had to come all the way up to Cambridge. Plus, I've never thought it's a good idea to take the last scrap off the table. You gotta let the other guy make money too if you want to succeed.

This is one of the few topics on which I've always disagreed with my father. From the time I was very young, he often took me on business appointments as he went about building his insurance business. From these experiences I learned the money in our family didn't grow on trees. This helped prevent me from becoming the sort of spoiled second-generation-type kid I've written about. I frequently take my kids to work with me for the same reason (and also because I like their company). A second thing I saw, though, was how my dad, who lost his own father at a young age and had to help support his household before he was even ten, would squeeze the last penny out of a business deal. This, I would tell him, was a bad idea. How was the other guy going to live? What level of service would he deliver? Wouldn't he turn around and leave you the first chance he got? Wouldn't it be better to spend a little more and get the guy's loyalty and build an enduring relationship? My father just said I was soft and kept doing it his way. For him, it works. He's first-generation. He doesn't have a huge organization of talented egos or dozens of key suppliers to cater to, but he doesn't need it. He's willing to do everything on his own and find a new supplier whenever an existing relationship ends.

I, having the benefit of being second-generation (yes, there are benefits), and perhaps, indeed, being a little soft, see things differently. On any individual deal I never make or extract quite as much as I could. In this way, I make less than I might have. On the other hand, I've had profitable relationships with some of my suppliers and agents that have lasted over twenty years (and I'm only about forty now, I remind you). I also have attracted an unbelievably great staff which has stayed with me for years. In this way, I think, on balance I'm much richer. You may not be able to immediately calculate the value of a relationship, an employee, or a potential referral, but they're part of your wealth, just as surely as money in the bank. The money can, after all, be lost, but some of the relationships might sustain you for a lifetime.

My great-aunt Anna (who died much too young at eighty-nine) used to say a good name is worth all the riches in the world. While in today's world of easy bankruptcies and easy credit this may be less applicable than in times past, the fundamental truth remains. The good opinion of the people around you is more important than the number of chips you have at any given minute.

This is not to say that you should be an easy-hearted fool who just gives everything away in business. Quite the contrary, you should be a cheap son of a bitch who fights for every nickel and gets a reputation for never being cheated. It's just that after you get done fighting and have determined exactly how far against the wall you can push the other guy, it's a good policy, if possible, to take a step back and give him some breathing room. Over the long run, you'll both breathe easier for it.

With the agency bankrolling me (even my test ads), business

started to run as smoothly as clockwork. Across America people were buying our imperial chopsticks, phone headrests, police warning light, and handwriting analysis. But mostly they bought our plants. The items sold year-round—spring, summer, winter, and fall. But it was in the fall, particularly in those months before Christmas, when things really went wild. Everyone, it seemed, was ordering our items to give as holiday gifts. Our big surge, though, came at least a month earlier than it did in stores. People knew they had to allow at least a month to receive items ordered from the paper and so by the last week in November the flood of orders would drop considerably. People would order anything, it seemed, as long as they were sure they'd have it in time to put under their Christmas tree. Ironically, the main thing we were sending people to put under their Christmas trees were trees. This gave me an idea.

Why not sell people the Christmas trees themselves? I mean, everybody would want a Christmas tree. Not the regular big, bulky *dead* tree you bought on the corner and had to throw away, but a real live baby Christmas tree, the kind you could decorate and put on the coffee table. The kind you could replant outdoors after Christmas instead of putting in the trash. The kind that would live and grow and that you could redecorate every year. The kind of tree that every day of the year would remind you of Christmas.

This time I'd finally done what Irving Berlin did when he wrote "White Christmas." I'd tapped into the deepest part of the American soul and I'd hit a wellspring. A Christmas tree with its own decorations (they were free, of course), which would live forever. Not all the nurseries in the world could fill the demand.

Thankfully, the agency was only able to place a quarter of the ads they wanted to because we had missed most pre-Christmas closing deadlines. In fact, only by guaranteeing in the ad that all orders postmarked by December 15 would be delivered in time for Christmas (provided the customer included $2 extra for the newly implemented Express Mail service) were we able to place ads as late as we did.

This time the mail didn't arrive by the tray or even the sack. It arrived by the truck. I kid you not. The local post office sent out a truck just to bring us our mail.

This time I wouldn't be caught unprepared again. I ordered every evergreen tree from every large nursery in three states flown in immediately. (No worrying about overordering. Any extras were destined to become bonsai trees.) I had thousands of strips of small cut-out decorations printed. I hired my sister's whole cheerleading squad to help with the shipping. I was on winter break from school and I'd supervise the shipping myself. This time there'd be no screwup. In the battle between Howard and any shipping Grinch who was planning to steal Christmas from my customers, Howard was going to win.

But even I couldn't have anticipated the tidal wave of orders. A wave that just kept getting bigger and bigger. In fact, people seemed to think that December 15 wasn't the final deadline to order. They seemed to think that was the day you had to order. And fully a third of everyone did. Thus, on December 20 as I sat surrounded by sacks of orders, all of which had to be shipped by five P.M. on December 23 to be received by Christmas, I could see I was in trouble.

I called in the reinforcements. Every nerd I ever knew in high school was offered a job. Every cheerleader in the Bronx was summoned. Even people walking down the street were offered jobs. Like a presidential candidate at the end of the campaign, we were going all-out. For the next seventy-two hours, no sleep. This was going to be a marathon. The trees would get there by Christmas.

We lived on McDonald's and beer. We were exhausted. We were tipsy. We couldn't think straight. Father Eric kept playing Burl Ives singing Christmas carols on his eight-track to keep our spirits up. Every time "Rudolph the Red-Nosed Reindeer" came on we all sang along. Everything anyone said appeared hysterically funny and we all kept going into fits of inappropriate laughter. We were working harder than the elves to get the trees out for Christmas. Suddenly the nerds, many of whom had never even been on a date, seemed very attractive and funny to the cheerleaders. This was some pajama party!

Keep packing. Just keep packing trees.

And then, halfway through, disaster struck. Just past two A.M. on the night of December 22, the decorations ran out. These little branches couldn't support real decorations, and who wanted a tree without decorations? The printers could never make more in time. Father Eric, who at twenty was quite the traditionalist (now, as an established pastor, he's an outspoken advocate for liturgical changes in the Episcopal Church), suggested we send out traditional decorations. What, I wanted to know, were traditional decorations? Traditional decorations, he told me, were popcorn and cranberries, which people could string on a thread and hang from their tree. They were, he went on, natural. They were inexpensive. Christmas didn't have to be all commercial and tinsel. It should be traditional.

I didn't need much convincing. Inexpensive! Of course I was for tradition. At three A.M., when the city's wholesale fruit market opened, Eric and the cheerleaders were there. Half an hour later our storefront was filled with the smell of popping corn. People stuffed Baggies with all the cranberries and popcorn they weren't eating with the beer or laughingly throwing at each other. By 5 P.M. on the twenty-third, we had done it! We'd shipped out every last tree. I went home to go to sleep. Some of the others were already sleeping on the floor. We did it! Triumph. Exhaustion. I'd think about it when I woke up.

Do you know what a postal processing machine does to cranberries and popcorn in Express Mail envelopes? Does "mush" mean anything to you? The evergreens were fine. G-d made these trees to resist heavy rain, sleet, and other stresses. He apparently didn't do the same with popcorn and cranberries. It probably never occurred to Him that some lunatic from the Bronx would decide to send thousands of them through the mail.

On the morning of December 24, when people opened the mail and saw the decorations, most of the people didn't worry, but were just glad to get their tree. And who knows, probably most of the popcorn and cranberries made it through all right. But some weren't so happy—enough so that pretty soon consumer protection agencies and reporters across America were hearing about the "outrageous fraud" we'd perpetrated. We'd sent people squished cranberries and popcorn in a plastic bag with a note that read, "traditional Christmas decorations." We were just trying to make fun of them. Something had to be done.

You can easily explain away how a chopstick could break in the mail or a pet plant fail to arrive. Just send a new chopstick or pet plant and everything's okay. But to deliberately go out and try to destroy Christmas—to send people cranberry mush and goad them with a cryptic note? There were no amends for this kind of outrage. This was a crime that needed to be punished. This was a crime that could get some assistant attorney general some real publicity and really launch his career.

Only our tens of thousands of Express Mail receipts, showing the volume of trees shipped and the fact that the ad never specified what kind of decorations were to be shipped, got us off the legal hook. But not before I got a really good scare. And this didn't stop the consumer reporters from having a field day with us.

The last straw came via my dorm room TV shortly after winter break. Sharon King, the local NBC affiliate's ace consumer reporter, was on with a really big story of a consumer fraud. You guessed it, our trees.

Seems some mother of a Vietnam soldier killed in action ordered a tree to plant and decorate at her son's grave. Imagine her distress when she got the tree and found crushed cranberry popcorn. Of course, she didn't plant the tree. She couldn't. She sent it to NBC. And there it was now, three weeks later, unwatered, almost dead. And there was the cranberry Baggie, now fermented, with the note: "Traditional Christmas decorations." "Let's all give a Bronx cheer for this company," the moderator intoned.

"Oh, come on! I can't believe this!" I yelled at the screen. "I didn't kill this woman's son. I only sent her a tree. What am I, the devil or something?" I'd just about had it with the mail-order business. This wasn't fun at all.

A few weeks later, Alfred Chandler, a DuPont heir and one of the most esteemed professors at the Harvard Business School, invited me into his office. (By now the administration was allowing me to take most of my courses there, even though I was an undergraduate.) "Jonas," he said, "in class you seem like a bright young man and I've heard you run a decent-sized business. Could you describe it to me?" I proudly told him, in detail, about the mail-order business. How I conceived the ads, tested them, found the merchandise; I told him about the agency, the shipping, everything. When I was done, he told me, "Really, you can do more with your life than that. Why, you're just one step above a pushcart peddler."

That hurt. More deeply than Professor Chandler could have imagined. Yeah, I was frustrated with the mail-order business. At best it was selling junk, and at worst it could get you into serious trouble. Not only that, but I wasn't there to watch it. Someone else was always losing the orders, not watering the trees, or failing to order enough decorations. The someone else was always in New York and I was always in Boston. I could have solved at least some of my problems by doing one simple thing: moving the mail-order business to Boston.

But I couldn't. For one thing, I didn't want to unemploy my old staff or break my family ties with New York. This was only part of the story, though. The bigger part is that I couldn't decide what I was. Part of me wanted to be a young, rough-edged hustling businessman, but part of me really did want to be Harvard—educated, cultured, above the fray, someone Professor Chandler could be proud of. I was leading a double life. And it was putting a tremendous strain on me. I wasn't giving all my heart to the mail-order business, but I wasn't giving it to Harvard, either. Everything was half-baked, tasteless, unsatisfying. Psychologically, I was coming apart. It had to be one way or the other. I chose Harvard. Who knew what a bad choice this would turn out to be?

I've since come to believe that the best thing in life is not to be compartmentalized. Not to be one person at work and a different one at home. Cheap one place, charitable elsewhere. Intellectual here, crude elsewhere. Associating with one group of people as co-workers and an entirely different type as friends. Not me. Not anymore. More than half of my friends work at IDT. My jeans are the same in both places. My house is not too much fancier than the office. I try to be consistent wherever I am.

I've read that Himmler would leave a concentration camp and hand out candy to the children gathered outside. He was obviously good at compartmentalizing. Not me. I won't buy a cheaper component at work if it comes from a totalitarian country any more than I'd buy "Made in China" shirts at home. It's not even that it's a virtue. I just can't take the strain of living behind different masks.

When it became clear to me that I couldn't live in two worlds, I chose Harvard, sort of. Sort of, I say, because I still wanted to be in business. Only this time, I'd go into a Harvard business. I'd hire Harvard men. We'd do Harvard-type things. No more pushcart peddler for me. We'd try again to be a legitimate advertising agency. I'd spend the summer working in New York, and then try to continue from Cambridge in September. I hired three sons of Harvard to begin my challenge to J. Walter Thompson and Young and Rubicam.

One of the guys I hired was a jock who was earning a good living babysitting and partying with the bored wives of Boston's financial elite. One of this young Casanova's demands (I kid you not) was that he had to take his bed with him wherever he went.

Superman goes nowhere without his cape; the Lone Ranger nowhere without his mask; Zorro nowhere without his sword; and my new director of marketing nowhere without his bed. (And to think I sometimes still complain about personnel problems!) Not only did we have to spend hours wrapping the maestro's mattress and bed before tying it triple to the roof of my car, but on the way down from Cambridge, when it began to rain, we had to spend hours in a Howard Johnson's as the car (and bed) sat dryly under an overhang waiting for the downpour to pass.

My only high point during this summer came during the Great Blackout of '77. As darkness fell (all of New York City was without power for close to twenty-four hours), rioting broke out in some deprived areas of the city. Some of this looting even extended to the Upper West Side, where Casanova and his bed were spending the summer.

Apparently the thought of rioting hordes scared him far more than Boston mutual fund managers returning home unexpectedly from the office, and he called me repeatedly. "What am I going to do? What am I going to do? Come save me!" he first demanded, later screamed, then cried.

"Listen, you're in a perfectly safe neighborhood," I assured him. "Okay, so some stores are being looted. The only thing you need to do is push your bed against the wall and pile all your furniture on it."

"Yeah, yeah. I'll do that," he panted.

I grinned all through the blackout.

As the summer drew to a close, we'd accomplished nothing but to seriously diminish my mail-order savings. All the Harvard men seemed to know how to do was have meetings and send memos. Boy, did they send memos. Only problem was they never landed any accounts, even with their great Harvard creative campaigns. They were always on the verge, while I was on the verge of wasting all my savings. At the end of the summer we went back to Cambridge with nothing to show for our efforts.

At first I was depressed, but I had my whole life ahead of me, and Harvard was almost behind me. And this time I was going to do it my way. No more double life. I was going back to New York in June and I was going into business. Which one? I didn't know. Just into business.

One last word on the problem of living in two worlds at the same time. Toward the end of my first year at Harvard, the *Crimson* (the official school newspaper) decided to do a story on student entrepreneurs attending the college. They were able to identify three. One was me.

Another student, who had gone into the stock brokerage business, was doing it the Harvard way. Football team jocks were selling his stock, economy majors were doing the analysis. English lit people were turning out the sales literature, and everyone was maintaining a full academic schedule. This was a pure Harvard operation. I mean, even when you went into his beautiful offices overlooking Harvard Square, the receptionist who greeted you was a Harvard cheerleader.

I heard from the guy years later. Things hadn't turned out so well for him at Harvard, and now he was down on his luck again, trying to sell salvage rights for abandoned oil wells.

Oh, what about the third guy? Well, he was smart. He realized you couldn't live in two worlds. He forgot about his Harvard degree and what that and all the Harvard contacts could mean to his career, and just dropped out. I knew some of his friends, but I never met him. I heard he was trying to get some of them to be partners and leave school with him. Maybe if he'd asked me, I would have gone. Too bad. Oh, his name? Bill Gates.

Chapter Four
Back to the Gutter

❖

Ilove going for rides in my car. If you ever need a lift or need to have anything delivered, just call me. I'm always thrilled to get on the road. And the longer the distance, the better. I love seeing the country and watching the trees go by. Other businessmen crowd the terminal at New York's LaGuardia, rushing to catch the next shuttle to Boston or Washington. Not me. I try to set my appointments later in the day so I'll have time to drive.

Of all the drives I've ever taken, though, there's one that stands out in my mind as the best. That was the final ride I took back to New York from college in June 1978. I had no idea where home was going to be. I would be staying just temporarily at my parents' till I could find a place of my own in the New York area. I also had little idea what I'd actually do once I got to New York. My businesses were all finished. All that was left from my once grand enterprise was one or two brochure distribution clients, who in spite of all our neglect steadfastly refused to cancel. The old '71 Plymouth Duster, with a mostly burned-out clutch and into which I'd squeezed all my possessions, wasn't much of a car.

But I was done with Harvard! I was free. I was young. I was healthy. I was ready for life to begin again. Like the wagon train pioneer of old, I was sure I was headed for the fertile promised valley. And every hill or lake or grove of flowering trees I passed seemed as beautiful to me in my Duster as it must've seemed to the pioneers from the wagons. You often hear people talk about being born-again Christians or born-again Jews, who've renounced their old lifestyle and embraced their new faith with such fervor that it's as if they've actually been born again. Well, I was a born-again schnook.

I'd left behind Harvard, elitism, graduate schools, liberal intellectuals, absentee management, Mafia funding, the whole ball of wax. Now I couldn't wait to start following the new path. I wanted to work my way up from the bottom as a working schnook. I wanted to answer my own single-line rotary phone in my own ramshackle office. I'd go to a secondhand store and buy a solid cheap used desk. I wanted to stay up late typing proposals with two fingers and, when they were accepted, push myself to do all the work alone so I could eke out a living. I wanted to slowly expand, first hiring a part-time secretary, then a full-time one. Eventually, salesmen, workers, skilled professionals would join me. We'd become big. We'd really make it. And I wouldn't owe anything to anyone, not Harvard, not anyone, 'cause I would've started from the bottom on my own. The bottom. What a great place. Could anything be more beautiful?

Even today when I pass used office furniture stores or go by overstated door plaques for obviously one-man enterprises in older buildings, I feel a thrill. I smell the mud at the bottom. New beginnings. Independence. Opportunity. You know, where the biggest tree starts to grow. From the dirt under the topsoil. I wanted to be like that tree. I was driving to New York so I could find a nice patch of dirt in which to plant myself.

I once read that whatever people really need, G-d gives in abundance. Air, water, the essentials, are plentiful and free. Grains, vegetables, fruit are usually cheap and just grow from the earth. The stuff we don't really need is rare and expensive.

I didn't think about a big fancy office, a prestigious position, or a Mercedes. All I wanted was a patch of dirt, a place to put my desk, and an opportunity. That was available everywhere.

I didn't even have to look. My old landlord gave me back my old space in his basement. No rent. I could pay something when I started making a living. The couple of brochure clients still around were happy to hear I was back. They said they'd recommend a couple of friends to use my hotel delivery service if I just started distributing efficiently again. No problem; what else did I have to do? I was back in the brochure business again. I even found a nice $250-a-month apartment. If I stuck to pasta, I could already support myself. Watch out, world, here I come!

Watch out, right. Not so fast. Used station wagons cost money. You have to work nineteen hours a day to distribute the brochures yourself all night and still be in the office all day to accept deliveries and sell your service to other clients. You have to bang your head against a lot of walls, make "cold calls" till your ego is shot, and still try to think of yourself as a tycoon in the making.

It helps to have a rich fantasy life. I talked to myself all the time. I turned car rides into wagon train expeditions, sales brush-offs into important opportunities, and the like. I guess I needed a lot of ego boosting, and who better to get it from than myself? On the other hand, it's important for people to dream and visualize success if they have any hope of achieving it. Peter the Great once dressed up in peasant clothes and went to Holland, where he wouldn't be recognized, to work in a shipyard and learn about real life without the impediments of having to be the Czar. It seems pompous or strange, I know, but for all the years I delivered brochures I imagined myself as a sort of corporate Peter the Great. Doormen might force me to use the servants' entrance. Stylishly dressed men and women might bump into me, knocking over my bundles, and walk away, treating me like furniture without even saying "I'm sorry." Former Harvard classmates, in town on business, would gawk and then feign nonrecognition as I knelt down filling the racks, but I was never embarrassed in the least. Under my deliveryman's disguise, I knew, lurked a future media magnate working his way up from the ground.

It was due to these deliveries that I actually made most of my sales.

In the various hotel lobbies I'd wind up finding varieties of brochures amateurishly self-distributed. Those businesses who'd gone to the effort of actually attempting to get their brochures into hotel lobbies on their own ended up being my easiest and most plentiful sales.

There is simply no substitute for being close to the market. I could have sat with my phone book for eternity and never figured out a calling list of places whose brochures I found in the lobbies. Most likely, even had I attempted a call, the receptionist wouldn't have let me through and I'd not have known to persevere in going after a sure slam dunk. Twenty years and hundreds of millions of dollars in sales later, I think this is still the cardinal rule of salesmanship and business: Stay close to the market and keep your ear to the ground.

There was one group of brochures that I periodically kept encountering and these were airline timetables and schedules. For the life of me, though, I could not get the airlines to sign on as my clients. Nevertheless, one or two older hotels had huge, ancient timetable racks tucked away in hidden corners of the lobby. From the look of the display, one would have thought that time and the hotel maintenance crew had forgotten this corner and that the schedules had been standing there for years. Surprisingly, though, the airlines schedules changed monthly. Who was putting them there?

For months no airline would take my calls. When they heard my call was related to brochure distribution, "We've already got that covered," they said. How could they consider themselves "covered," though, when only maybe two out of a hundred hotels in New York had their schedules? And those two were on the verge of closing for lack of business.

Finally, one airline executive told me they used a firm called Timetable & Folder Distributors, who handled their distribution for the whole mid-Atlantic region.

"But they're not doing anything," I protested. I'd seen unopened bundles of airline brochures in garbage pails behind hotel desks. "Everything is just getting dumped."

"Couldn't be," he told me. "We've been using these guys for as long as anyone can remember. Anyway, I can't really waste time wor-rying about brochures. We have more important marketing concerns. Sorry." And that was it. He didn't care what kind of job they were do-ing or what the airline was charged. And he was not alone. All the others felt the same way.

Maybe if I couldn't get the airlines as clients directly, I could con-vince Timetable to subcontract their distribution to me so that the material actually got displayed. I made an appointment and went to see them. I was amazed. It was as if you'd entered a time warp. The office filled the same floor they'd occupied in a lower Manhattan loft building for close to fifty years. The desks were all oak. The switch-board still required an operator to plug in wires to connect calls and there was a cavernous area still filled with boxes of brochures for tourist attractions or railroads that had been out of business for decades.

There was another strange thing. There were hardly any people to fill all the desks and packing stations. It was like a neutron bomb had wiped out all the people decades ago and left the facilities intact. Only a couple of women had apparently survived and kept the memory alive, running to plug in the switchboard before running back to an-swer the phone. No one ever made a sales call here. No one ever vis-ited. Not even the directors of the company.

Today, though, was a red-letter day for the staff. They were getting a visitor. Someone who wanted to do business with them. This was such an unusual occurrence that the firm's president, Herman Mehr, an elderly attorney who ordinarily showed up at the offices only for the nonattended annual shareholders' meeting, was today sitting at the ornate half-century-old chairman's desk waiting to see me.

"Mr. Mehr," I began, "I'm your competitor. I distribute brochures to all the hotels in New York. Here are photos of my displays and a list of my clients. You're in none of these hotels. You've just got one old rack in the Commodore and one in the Taft. Yet you've got all the airlines and I don't. I tried to get them from you, but I couldn't.

Sooner or later, though, we both know you're gonna lose them when someone up at marketing walks into a lobby and finds out your whole service is phony. Plus, you're obviously paying the driver plenty to run around and give out the packets, which are only getting thrown away. Why not pay the money to me and I'll give you real distribution?"

"I've got a different idea, young man," he said. "You seem full of energy. Why don't you just give me a hundred thousand dollars and buy the company, and you can do whatever you want? Then we can close down this money-losing operation, make a distribution to shareholders, sell the corporate assets, and fund everyone's pension plan so me and the girls can retire. Is the old man moving too fast for you?" He chuckled.

Mr. Mehr was practically dancing around the desk. Like Sleeping Beauty waiting for the prince, he must have spent decades, waiting, hoping, and praying for a competitor to emerge to buy him out. Now the prince had finally shown, and he was thrilled. "Let me see the books," I said.

The books showed that even though Timetable hadn't raised their prices in a decade, they were still taking in thousands a month from the airlines. All this money, though, was being spent distributing the brochures to hundreds of rural cities the airlines didn't even fly to. The balance was going to pay for the loft and the elderly dowagers who answered the phone, did the books, and sent out the bills. My free basement in the Bronx could easily replace the loft and an extra half hour's work a month could more than replace the output of Timetable's aged clerical staff. That would instantly put us in the black.

"Why are you distributing to all these rural towns?" I asked.

"Because we always have," he rejoindered.

"But why? You're distributing for the big airlines and they don't fly anywhere near these places."

"Well," he said, "this company was originally owned by the

railroads. They had to divest us after the 1919 antitrust action, but they remained our main accounts. And there were so many of them, over a hundred. That's why we got such big racks. Anyway, everywhere in the mid-Atlantic states where there was a railroad station, that's where we distributed. You shoulda seen the company then! We were really pumping. We had fleets of trucks, our own pier, offices all over the place. We were hot. Then the railroads started to go under. We got some airlines to replace them, but for every new airline that started, ten railroads went under. The company just lost its drive and everyone left."

"But why didn't you go after other kinds of tourism accounts?"

"I don't know. It just seemed low-class. We were all transportation guys, after all."

"Well, why didn't you just get rid of the rural areas and do a better job on the cities to suit the airlines?"

"Oh, I don't know," he said. "There were so few airlines and they just paid their bills and didn't ask any questions. We didn't want to shake them up by raising prices or changing distribution. They might have quit if we did, you know."

Ridiculous, I thought. Obviously the airlines only cared about New York, Washington, and maybe Philadelphia—the big cities they flew to. Seriously, was anyone going to take a timetable from a motel in Utica, and drive six hours to New York to catch a flight? Was any United Airlines sales director ever going to care about a motel in Utica? Obviously not. They wanted their stuff at the Hilton, Sheraton, and Holiday Inns near the airport. I could ditch Timetable's whole distribution system and do it all myself. If I bought this company, it would be 100 percent profit. Man, I wanted it bad.

Problem was, I'd lost almost all my money on the Harvard advertising agency fiasco.

"Well, a hundred thousand seems like an awful lot of money when all these airlines are about to quit," I said.

"Quit?" he said. "Who said they're quitting?"

"Why, you just did," I responded. "Not that I didn't know anyway. I mean, most of the guys I talked to said they might cut this out of their budget anyway."

This wasn't exactly true, but Mehr was clearly out of touch and easily alarmable.

"Look," I said, "I tell you what. I'll give you five thousand down and half of everything I take in for the next three years. If most of the accounts stay, that'll be even more than you're asking. You can have our payment, go right to the stockholders so you can dissolve the company now and sell the assets for yourself. I'll even base your fifty percent on the current billing rates so if we have to cut prices, you'll be protected." (I was, of course, intending to raise prices and didn't want to have to split the additional income.)

"I'll take it," he said.

Right away I realized I could have offered less, but in retrospect it was one of the best deals of my life, so I'm not complaining.

"There are certain assets I have to get, though."

"And what's that?" he asked.

"A van and some packing tables," I said, figuring that with the bigger operation I'd need them.

"Fine," he answered, glad I didn't want anything big.

"That's not all," I said. "I also want your desk and the corporate minute books going back to the beginning."

"Why would you want that?" he asked.

"If I'm buying this company, I want to know everything about it. About its history. What it did right. What it did wrong. Sixty years in business is a long tradition. It's my tradition now. That's why I gotta have the desk too."

"Fine," he said. "Is that all?"

"That's it."

"Then the deal's final?"

"Final," I agreed.

Right there he wrote up the contract and I gave him a personal check for the five grand. Afterward he told me, "You know, you could've gotten a lot more out of me than an old desk and some musty corporate books."

"Guess I'm not that sharp," I responded.

Maybe not sharp, but suddenly almost rich. Within two months we had stepped up urban distribution and gotten rid of the rural service. The airlines agreed to let us double their prices. Then they started introducing me to the competing sales managers whose airlines were not yet my accounts, and business doubled again.

Raising the prices when I changed the distribution schedule and getting the sales managers to bring in their industry colleagues wasn't an original idea. Timetable had done the same thing with the railroads thirty years before. I read about it in those worthless musty books the first night I bought the company.

I probably learned more from those books than in all my classes at Harvard. How to make a public company grow and how, if you don't keep up with the times and ignore the market, you can sink so low a boy barely out of school can buy you for five grand. Some of these lessons I wouldn't get to use till I was running my own public company decades later. Most, though, were applicable right away. Those books contained the history of an entire industry. All of their innovations and failures, all their great ideas and ridiculous notions were there for the reading. The corporate minutes from day one.

The most interesting thing I learned from taking over Timetable, though, was the tremendous value of hard-core clients. Most people looking at Timetable's business would have said, "What a disaster. Almost everyone's quit. This business is finished."

I saw the opposite. "What a great business. They've had these airline clients for thirty years, and no matter how bad the service is, they won't quit. You could probably break into the president's office, pee on the rug, and they'd just keep paying the bills. Imagine what you could make off these guys if you really serviced them!"

Business books nowadays all tell you: If you want to succeed and get or keep clients, you gotta be the best. You gotta anticipate their every need. You gotta stay close to them and spare no expense keeping them happy.

Bullshit. You heard me. Bullshit. I know this is the part of the book that is going to get quoted and taken out of context to portray me and IDT as a bunch of corporate ogres who mistreat our clients, but somebody needs to tell the truth. Not every client needs you to give him your heart, liver, and kidneys. In fact, if you spend all your money delivering unnecessarily high levels of service to every account, you will be broke and will deliver service to no one.

Clients are just like everyone else. They can be plotted on a bell curve. A few, at one extreme, require extraordinary amounts of attention. To keep these guys happy you have to literally anticipate their every need. You have to spend a fortune on them. Unless you're selling extremely high-margin luxury wares, you'll find that servicing clients whose demands put them at this end of the spectrum is a recipe for nothing but ulcers and insolvency.

In the middle of the curve are the vast majority of clients. They require a moderate amount of attention. Keep them on hold for over twenty minutes waiting for tech support and you'll lose most of them. There's no need to overstaff, though, in order to answer every phone on the first ring. They're not prima donnas; they'll gladly wait a minute or two on hold while you play them a pleasant message explaining that they'll be taken care of very shortly. These clients are profitable; they're the bread and butter of any business.

The real prize clients, though, are the few at the opposite extreme of the bell curve. They're the ones who pay no matter what. You can keep them holding for hours and they'll apologize for interrupting you when you answer. In truth, though, this rarely happens because they almost never call. They don't want to bother you. They solve their problems on their own. They may only log on to computer service for a few minutes a month, but they gladly pay as if they were on for hours a day. Servicing these clients costs you almost nothing, and they'll usually stay with you forever. These clients are often the ones that constitute your entire profit margin.

Think about it. In a typical service business maybe 10 percent of your gross take winds up as profit. And to do that well is rare. Here you can clearly see that it's really the few accounts at the far end of the spectrum—the ones who make no demands—who actually constitute the entire profitability of most service businesses. Everyone else is just a break-even or money-losing proposition.

The problem is that there's really no way when you're building a business to target getting only these kinds of clients. What are you supposed to do? Run ads saying, "We offer lousy, second-rate service, and if you're willing to put up with that, we're your guys"? Or perhaps, "A classified entrepreneur seeks sugar daddy clients who will pay their bills no matter what, for a long-term, financially secure relationship"? Obviously, this is foolish. the super-tolerant clients, like everyone else, sign up only because they feel your service gives them the most value for their money. It's only over time that their non-demanding status emerges.

Many businesses, however, that have been around a long time, particularly those whose problems have driven the most demanding accounts away, are huge repositories of just this sort of low-maintenance account. Often the business is losing money only because it is still trying to provide a service level to satisfy clients who are long gone. What a potential gold mine!

A normal business insists on starting by providing a high enough service level to attract all classes of new accounts. Usually, it loses money until it has accumulated enough of the nondemanding accounts to make a profit. In the case of a business with a long-established customer base you have the opposite case. You can actually lower the amount of money you spend to the point where the business is profitable. Then you can reinvest a part of the money this solidly profitable base produces to start offering premium service to new sign-ups and your existing base as well. Everyone will be delighted with your service and the business will even start to grow, attracting a certain percentage of even more of the profitable, low-maintenance accounts.

The lessons I learned acquiring Timetable I used many years later in the telecommunications business. When I bought the Genie on-line service from General Electric, everyone thought I'd gone nuts. America Online had clearly killed Genie in the on-line war. Everyone pointed out the over half a million clients who had quit Genie over the past three years. The service was a dinosaur. Could I possibly find a worse sinking ship to buy into? I, however, didn't care about the hundreds of thousands of clients who'd quit Genie. I was looking at the tens of thousands of clients who'd remained. These guys had been on for years. Many owned old computers that wouldn't work on any of the other modernized services. Sure, Genie was losing money because it was trying to replicate all AOL's newsfeeds and proprietary content. When I looked at the usage figure, though, I discovered no one was accessing this content anyway. All our remaining users wanted was to be able to send E-mail, chat, play games, and get on the net. These services cost almost nothing to provide.

I took over Genie, cut the expensive stuff no one wanted, polished up the user interface, and raised prices. Most users stayed right on with us and suddenly we were making millions in profit on the dog everyone had laughed at. Soon we even started getting more accounts by going after the niche market of machines that only have an ability to show text without graphics. We may not be AOL, but unlike them, we make money every quarter.

Similarly, when people advised us to abandon the Internet business, I looked at how many long-term users we had and decided to cut back and just service them. Without the huge expense associated with holding the hands of new users, we turned very profitable. When some of the profits were plowed back into the service, we suddenly became the best in the country. Discerning clients who were already Internet savvy then started coming to us.

Much of what I did in the Internet business was based on what I learned from the Timetable books. I'd absorbed it all like a sponge. When IDT went public in 1995, I went back to the Timetable minutes once again for guidance. The directors of Timetable and Folder Distributors, Inc., held my hand across five decades and helped me make the critical decisions.

Chapter Five
One Step Above the Pushcart

❖

Timetable's acquisition and its subsequent growth generated so much work that I started to get overwhelmed. I now had to deliver brochures not only in New York, but in Philadelphia and Washington as well. I would drive two hundred and fifty miles to Washington, work twenty-four hours delivering all my brochures, detour fifty miles to spend twelve hours delivering in Philadelphia, and then return to New York. I'd work all day and into the night in the office talking to airlines and tourist attractions and then spend the whole late night and early morning for three days delivering in the city. Fridays I'd work a full day and then drive two hundred miles to Boston to see Debbie, making sure to return by three A.M. Sunday morning so I could get in a full day's work on Monday before leaving for Washington again.

I know I said I love to drive, but this was getting to be too much, even for me. I was on the way to putting a hundred thousand miles a year on my car. Half the time I was on the road. I was so tired I kept seeing spooks running across the highway. I'd slap myself to stay awake. One time a state trooper pulled up as I was stopped along Interstate 95 in Delaware.

"Why," he wanted to know, "are you doing push-ups on the shoulder of the road at two A.M. in the middle of a blizzard?"

"I'm just trying to stay awake, Officer, so I can finish my deliveries."

"Son, I think maybe you're working just a little too hard," he said, laughing, before driving off.

I was. Maximizing profits by doing the work myself was one thing, but I could barely function anymore. Instead of pumping out sales calls, I'd sometimes slump over my desk and just fall asleep for an hour or more. I hired some deliverymen to help me. Father Eric signed back on. I still had to go out and supervise, but at least I wasn't so tired that I slept on my desk. Now I could make sales calls all day. As more clients now started to sign, I could again no longer keep up with things. I needed someone to share the management burdens.

At just that time a little Kosher dairy restaurant on Pelham Parkway in the Bronx, where I used to eat lunch every day, was going out of business. A few years before this, the owner had given up managing a chain of nursing homes to pursue the dream of owning his own business. For a while he had prospered till demographic changes in the neighborhood left him without clients. Wow, I thought, someone who could manage a chain of nursing homes and run his own restaurant for years was a versatile manager and could probably help me run my brochure business. I was right. Jerry Kleinman streamlined our operations, sold accounts, and took some of the pressure off me. Soon I actually had some leisure time. At first I used this time to acquire my competitors, who were delivering brochures in Philadelphia and Washington, D.C. Soon, with a virtual monopoly on our service and Jerry signing every new prospect who might appear, I was looking for something to occupy my time.

From all the years I'd spent reading every tabloid, newspaper, magazine, or periodical I could get my hands on for the mail-order business, I had begun to dream of launching my own magazine. At Harvard I had helped to found an alternative student newspaper, and I had even been involved in a similar project back in high school at Bronx Science. My dream of being in business—any business—had become more specific. I wanted to be a publisher. Now, with the cash from the brochure business, I could pursue my dreams. I bought a couple of nearly bankrupt trade journals, beginning with the *Auto and Plate Glass Journal*. I had visions of grandeur, but nobody wanted exposés on glass, or editorial opinions about the industry. They wanted pictures, which Father Eric and his cheap 35-millimeter camera dutifully provided, of windshield installation procedures and diagrams. I traveled all over the East and Midwest, driving from New York to Wisconsin and back a half dozen times, in pursuit of advertisers. Sure it was profitable, but the glamour of being a real publisher eluded me. Then I bought a magazine for New York taxi drivers. Really it was just a glorified airline brochure that told drivers when flights from Saudi Arabia or Pakistan were arriving in the middle of the night so they could pick up unsuspecting foreigners and give them an expensive "tour" of the city on the way from the airport to their hotels. I thought I'd spruce it up, but just selling advertising in this industry really took away my illusions. I could barely get taxi mechanics out from under the hood long enough to persuade them to advertise with me.

I had hoped to put together a string of little magazines and then trade up to something bigger, but prices for publications were going through the roof and I was always being outbid by larger publishers. My few publications were taking all my time and, relative to the brochure business, generating little profit. I was aware that the main asset I had if I wanted to get ahead was my own time. Putting out marginally profitable magazines for auto glass installers and taxi drivers didn't seem the best use of my time, if it couldn't serve as a base to expand to something more exciting and lucrative. Sadly I accepted the reality that publishing a few trade journals was not going to prepare me to buy the *New York Times* or the *Washington Post* down the line, as I might have dreamed. So I put my trade journals up for sale. Sure enough, a large publisher bought me out for far more than I could ever have made running the business.

At just about this time my wife (See? Perseverance pays. Debbie eventually agreed to marry me) gave me the great news that she was pregnant. I was so excited. It seemed all I wanted my whole life was to push my newborn son (Yeah, I was a sexist. I didn't know yet how great it was to have daughters) in a carriage. I was on cloud nine for a whole day. Then, like most expectant fathers, I went into a panic. My particular panic centered on where our new baby would live. We were living in a one-bedroom apartment. Where would my son put his baseball cards and hang his glove? Where would I put his bookcase? The fact that newborn infants neither read, play second base, nor trade baseball cards did not even occur to me. I was loony. I had to find a new apartment immediately. Couldn't take any chances on Junior going practically homeless.

In my neighborhood, though, nothing was for rent. Everything was being co-oped. This is a process in which the owners of rent-controlled buildings are allowed to sell shares in the building equivalent to the value of individual apartment units at their fair market value, and usually this earned big profits. In order to do this legally, however, they needed 50 percent of the tenants in the building to agree to buy their own apartments. This could be achieved only by selling to tenants in occupancy at 50 percent discount of market value or better. The real profit would then come from the owner selling vacant or vacated apartments.

This system meant the owner would make a lot of money. Tenants could make a lot of money by buying their apartments at a fraction of the price landlords could charge in the general market. Therefore landlords wouldn't rent vacant apartments. They'd all be hoarded. If you wanted an apartment, you'd have to buy it and pay through the nose. Many tenants, though, didn't have the money to buy or—in the case of my neighborhood, where Japanese corporate employees lived on temporary stays in America—were afraid of getting involved in a market with which they were unfamiliar.

Desperate to get Junior an apartment, and unable or unwilling to pay the exorbitant market rates, I figured out that if I paid one of these Japanese workers a fee I could buy the apartment in his name at a discount and then sell it to myself without having to pay a markup. Once the occupant returned as scheduled to Japan, the apartment would be mine. The Japanese, though, were afraid to get involved with a system they didn't feel comfortable with. But if I got a Japanese attorney to hold their hand, then they wouldn't be that scared at all. The Japanese Embassy directed me to such an attorney, and I soon had my apartment.

A funny thing happened, though. They say each child brings his own luck. Well, Junior's started before he was born. A landlord friend of my father's agreed to very inexpensively rent us a much nicer apartment than the one I'd bought from the Japanese guy. Now I was stuck with two apartments. Well, maybe not exactly stuck. I was soon able to sell the first apartment for twice what I paid. This was almost as much as you'd make in a whole year of brochure distribution. It almost felt like stealing, but nobody got hurt. Everybody was happy— the Japanese guys, the landlords, and most of all, me.

I had a lot of time on my hands and making money like this seemed as good a way to keep busy as any. Soon I was buying every Japanese apartment I could get my hands on. In fact, anytime any tenant in the neighborhood wanted to make some quick money without taking a risk, I'd buy that tenant out. It was great. Like shooting fish in a barrel. I more than doubled my money every time. Sure, it was temporary. Once everything was co-oped in a couple of years, the whole game, we all knew, was sure to end. But what a great way to make hay while the sun shines! Anyway, like I said, I needed something to do, with Jerry managing the brochure business. I wound up making way more off co-ops than I did from brochures. Did I work harder at it? No. Did I put more creativity into it? No. Did I need to set up a great organization to do it? No again. I was just in the right place at the right time. I was never really able to tell myself what a great talent I was for succeeding at this because I have little capacity for self-deception. Seeing how hard it was making money in real business and how easy it was coming here made me actually feel guilty about the profits.

There is no denying the lesson that your chances of success are much enhanced if you manage to catch the right wave. A rising tide, like they say, raises all ships. People who've gotten in on any boom early, be it oil, real estate, stocks, or semiconductors, have prospered out of all proportion to normal businesspeople. These great waves have usually been caused by some massive shift in the structure of society. The baby boom, information age, beginning or end of inflation or the cold war have not only changed society, they've made many of the first guys to recognize their financial implications rich. The change in New York City's better housing stock from rental to tenant ownership was a seismic event in that market. Once I'd gotten in on it, I was always looking for the next great wave. The deregulation of the entire world's communications network may well turn out to be the biggest structural shift in the history of business. It clearly makes anything as small as a shift in the ownership structure of New York apartment buildings seem like a joke by comparison. IDT is, in my biased opinion, a great company. Our stature, though, has clearly been increased a hundredfold by the fact that we were surfing on top of the biggest tidal wave ever.

Back to the co-oping, though. Just as everyone predicted, the conversion market eventually petered out. Just then, fortunately, a new opportunity presented itself. One that would let me fulfill my dream of becoming a publisher. We had, by this time, expanded our brochure distribution routes to include not only hotels, but military bases. In hotels, you find a few independently distributed brochures for establishments that are trying to attract travelers. The travel and recreation offices at the military bases, though, were literally filled with every kind of leaflet imaginable, offering discounts to uniformed personnel. Unlike normal travel brochures, which are always four inches wide by nine inches high, the literature at the army bases wouldn't fit into any of our standard displays.

A thought occurred to me to reprint the various establishments' special military offerings in some nice indexed type of directory, which we'd give away to every enlisted man or woman. Every soldier would want one, since it would tell him how to save money. The bases would love them because it would improve morale and eliminate clutter at the travel offices. And the advertisers would love it, since we would charge them much less than their current combined printing and distribution cost. The directory was an immediate hit. Hundreds of clients signed up almost immediately. This, of course, made me happiest of everybody. As word of the directories' tremendous business-generating success got out, it looked like the advertising for our second edition might more than double. Not only that, but letters of thanks from soldiers and requests for more books from the bases were pouring in daily. Everybody loved us, and we were making money hand over fist. It was like someone had given us the key to the mint and was letting us print our own currency. In fact, to make the directory look even more official, we actually reprinted on its cover the great seal of the United States, which we copied off a real dollar bill.

That was how they got us. Not everyone, you see, was so happy about the success of our directories. There was one party in Washington who hated our book, a competitor who put out a similar book of their own. At first I didn't even know this competitor's book existed. We gave away thousands of books for free weekly, while the competitor charged over $10 for their guide. It was, therefore, rarely seen. Even if you got a copy, you'd find it was complicated to understand and printed on poor paper.

Under normal circumstances such a poor competitor would usually change tactics and improve their product. This one was obstinate. They didn't care what the market wanted; they just kept up with their old book. That was fine with us. If they were going to let us completely dominate the market, I wasn't going to complain. Under normal circumstances, a dumb competitor like this would eventually go out of business.

This one was different, though. There was no way they were going under. The competitor had a rich uncle, you see, who just kept funding whatever operation deficit they ran up. A very, very rich uncle. Uncle Sam, to be precise.

Our competitor, you see, was the General Services Administration, a branch of the U.S. government. The bureaucrats there had been charged with putting out a directory similar to ours. This they had done for years. Hundreds of people were involved in the production. They got paid well, traveled a lot, and had a great benefits package. The fact that people never used the directory was never a matter of great concern. I mean, the less copies printed and given away, the less money needed for staff. If anyone wanted a copy, they could buy it.

Suddenly, though, their directory was not only poorly circulated, it had become completely obsolete. Our directory had replaced it entirely. Many bases didn't even bother keeping a reference copy of the "official" directory anymore. Word started getting around that the army and navy guys didn't need the old directory, and suddenly the bureaucrats realized their jobs were in danger.

Official letters started going from the GSA informing our advertisers and prospective advertisers not to use our book. It was unauthorized, they said. It was not the official U.S. government directory, they said. It might be banned from government offices, they said. Many prospects decided, on the basis of these official communiqués, that we were a scam and wouldn't sign up. Even some of our current advertisers, whose businesses were literally packed with uniformed personnel thanks to our ads, refused to pay their bills on the basis of the GSA letters.

Many prospects, on reading the letters of praise from hundreds of base officials, signed with us anyway or renewed. No doubt about it, the GSA was hurting us, but we were growing anyway. Better, we thought, not to start a head-on legal fight with them. They had unlimited resources. Who knew what might happen? Anyway, it still seemed we had the keys to the mint. The presses that were running off the dollar bills might have been slowed, but our books, which produced our currency, still looked mighty good to us.

When the GSA examined our books they looked pretty good to them, too. In fact, they looked so good the next thing we knew the GSA was accusing us of counterfeiting. We'd reprinted the great seal of the United States without permission. This was a felony. Same as printing money. Treasury would have to be called. Jail time and big fines for everybody. Of course, if we agreed to just stop printing the books, everything might be forgotten. I could stay free with my family instead of being thrown in with the other inmates.

Counterfeiting? Felonies? Jail time? Was this book really worth it? I didn't think so. I had really stepped on the wrong toes. I figured I could live without the publishing money. The brochures were still doing fine. I didn't want to go to prison.

But this was just wrong. It sounded strange, I know, but I felt some great principle was being violated. This wasn't the Soviet Union. The U.S. government can't just make up a story that someone's a counterfeiter and throw him in jail. What about the protection of the individual, the Bill of Rights, the Constitution? What about all the army guys who loved the book? I was doing the country a service. This was insane. If I gave in and just quit, then I'd be doing the wrong thing as a citizen. I'd just be agreeing to an injustice. I'd be accepting that the United States wasn't special; it was just the little guy had no rights like everyone else. How could I live with myself if I just admitted I was a counterfeiter to get out of this?

I'd write the President. And while I'm at it, I'm gonna write my senator and congressman, too. In fact, I'll call my congressman. Know what? I'll write every senator and congressman. And I'll call all their offices. That'll give the GSA something to think about. Just who the hell do they think they are, anyway, allowing this to happen while they're supposedly trying to cut the deficit? I'll let them know how a private company's being persecuted for trying to give servicemen something for free that the GSA is gouging them for after wasting millions in government money producing it. And while I'm at it, I think I'll contact the press too.

America came through for me. Several of the senators and

congressmen actually sent letters to the GSA asking them to explain their position. Needed it for their investigation, they said. And could the GSA explain why it was charging for the books after using all the taxpayers' money, anyway? Could this be cause for an investigation?

The GSA turned out not to be that tough, after all. Prison time, counterfeiting, did I really think they meant that? Of course not. They were just quoting from the law. You know how sometimes these junior bureaucrats run amuck and do things on their own. It was a terrible mistake. They'd even send out a second letter rescinding it.

As for the seal of the United States. Well, you know, the law is the law. You guys really shouldn't have used it. Now that it's on the record, we have to come up with some way to solve this. We can't give you authorization to just use the great seal of the United States. You're not the mint, you know. Maybe you could just destroy all the books and reprint them.

Reprint them all? Are you kidding? What if we just print a sticker and paste it over the great seal? Do you guys own the flag, too? No? You mean if we print a flag it's not counterfeiting? Okay, good. Just wanted to be sure. Then we'll agree to print a hundred thousand flag stickers and put them on each book. Yes, we agree to do that. You can just send the release to my lawyer along with the retraction letter and we'll sign off on it.

It wasn't quite all behind us, though. Do you know how long it takes to stick a hundred thousand American flag decals on the covers of directories? For weeks we didn't do anything else. Then we started to sell ads again.

The GSA hadn't turned out to be so tough because we found someone bigger whom they were afraid of to put them in their place. This is how the world works. Once you get really big, you become just a part of the pecking order. You've got to knuckle under to forces more powerful than you if you want to keep your position. The GSA was also one of the most incompetent competitors we'd ever faced. They were much too big and bureaucratic to respond to us. Years later, other private publishers moved into our market and gave us more of a run for our money. The GSA, though, was never able to respond.

Many people, years later, likened IDT's fight with AT&T to the struggle of David versus Goliath. Everyone was surprised David won, but as in the original struggle, Goliath never had a chance. He was big and lumbering and had to do whatever his Philistine commander told him to do. David, on the other hand, was small, quick, smart, and had complete freedom of action. Goliath probably never saw the stone coming.

In our fight with AT&T we used everything we had against them. This time, we were able to get direct access to the White House. It was really like being up against the GSA all over again. We had a much superior product at a much lower price, and our competitor's only recourse was to try to have our activities declared illegal. The amazing thing is that people went right on placing their bets with Goliath. Maybe if they read the Bible instead of the business pages, they could get a better return on their investments.

When I thought about it, the GSA did have a point, and it would be useful to us. Part of the reason our book was such a success is that it seemed "official." Were there any other industries with large numbers of suppliers and the need for an "official" directory? Dozens of possibilities occurred to me. The most appealing was to start an official directory to cater to the Japanese tourism industry, which had suddenly sprung into prominence, sending close to ten million travelers a year overseas. Why, if I just opened a Tokyo "headquarters" office and put out a Japanese-language directory, tourism-oriented businesses around the world would soon be advertising with me. Sure enough, in no time at all the Japanese directory had surpassed our military book in revenues. What a great formula. I could hardly wait to start the next publication.

A key to success is not always having dozens of ideas, but always exploiting the few truly good ones you do have in every place they can be applied. Like McDonald's, if you find a formula that works in one locale, try to apply it around the world. In order to do this you have to really examine your business and try to find the key ingredient that makes it work. In the mail-order business, for instance, it wasn't that people wanted to buy Venus's-flytraps; they liked the idea of a plant with a story. Realizing this enabled us to sell a whole variety of "pet plants" and bonsai trees for years rather than having just one hot item. Similarly, in the brochure business, we were always looking for new places like military bases to distribute, rather than just handling hotels.

Many businesses often contain successful formulas that, if exploited in other areas, would let them grow really large. Often, the very entrepreneurs who came up with the business don't recognize these formulas as a template on which more can be built. Often, the entrepreneur is simply overwhelmed just taking care of what he's already created. Sure, it's a great idea to turn your single successful hamburger stand into the McDonald's chain. But guess who didn't? The McDonalds themselves. These two brothers were so overwhelmed flipping burgers and making shakes they couldn't even think of expanding. To do so they'd have had to build an organization. Instead, they sold out to Ray Kroc. He built the organization and he made the fortune.

Chapter Six
Gold in the Sewer

❖

Seeing all the possibilities my new publishing formula opened, I realized it was time to start building a real organization. In fact, it was way past time. Between the translating, advertising, sales, billing, production, and distribution, I was beginning to feel like I had in the old days, putting a hundred thousand miles a year on the car. Actually, maybe a little worse. I wasn't getting any younger, you see. But how to build an organization? Start with one good person. I had Jerry in brochures. Now it was time to find a partner to grow with publishing.

Ever notice when you look at any of the really great accomplishments in history, like the birth of the American nation, it seems there are not one, but several extraordinary personalities who were contributors? Just look at Washington, Adams, Jefferson, Franklin. Has the world ever seen such an assemblage of statesmen and intellectuals since? Many people would look at this and say it was the times, the events, that brought out the greatness in these men. Certainly true. Still, I can't help but think that in the assemblage of the collective talents a spark was created, or rather the energy level caused a sort of spontaneous combustion that lit up the world and drove the events.

Similarly, at the beginning of any great business enterprise you find this same sort of gathering of unusual talent occurring. It's not something that's planned. In the beginning it just sort of happens. And then more and more talent gets attracted to the exciting new projects, as moths are attracted to light, and suddenly the combustion just happens and you know you're dealing with something extraordinary.

But where was I going to find these kinds of great people? How would I ever attract them to a still small, relatively unexciting business like mine? Truly talented, already successful people were, undoubtedly, happy doing what they were doing. They either owned their own enterprises or were so valued and well taken care of by their present employers you'd never lure them away.

If they were already lucky enough to be really successful in their chosen field, that is. There were, I realized, two other possibilities. The first was someone may simply have chosen the wrong field to go into. It is certainly no harder to imagine a young person selecting the wrong profession than it would be to imagine that person marrying the wrong individual. Who really, after all, has any experience the first time they make one of these momentous decisions? You could easily wind up in a field that is unrewarding or where your potential is neither recognized, appreciated, nor utilized.

The fact that a talented, energetic person makes a bad career choice does not diminish him as a person. Like the hardy blade of grass that will crack through a concrete sidewalk to reach the light, so will this person's unrealized potential break into view, if not in his professional life then in his nonwork undertakings, such as hobbies, social activities, charitable work. Show me a postman who, in his spare time, has organized and run a large Little League team, for example, and I'll show you someone who could be managing a large number of people if he weren't delivering mail.

(Technical people are an exception to this rule. You can't turn a mailman into an engineer overnight, no matter how talented he is. When it comes to technical personnel, the best move is to hire the best you can get. David Turock, who warrants a separate book just about him, and Jeff Goldberg, two leaders of our technical team, were widely regarded as the industry gurus in their respective fields even before we hired them.)

The first possibility was to find a young lion cub who'd somehow wound up in a cage. I'd just have to convince him that our company was his natural habitat, and when running free he could become the king of the jungle he was destined to be.

The second possibility was to find someone who'd actually chosen the right field, started to succeed in a big way, but due to bad luck had failed. Failed big. In fact, the bigger the failure, the more I'd know I'd found the right person. Because generally it's the greatest undertakings with the most talent and effort poured into them that result in the greatest disasters when something fails at the wrong moment. I call this my spectacular failure theory.

I'd found over the years in business that talent is no guarantee of success. Sometimes you just need luck. The very nature of being an entrepreneur is to take a risk when most others decide to play it safe. To push the envelope. To go into uncharted territory. Sure, you can't just be foolhardy, and it's wise to do everything you can to protect yourself and provide a fallback position, but there are just times you're going to be exposed and if the rope snaps at the wrong minute, you're history. If this happens later in one's career, there are generally other past successes the unlucky gambler can fall back to and regroup. Failure earlier along (and due to inexperience and the daring of youth, this is precisely when most failures occur) is likely to prove devastating, leaving the one-time high flyer ruined and depressed.

What a great time to hire someone. You can get him cheap. He'll always be grateful to you (and loyal) for picking him up when he was down. And you're not getting an ordinary person, but someone of extraordinary ability. Someone who can think independently. Someone with the ability to bring together a whole set of disparate resources in order to make it. Someone who at one time soared above the ordinary. But he crashed, you say? So what? I answer. Who hasn't failed? Only the person who never tried. When confronting these people and listening to their stories, I realize how easy it would be for our roles to be reversed. My luck was just better, I realize, or I was just a little more cautious.

I can't really tell you which of my two theories—the spectacular failure or the lion cage—yields the best people.

With the first employees I hired for Timetable, I hadn't yet honed these theories, I just got lucky. But to give you some examples from IDT, let me tell you about two of my earliest hires who helped shape the company.

David Barth was a young CPA at Ernst & Young who felt trapped in that hierarchial environment. You could see the young lion behind the accountant's glasses when he took an unpaid leave to start up and run a camp for underprivileged kids in Russia with hundreds of participants. This lion was not only young, but he had integrity, soul, and passion, which he was eager to apply to a venture that challenged him. We hired him away for half his Ernst salary to join our then two-man company. He subsequently, at different times, has served as the company's sales manager, telecom director, Internet coordinator, and controller. Wherever there's a problem, we just plug David in. Our solvency is due in large part to his efforts.

On the other end of the spectrum, Jonathan Rand was a truly spectacular failure, through no fault of his own. The *Campus Connection* magazine he started in his University of Pennsylvania dorm grew to a national chain. At its height, it had a sales force on a hundred campuses, a slew of national advertisers, and a circulation in the millions. A public offering was just around the corner when *Esquire*'s parent company entered the market and, after years of cutthroat competition, bled Jonathan's company white and forced a sale of the publication.

Jonathan, who also took a pay cut to join our five-person enterprise, has been our international sales director, CFO, and human relations director. Whenever energy, organization, and enthusiasm needs to be instilled into the company, we just wind Jonathan up and, like the Energizer bunny, he keeps going, and going, and going.

To me, though, the most spectacular failure we ever hired (I laugh to think anyone has the nerve to use this appellation) is our current chief operating officer and real mastermind behind IDT, Howie Balter. He's the one who really runs the company day to day. Howie had been a major New York City property developer in the eighties, converting old factory buildings into luxury condominiums. He had millions in credit lines from the big banks, dozens of construction crews reporting to him, and he was making money hand over fist. Not content to rest on his laurels, he plowed everything back into further expansion.

Then, suddenly, the real estate market crashed, with Howie's company and all his fiscal net worth along with it. The first time I interviewed him it was as a favor to a friend who asked if I could give him a job because it was difficult for him to support his wife and three kids doing small home repairs.

Can you imagine it? This guy with an advanced math degree, advanced rabbinical training, a huge intellect, tremendous street smarts, who'd been one of the city's big real estate developers, was fixing people's porches, and wanted a real opportunity? I'd have given him a job anyway, just as a good deed, even if he had no qualifications. But could this be real? Talk about finding gold in the sewer! Sure, he was a little depressed when he first started. But how'd you feel if you'd lost all that?

Early in IDT's history, Howie made some decisions that totally changed the focus and direction of the company. He singlehandedly put us in the business of selling our own phone service, rather than just being a middleman. It was risky. It was revolutionary. It put us head to head against AT&T and the other giants of the industry. But Howie said he'd put his own credibility on the line and pay for the loss himself if it didn't work. Now, this was confidence. (Of course, he had no money to pay with, but let's forget about details.) If Howie was so sure, I had to give him a free hand to try. It worked. The rest, as they say, is history. Howie's run and built everything in the company. To even list his accomplishments would demean him. Basically, IDT is his accomplishment. I just came along for the ride.

In spite of his loyalty and big equity stake in the company, headhunters call him weekly, trying to get him to leave and take over one large public company or another. Frankly, I don't think this is fair. I think that if the headhunters really wanted to earn their money, they should have to look in the sewers and cages like I did.

Eventually, of course, as we grew and succeeded, it became easier to attract top people, and the personnel process stopped being mainly a scavenger hunt. Still, though, the old rules continue to cast their shadow and our top hires still come from unlikely places rather than from the ranks of our competitors. Hal Brecher, our executive VP of operations and a member of our board, is such a person. We searched through the ranks of all the telecom firms we knew and couldn't find a candidate as good as Hal. The only drawback was that he knew nothing of our industry, having run a very large family-owned mail-order business for a decade. When the family wasn't going to let Hal have an equity position, it became clear to him late in the game that he'd chosen the wrong profession.

I certainly wasn't one to discriminate against mail-order men, though. The field has turned out some of the best guys I know (if you know what I mean). The mail-order industry's loss was our gain. Sure, it took probably three months till Hal had learned enough to function in his new role, but what's three months when you're hoping someone will stay a lifetime?

Jim Courter, our president, was surely our most unusual hire. By the time Jim and I first met in mid-1992, Jim was in my opinion a national hero. Congress and President Bush, unable to decide which of America's military bases to close because of the political pressure exerted by each state and community to keep its bases open, had turned the entire problem over to Jim. He and the committee he chaired were to have sole discretion to decide in the interest of national defense what to keep and what to scrap. The job seemed undoable and was thankless. Editorial writers railed that this undertaking would surely succumb to political pressure and fall apart. Yet the blue-ribbon panel Jim assembled, the impartial inquiries and hearings they held across the country, the judicious and impartial manner of the deliberations, had won over all segments of the political spectrum. As a result, the country was able to save billions annually without sacrificing military preparedness. Jim's stature was such that Bill Clinton, who would be elected that fall, reappointed him to the same crucial position for a second time.

This reappointment was remarkable because Jim was, at that time, the most popular Republican in the state of New Jersey. We couldn't even walk down the street from my office to get a slice of pizza without half a dozen people running up to shake his hand. And small wonder; only a couple of years before, Jim had lost a hotly contested election to be New Jersey's governor. The new governor's disappointing performance contrasted starkly with the stellar reviews Jim was now getting. The citizenry seemed to be longing to reconnect with him. I was floored. It was like going to have pizza with a movie star. Jim, however, having already been in the public eye for decades, including a twelve-year stint in Congress, was unfazed. He wanted to talk about my fledgling business.

"You," he told me, "are a hero. You're changing the world by going out there and cutting international phone rates. What an honor it was for me to visit your switching center. Who would've imagined such a world-changing undertaking is happening right here, today?"

Now, wait a minute, I thought. This guy is serious. He's been in Congress for twelve years. He's met with presidents and prime ministers. Now he's telling me a little eight-by-ten closet I showed him with some modems we reprogrammed to circumvent foreign phone companies is changing the world? This guy really is some politician.

As we talked for hours that day, though, I became completely taken with Jim's sincerity and idealism. He'd gone into politics because he believed in liberty and free enterprise. Much of political life, though, he found was just posturing and political gamesmanship. The real people who changed the world, he'd come to feel, were the free enterprise visionaries who made things happen. His only role was to protect them and the country from forces who wanted to limit freedom. Frankly, he said, he thought what I was doing was much more significant than being in politics. Wow, I thought. Up till that moment I'd gladly have traded all my businesses to be in Congress. Yet Jim had a point.

I wondered if he really was so enthusiastic or if it was just talk.

"Would you like to invest?" I asked.

"Boy, if you'd let me, I'd scrape up every penny I could."

Jim bought 1 percent of the company. I really didn't want to sell it to him. I didn't know how long we'd last. Rich real estate guys with a hundred million or more, sure, I'd take their money. But Jim Courter, how could I do this to him? Jim wasn't a rich guy. He drove a weather-beaten Oldsmobile. The next week three-quarters of the money arrived with a note that he'd send the rest when he got his tax refund. Poor Jim, I thought. This is like robbing an overidealistic orphan.

"Take the money back," I suggested. "This is way too risky."

"Don't worry. I have complete faith in you," he countered. "If this doesn't work out, I have no problems taking the loss."

"Fine," I relented. "But at least don't send the last twenty-five percent. Let me take it in legal services from you."

So far he's made better than 1,000 percent return on the money he gave up. I, however, earned far more on the 25 percent I didn't take. Jim became not only an investor and our lawyer, but our protector, counselor, and advisor in every major deal or crisis we subsequently had to handle. Whatever the situation, once I'd call Jim, things would improve. Not only things, but my mood as well. Of all the people I'd talk to in business, it was soon clear to me that the one I enjoyed talking to and being with the most was Jim. In spite of the vast difference in our backgrounds, ages, and experience, we were kindred spirits.

When we went public, Howie and I both realized we needed someone corporate and polished to share the burden of running the company with us. We interviewed many present and former CEOs and COOs from larger, more well known companies. They were all polished, but they left us cold. There was no chemistry. No spark. Not knowing where to turn, I went to Jim. Could he help us in the search? Did he know of someone?

After a supper meeting Jim had arranged for me to attend with George Soros, Jim said he needed to speak with me privately.

"I've really thought over your problem about finding the perfect president," he said, "and I have an unorthodox idea I'd like you to think about before responding."

Okay, I thought. I'm ready for anything.

"How about me?" he asked.

This I wasn't ready for. "You know we can't pay you even close to what you're worth, just a normal salary and a bunch of options."

"I've worked out the finances," he replied.

"Jim, are you sure?" I asked.

"I'm sure," he replied. "Now it's up to you."

"Give me a week," I said. "I'd love to work with you, but in fairness to both of us, I just need to think it through."

I talked it over with my wife. Jim had no corporate experience. Wall Street would be unimpressed and think he was just a figurehead. He wasn't a telecom expert. He had no experience managing a large public company. His style was different than ours. Would our team accept him? At any moment he could be named to the Cabinet and he'd be gone.

On the other hand, I liked him. He'd founded a large law firm of his own and built it up before going to Congress. That's like being in business, right? He had tremendous contacts who might eventually wind up being partners or investors. He could get us in with foreign governments. What we were doing was so new, no one had experience, anyway. And he did fit our profile. He did have a spectacular failure, if you count narrowly losing a governor's race and not becoming President of the United States as a failure. And clearly, he was a lion in a cage. Being a Washington lobbyist just didn't suit him. Plus, I liked him. It just felt right.

Sometimes logic and Wall Street don't matter. Sometimes you've got to go on instinct. It was one in the morning, and I'd been moody over this decision for days. Our bankers and board had advised against it. Howie said he sort of liked it but it was up to me. I'd talked to my wife and argued both sides till she no longer knew what to think. Then, suddenly, at one A.M. it became clear.

"This is a once-in-a-lifetime chance," I said. "I'm not letting it go."

"Are you sure?" she said.

"Yeah, I'm sure," I answered.

"Then let's go to sleep."

The next day Jim came over and we wrote an agreement on notebook paper. The deal was done.

Jim wound up being a sensational president, probably the best in our industry. The headhunters are after him now, also. Just goes to show you, you can't keep a good man down. If someone rises to the top in one field, it's usually no accident. Put him in another, and he'll rise there as well.

It's all sort of logical when you think about it. Just find someone who's shown a lot of promise in some sort of undertaking. Move him into your field, give him some support and love, and he'll succeed for you. Success, in short, is an absolutely accurate predictor of who will succeed. That's absolute rule No. 2. Oh, I forgot to mention absolute rule No. 1: There is no such thing in business as an absolute rule. Every rule has an exception.

Our most notable exception is Michael Fischberger, the most senior divisional manager in our company, and everyone's universal choice as most decent human being on earth and the one least likely to succeed.

I mean, in terms of obvious lack of potential, it's hard to top this guy. We hired him as a favor to his family. They were just happy for him to have an indoor job. Prior to his coming to us, he'd spent a couple of years working in construction, where he'd advanced from filling wheelbarrows to pushing them. Burdened by a learning disability that made school a nightmare for him, the only hint Fish ever gave of his future managerial cunning was in hiring older friends to sneak out of school and steal his report card, after the postman delivered it but before his parents got home. Even at this, though, he failed. He paid the thieves in advance, thus allowing them to stop for pizza before his tattletale sister arrived home and spotted the dismal report card in the box.

As a young person he started no business, chaired no organization, and captained no teams. From all reports (drawn largely from himself), his parents were already mourning over his failure before he'd even accomplished it. If ever a person was made to be the assistant of the assistant of the assistant manager of tech support, Fish was the man. And it was to that position we assigned him, hoping ardently we wouldn't have to demote him lower.

A funny thing happened, though. He did a really good job. Show up late at night, after all the assistants to the assistants, senior assistants, and managers were gone, and there was Fish working. We started talking, and after a little while I realized he wasn't dumb at all. In fact, he was incredibly smart. Whenever a problem came up, he was the only one who knew how to solve it. So, what the hell? We moved him up, and up again.

When the position opened up to put someone in charge of handling Internet sales, we couldn't find anyone who was qualified. We took a gamble. We gave the job to Fish.

Because he was not computer-literate, he'd just make a little mark in his book every time someone signed up. At the end of each day he'd tally the marks to tell us how well we were doing.

And guess what? Soon the marks started to really add up. We were making real money. I thought I'd better get a real manager in and get Fish out before he messed it up. Maybe put him in charge of tech support. Sure, he didn't know squat about computers, but he'd learn.

Nine months later the Internet business was collapsing. Sales and technology were out of control. The only thing that was working was tech support, with everyone happy and motivated and willing to be underpaid, as long as they could work for Fish. Go figure. So we put him in charge of the whole division. Soon everything Fish was running was making money, and everyone was happy. So we increased his responsibility. Over two hundred people are now working for Fish. We won't ever make a decision without his input. Usually, he has no opinion. He can see it both ways. But whenever he has an opinion, that's it. We all go along. Everyone's come to know that Fish is always right. Not only that, but he is a real *mensch,* the kind of man you'd be proud to have your son grow up to become, the kind of manager who shows respect to the people who work for him, and receives it in return. Fish has a gift for knowing how to treat people and motivate them. His staff would walk through fire for him.

Funny thing. Fish's in-laws and parents are always so nice to me. They must think I'm still doing him a favor. If not for me, I'm sure they think, he'd be back behind the wheelbarrow. By all means use logic and borrow my rules. But keep your eyes open because you just never know where the gems will be found.

Chapter Seven
Conducting the Orchestra

❖

I'd have had no stories about Fish, or for that matter Dave Barth, Jonathan Rand, Howie, or Jim if I'd stayed overwhelmed with my brochures and directories. As you remember, that's what got me started on this whole topic of hiring. It was still 1988, four years before I ever met Jim. I needed to hire a second, a partner, someone who could help me expand out of my basement and become big. Someone with real ambition and talent who'd work for peanuts and finally help me get to a higher level. In some of life's most crucial decisions, like getting married, you look around, see what's available, listen to your logic, hunches, and emotion, and then you throw the dice. Sometimes you win. Sometimes you lose.

I chose Marc Knoller, a junior loan officer at a big bank. He was nothing in business, but the hardest worker anybody had ever seen on communal and charitable projects. So I threw the dice and I asked him. Right away, I regretted taking the gamble, for his sake. I tried to rescind the offer.

"It'll never work," I told him. "You'll be out on the street. You've got a family. Keep the safe bank position."

"Too late," he told me. "You got me thinking. I'm tired of the safe life. I want to gamble too. And I want to do it with you. Don't worry if I'll succeed. I guarantee I will."

Oh, great, I thought. I'm finished. Now I've got some bank clerk who suddenly thinks he's Indiana Jones and there's no turning back. This'll never work. I should have played it safe. I'd been a fool and thrown the dice. Now they were out of my hands and tumbling down the felt. As I said good-bye to my savings, I had no idea I'd finally hit the jackpot.

This was my state of mind in 1988. Things were going well and I just wanted things to keep getting a little better each day, without confronting any huge challenges or chances of rejection head-on. There are just lots of big opportunities with low probabilities of success you don't pursue to save your energy for surer bets.

Rejection didn't seem to matter to Marc. Exhaustion didn't seem to exist for him. Hard work, intelligence, loyalty, success, and frugality were his only concerns. I mean, the man started calling people at eight in the morning. I never saw him eat, and he'd stay at it until there was nobody left to call at night. Fear didn't seem to faze him. I was afraid to call the really big ad agencies and global corporations. They'd never advertise with me. They'd just laugh. Marc called them, and called them, and called them. And suddenly the contracts started rolling in, not just from America, but from around the world.

Our two publications grew to a dozen. The few hundred advertisers swelled to several thousand. The revenue climbed. Our staff grew. Where once I'd always played it conservative, with Marc as a partner I'd started to grow more venturesome.

Before Marc came along, I was a visionary without a staff. A general without an army. A conductor with no orchestra. Marc was the staff, the army, the orchestra. To this day, he runs the publishing business, allowing me to concentrate on IDT, and at the same time he serves as IDT's chief troubleshooter and a member of its board. Marc overseeing expansion is what gave me the whole idea for the callback business in the first place. And his one-man, year-long campaign to sell the new concept in the face of continual multiple daily rejections is what finally allowed us to break through and succeed.

If you think I seem to be saying I had a lot of inadequacies which Marc compensated for, and that's what allowed us to really succeed, you're right. Could I have accomplished what we have so far by myself with so many shortcomings? Of course not. Am I ashamed that I needed Marc and others to compensate for my shortcomings? Certainly not. I'm not perfect. If I were, I wouldn't be human.

Even if you were perfect in every way, which no one is, you still couldn't be really perfect because at different stages of your life you'd still be lacking in attributes you'll have more of at a later stage. This is the human condition. We all go through this journey, trying to do the best with the shortcomings we have. No one has it all. The best you can do is accept your limitations and accentuate the positive. This, however, is only true on an individual level.

A company actually can pursue perfection. Is the company lacking in vigor? Hire young lions and set them free. Is it short on brainpower? Convince some real geniuses they'll be able to really make their mark with you and you'll soon have your own brain trust. Are you short on stature and people skills? Maybe get a former congressman on board. Whatever your limitations are as an individual can be compensated for by a great organization.

You can come close to creating perfection: a "perfect" society of diverse individuals with diverse strengths coming together to create something really great. The strength comes from the diversity. The whole is truly greater than the sum of its parts.

What's true of a company is true of society in general. Most countries reject immigration and the diversity it brings. Their population resents the strengths outsiders bring with them, which in many cases allows them to outperform large segments of the already existing population. Rather than admit this, though, they harp on the unique shortcomings of the foreigners, the friction and changes that their different outlooks will impose on society. Then they throw them out. You know who loses? Society. The diversity would have enriched it and made it stronger. Look at the American experiment. After everybody's spoken all the slander they want against us, there's one undeniable reality. We've succeeded. Are things perfect? Do we all fit together without problems? Are there no tensions? Of course there are. It's how our society deals with those tensions and gets everyone to work together that is the key to the nation's success.

And, I might add, the key to a business's success as well. People's diverse abilities are only able to come out when you give them the freedom to act. Obviously, however, when so many talented and different individuals all start expressing themselves at the same time, what comes out is likely to sound like a confusion of noise from diverse instruments rather than an orchestra playing. The leader's job, at some point, is to stop playing an instrument and be the conductor.

I often thought it was wrong the way conductors like Leonard Bernstein or Zubin Mehta get so much glory. What do they do, after all? The composer wrote the music; the artists perform it. The conductors are just waving a stick. But now that I run a large company, I think differently. What a job! To know when to allow an artist to solo, and when to go with the group. When to follow the music as written, and when to go with the spirit of the orchestra.

In business it's even more complicated. We don't even have a score to play from. Everything's changing moment by moment, so we actually have to improvise the movements as the performance goes on. If someone can manage to coordinate all this and have it all come off, even if he's working with the best musicians or executives in the world, maybe it's okay to take a little bow at the end of the performance.

I'm not ready to take any bow yet. The performance is still going on, and any minute we might all go off key. With the performers I'm working with, I'm sure we'll correct it. But you can't risk facing the audience or taking your eye off the orchestra. Not that there yet was any orchestra when Marc first joined or for a long time thereafter. Sure, we dreamed of Carnegie Hall, but at the time we were just a little chamber music group, distributing brochures and expanding our publishing interests. Like most chamber music groups, we just loved what we were doing. Carnegie Hall was just a dream.

Chapter Eight
Us Against the World's Phone Monopolies

❖

I never intended to go into the international telephone business. I wound up in it by accident because I was cheap and I was desperate.

My desperation sprang from the fact that Marc Knoller, my right hand, informed me that he intended to move his family to Israel. I was in a panic. He was irreplaceable. Without him I'd be back to running a marginal publishing business.

I was on the horns of a dilemma, however. He didn't want to leave for a better opportunity. He wanted to move for reasons of religious principle. I didn't think it would be right to try to make him stay against his conscience. I also didn't think it would be productive. The secret to getting magic people like Marc to work with you is to share your dreams with them, to become spiritual partners, so to speak. Such a relationship is impossible if one party is being forced into it against his will. And without the relationship, the magic effort people put out when they feel they're working for themselves stops being exerted. Then the magic dies.

I know this sounds corny, but I don't believe there's any power on earth as strong as a motivated human soul. This is what gives mothers, literally, the strength to lift a car that is crushing their child. It is also the power uniquely successful people have to achieve undreamed-of accomplishments. A soul, however, is not for hire. You can hire a person's body or mind, but the soul will only work for itself. The only way, therefore, to engage a person's soul in an undertaking is to set things up in such a way that the person honestly feels as if he's working for himself. Then he'll put his soul into it. And watch out. Something that feels like fingernails on a blackboard to me is when I hear someone from IDT, especially a senior person, say he works for Howard Jonas. I always correct him, and ask him not to say that again. Rather, I ask him to say that he works *with* Howard Jonas. I similarly make sure to use the same words myself, and never say someone works *for* me.

This is not just a game of modesty, it's how I really feel. We're all part of a team and I need the people I hire as much as they need me. Besides that, what am I? Some kind of an overlord on a plantation in charge of a bunch of slaves? Who wants that? It's much more exciting and productive to be working with a group of highly motivated, independent people, especially when you can feel the fire burning in their souls.

On the other hand, without Marc there was no magic. So I proposed the only deal I could. Marc could open his own office in Israel, or nearby Italy, and continue his sales efforts from there. After all, about half of our advertising came from overseas anyway. So what did it really matter if the sales were done from Europe or America? We'd simply reverse the process. Previously, we'd sold about half our ads to Europeans from America. Now we'd sell half our ads to Americans from Europe.

Marc thought it was a great idea. With the much lower living costs in Israel he'd be almost rich on his American pay. The time zone problem also didn't matter, since Marc normally worked till past midnight. When Marc took a vacation in 1989, we decided to test out how doing sales from Israel would work. It worked great. In fact, without having to deal with administrative work back in the States, his sales actually went up.

Everything seemed great until I saw my telephone bill. It was five times higher than it would have been had he made all the calls from the States. There is competition for long-distance service in the United States, but overseas there were only state-owned monopolies. The differential was staggering, and it was going to have to come from my pocket. The lessons learned at the hot dog stand, such as not over-paying for supplies, were not forgotten. Either I had to solve this problem or give up on Marc's overseas expansions.

Why not bypass the European phone lines altogether? We could adapt the system I had used with my parents when I was in college. I'd call collect, using a code name, and they would refuse the charges. Then they'd call me back. Essentially, callback worked on the same principle. The European user would call a number in the States, and an operator would recognize his signal. Then he'd hang up, and within a few seconds he'd be "called back" with an open, American line over which to make his calls. Instead of paying for a call from France to New York, as an example, he would be using an American line, and his bill would reflect the cost of a call from New York to Paris instead. Depending on the country, he could save more than half the cost of his international phone calls. At first this whole process was done manually, with operators placing the return call. They had to work around the clock to accommodate different time zones. Eventually I designed a box and with the help of a computer engineer built one that mechanized the process and automatically redialed the caller. My phone bills were now manageable, and the callback industry had been born.

The lesson I learned from this is that if you look hard enough, you'll usually find a way to circumvent obstacles. In fact, sometimes you can do this so effectively, and get such a big advantage over your competition by doing so, that it actually pays to go out looking for obstacles to circumvent.

About six months after inventing the callback system, I was on vacation with my family in Israel. Here I used the callback system many times myself in the presence of others. Almost everyone who saw this was amazed and told me they wished they could use my system to cut their own bills. Although I was flattered, I couldn't accommodate them, since I only had enough callback equipment for my own purposes.

Late one night, as I was driving past the Dead Sea to the vacation resort of Eilat, I had a stunning revelation: There were no limits! I was so excited I couldn't drive anymore. I stopped the car, jumped out, and woke up my passengers, my best friend, Simon, and my wife, Debbie. "I've got it!" I told them. "We'll start an international phone company! We'll change telecommunications forever!" What did they think? My wife said it sounded like a good idea. Simon nodded his approval. "We're going to be bigger than AT&T," I shouted. "We're going to be rich!"

"That's great," my wife said, but could I please get back in the car and keep driving before the kids woke up?

I did, but I was still on fire. Within days I had, via telephone, redeployed Marc and half my office staff to start working on the details of setting up a phone company. It seemed like taking candy from a baby. I came back from Israel ready to take on the world.

It was an exciting time for us. If a person really believes in something and is willing to exert leadership, anything is possible and everyone will follow no matter how far-fetched the idea. Sometimes, though, these far-fetched "visionary" ideas just don't work out in the real world. And as I began to turn my dream into a marketable reality, this began to look like one of those times.

First of all, I discovered tremendous resistance on the part of consumers to use a system that they perceived as cumbersome and time-consuming. Some Fortune 500 firms felt it was legally questionable, to boot. People take telephones for granted. Of all the instant things in our society, the telephone is probably the most incredible, and the one we get most annoyed about when there's any glitch. To have to wait for a callback, or a dial tone, even if it took only nine seconds, was a tough thing to sell. Not only that, but since the people who could really benefit from this were all living and working in Europe, just reaching them to pitch the idea posed a problem. Setting up an international sales force proved to be virtually impossible. Whatever lessons about absentee management I hadn't fully absorbed from my years in Harvard were now driven home twice as hard, as my sales managers in France and Spain ripped me off to the tune of hundreds of thousands of dollars. The idea of callback was brilliant; putting it into practice almost put us under.

A little more than one year after my "revelation" at the Dead Sea I was just about ready to quit the phone business. The year was 1991, and it had been a disaster. My staff was dispirited. This was pure folly.

There were one or two bright spots. The three-man Olympic setup team from NBC was using our system from Barcelona, and we had miraculously secured a small exhibit space at Telecom '91, the grand international telecommunications show in Geneva. But basically the business was a failure. I told my wife I wanted to quit and skip Geneva. She counseled me to go to Geneva, since the fees we'd paid were nonrefundable and not going would have been throwing money away. "Go to Telecom for the fun of it," she said. "Get the phone business out of your system, and then if you have to you can quit." Thus began six days that changed my life, and perhaps the international telecommunications business, forever.

Once every four years the international telecommunications industry—under the sponsorship of the UN—stages a grand industry conference and exhibition in Geneva called Telecom. This beautiful and normally peaceful little city on the shores of Lake Geneva is home to Swiss bankers, exiled potentates, and flocks of swans. It also houses many of the UN's quiet administrative offices, including those that regulate international communication.

But when Telecom happens, the city is transformed into a beehive of activity. Every one of the world's major telecommunications and computer companies sets up a huge exhibition at the convention center. These multimillion-dollar exhibits stay up for just a week, but are planned out years in advance. In the aggregate, almost a billion dollars is spent on this week-long extravagance. Major firms time their research and roll out new products to coincide with the exhibition. Exhibition space is sold out three years in advance. Over a hundred thousand visitors show up for Telecom and hotel rooms are sold out for a radius of seven miles, with visitors being whisked in on high-speed trains. In the exhibit areas, extravagant gifts are given away to potential clients, and multimedia extravaganzas of Hollywood proportions are staged in the pavilions of the large companies.

It was to this exhibition that Marc Knoller (the only other person still working with me on the callback business) and I arrived with our homemade four-foot folding exhibition booth in a suitcase to push the product we no longer believed would transform the industry. On the Swissair flight, we discussed which publications he would be in charge of when we gave up the phone company upon our return. We were pretty well resigned to defeat, but the excitement of the trip and the spirit of the exhibition soon had us revved up again for one more great try.

Then we saw our exhibit area. We were placed in the Telecom equivalent of Siberia, miles from the main exhibit area, with other small American companies. While thousands thronged to the indoor fireworks and bands at the IBM, AT&T, and Alcatel booths, or lined up to receive free cameras from Canon, only a few lost or intrepid souls wandered to our area of the exhibit floor. Action was called for, and I had an idea.

All visitors to the exhibition had to come in through the grand entranceway. Here each visitor received a copy of the show's own daily newspaper, as they moved on to a set of escalators that whisked them to the main exhibit hall. In the main hall they were greeted by stunning models who were beautifully dressed in the national costumes of their home countries or the sharply fitting uniforms of their sponsor companies. These models handed each visitor literature encouraging them to visit the booths of the companies they were working for.

The impressive displays these large companies staged were actually more a sign of their vulnerability than of their technological superiority in the marketplace. While big executives of the "important" companies were staying at luxury hotels and partying into the night, Marc and I had managed to secure an austere, empty one-bedroom apartment that had been unexpectedly vacated. Unfortunately, the former tenant had flown the coop, stiffing not only the landlord, but the telephone, gas, and electric companies as well. Ironically, while we were attending this futurist telecom extravaganza, we were without basic phone service once we left our exhibit booth. Not only that, but we ate all our meals by candlelight, after we had heated them up on Sterno. No doubt there are romantic occasions when a candlelight dinner in Geneva might be wonderful, but this was decidedly not one of those times. After several nights of tuna fish and soup in a cup, Marc and I decided to go downtown to see how the other half lived.

If anything, what was going on at night was even more mind-boggling than the excesses we witnessed by day. Huge yachts, adorned with the names of their corporate sponsors, floated majestically in the lake, while tuxedoed men, and women in haute couture gowns, danced and laughed on the decks. We thought this was unbelievable, until we came to the Grand Casino, where AT&T was holding its reception.

It is almost pointless to try to describe the elegance and splendor of the setting. This affair was clearly on par with a royal wedding. All guests was presented with a piece of Baccarat crystal as they exited, and were whisked away in a private limousine, courtesy of AT&T. Those guests who preferred to stroll in the moonlight first were discreetly followed by an AT&T observer, who radioed to the waiting limo driver when he thought the opportune moment for taking the guests home had arrived.

At first this all frightened me deeply. How could I ever hope to compete against people who could afford to spend money like this? Then I turned it around. How could companies that wasted money for their own self-aggrandizement ever hope to compete against me?

Their wealth, their bloated, grotesque display of it, distorted their corporate focus. The competition between the giant telecom companies centered more on how to impress the clients than on how to improve service or lower prices. Telecommunications is a very thin-margin business. These obscene expenditures only raised the overhead of the giant companies to the extent that they were not in a position to lower prices and rejoin the competitive fray. The one-upmanship that the big guys played with one another made them ripe for the picking from an upstart, downscale company like IDT.

As a matter of policy, we still use our same old folding display whenever we attend a trade show. We try to offer our clients great service and innovation, but there are no free drinks at the IDT booth. At the time, though, I wasn't interested in making any stands on principle, or on the virtues of corporate frugality. I just wanted people to come to our booth. So I put on my IDT baseball cap and told Marc that it was my intention to join these lovely women and give out our literature to incoming visitors. Marc greeted my plan skeptically. "You're ugly," he said. "Well, there's only two of us here, and you're not any better looking," I replied. I left Marc alone at the booth and went to join the models handing out literature.

It wasn't my looks, however, that landed me in hot water. The small press notices our callback services had generated by servicing the NBC Olympics contingent had aroused the ire of some of Europe's largest phone monopolies. True, we were almost broke and had almost no clients, but a monopoly can never be too careful, and instinctively feels the need to squelch any would-be competitors in even their most fetal state. I had not realized how threatening our fledgling efforts were to them.

It must have been this open-minded spirit that caused the gentleman at France Telecom to point me out to the huge Swiss policeman who stood at attention by the entranceway. A moment later, I was surrounded by gendarmes, and they informed me that it was illegal to distribute literature at the entrance to the exhibit hall. But, I pointed out, everybody here is doing the same thing. The others, I was informed, were handing out literature for approved companies, while I was from an outlaw, impudent organization and didn't belong in the exhibit hall. My exhibitor badge was confiscated and two huge gendarmes grabbed my arms, carried me down the escalator, and deposited me outside the exhibit hall. It was like a scene from *Curious George*. Out of the corner of my eye I saw a third policeman on the radio to his fellow officers in an apparent effort to see that I was not readmitted.

I was really stuck now. I couldn't even get back to my own booth. No matter what exhibit door I tried to come in, there were polite but implacable huge policemen refusing me entry. I was desperate. As I walked in circles outside the convention center, I suddenly had an idea—the press door! Using my American publishing credentials, I was able to secure entry to the press room. Here business journalists from around the world were drinking coffee and tapping out their stories on courtesy computer terminals. There were rows of pigeon-holes where large companies could leave press releases or messages for those reporters they wanted to reach.

This, I realized, was not such a bad place to be. I immediately started filling all the pigeonholes with my literature, and when I finished that, I attempted to reenter the exhibit floor through the press corridor. It is no wonder that no invader has penetrated Swiss territory for hundreds of years. The moment I left the press room I was spotted and a phalanx of gendarmes ran to apprehend me. Naturally, I ran back into the press room with the guards in pursuit. Just as they were about to grab me, I began shouting to the assembled journalists. "They're trying to get me. They're trying to shut me up. They want to squelch international telephone competition. No matter what they do to me, you've got to get the story out." I threw all my remaining literature up in the air, confettilike, to the reporters as I was ejected finally, and much more roughly, from the exhibit hall.

Back in the press room, however, the reporters were apparently electrified. This sort of thing may be commonplace for reporters covering wars, freedom fighters, or international terrorism, but it doesn't happen too often at business conventions. Here was a chance for the reporters who had the boring bad luck to be there to be real reporters, not just to regurgitate press releases. The effect was immediate and seismic.

Reporters descended on Marc back in our booth demanding to know how we had broken the high international telephone rate monopoly. Others demanded to know the nature of the conspiracy against us. Some actually filed their stories from our booth using our callback system. One reporter from the *New York Times* went to interview the director general of France Telecom, and was told that he was forbidden to write about IDT. The French press that the director general was used to dealing with may be cowed by this kind of directive, but it didn't fly with the *New York Times*.

Two days later we were the cover story in the Telecom show's daily paper. I was readmitted to the exhibition and returned as a sort of hero. Thousands of people flocked to our booth. The other small American companies near us were delirious. Throngs of people, unable to fight their way to our booth, quickly started buying everything our fellow Americans had to sell. Within days we had sold more service than we ever dared imagine and had lined up distributors around the world. We were jubilant. Victory had been seized from the jaws of defeat.

The small American firms that surrounded us at the convention were a story in themselves. Though the crowds were attracted to the flashy shows in the center of the exhibit floor, the companies who were developing the exciting new technologies that proved to be the engine of growth for the entire industry were all right around us.

Even I didn't realize to what extent this was true. There was a booth across from us run by a small New Jersey firm called Dialogic. Sitting across the aisle for an entire week, I noticed a particularly energetic tall saleswoman who was working Dialogic's booth. What was particularly striking about this woman was that the colors of her high heels and lipstick were always perfectly matched—bright red high heels, bright red lipstick on Monday; on Tuesday orange high heels, orange lipstick; on Wednesday hot pink high heels, hot pink lipstick; and so on. I was so impressed by her ability to match colors that I missed out on discovering one of the world's greatest companies years before it became famous. Dialogic is now one of the hottest companies on Wall Street. Unfortunately, I noticed the lipstick, but never bought their stock. Today, any company that wants to control telephone switching with a personal computer is familiar with Dialogic cards. These essential computer peripherals have revolutionized telecommunications.

Dialogic and other small to mid-sized companies that we saw in Geneva were responding to the real needs of advancing technology, which demanded that everything that had been done on a million-dollar mainframe yesterday had to be done by a thousand-dollar PC today. This is business technology at its purest, responding to the real needs of the market. This is in sharp contrast to another form of expensive self-aggrandizement I've enjoyed watching big companies pursue. That is, they try to establish themselves as the leaders in whatever the latest trendy new technology seems to be. These companies will spend billions of dollars providing "interactive" cable services to a few hundred cable subscribers in some test market. They run to tell eager Wall Street analysts that their company is leading in the latest hot technology and so they're definitely the company to stay with. Usually these same companies totally ignore improving and concentrating on their core product line.

To give just a couple of examples, consider the automobile industry. While Japanese automakers were looking for ways to improve the fuel efficiency and reliability of their cars, General Motors was using its high cash surpluses garnered from the sales of soon-to-be-outdated gas guzzlers to purchase Hughes Aircraft. Honda, in the meantime, had in 1976 invented a totally new process that pushed gas mileage through the roof, allowing Honda, up to then principally a maker of motorcycles, to leapfrog the American automakers with the Accord, eventually displacing the Oldsmobile Cutlass as America's most purchased car.

Similarly, while Toyota and other Japanese automakers were conducting intensive focus groups with American consumers to find out what amenities would persuade them to buy their cars, Ford executives in Dearborn were completely in the dark as to what consumers wanted. It was not until the early 1980s that Ford executives instituted consumer focus groups to find out how people actually felt about Ford cars. It is interesting to note that by the time these groups were held in Marin County, California in the early eighties, domestic car market shares in that area had fallen drastically—Ford's included. The situation was so bad that in some groups local citizens were unable to express any opinion on Ford products. Not only did *none* of the participants own a Ford, but not one of the participants even knew a person who owned a Ford.

Perhaps, though, one of the strangest cases of a large company that lost focus was Xerox. This office products giant actually set up the most advanced private computer research facility in the world in Palo Alto. The remarkable group of scientists they assembled there actually invented and were developing the technologies on which Windows software, the Macintosh computer, and laser printing were based. Had Xerox seen these projects through to their conclusions, the company would today be the dominant player not only in copying products, but in computer hardware, software, and imaging as well. At that time, though, diversification conglomerates and stock swaps were the rage on Wall Street, while new technologies were ho-hum—exactly the opposite of today. Therefore, the powers-that-were at Xerox corporate headquarters tried to impress Wall Street, rather than do what was best for their own company. The remote executives in Rochester pursued a course of unfocused diversification and stock market maneuvering. The industry Xerox gave birth to is today dominated by Hewlett-Packard and two previously unknown companies whose chief executives had the good fortune to learn early about the new technologies at Palo Alto that weren't being developed. Those two chief executives were Steve Jobs and Bill Gates. Their companies, Apple and Microsoft, are where they are today because Xerox execs in Rochester had more important things to think about than office products.

About a year ago, while attending a gathering of the Royal Society for International Affairs in London at which I was to speak, I heard speaker after speaker from the world's largest telephone companies on the wonders of interactive cable and broadband media services. One after another they told how their companies were spending almost all of their multimillion-dollar development budgets pursuing these futuristic services. All of them said that in the future telephone calls would be unimportant, and actual calls would ride the network for free. Once again, I was alarmed. How could I hope to compete without spending billions on interactive cable technology too? Then I realized these guys didn't know what they were talking about. They were so busy worrying about becoming obsolete by not leading the market in interactive cable and other futuristic technology that they hadn't stopped to consider if anyone really wants it. In fact, like the automakers who didn't improve their core product, but researched electric cars or diversified into aeronautics, they were vulnerable to be beaten by upstarts like us. When my time came to speak about the future of telecommunications, I had one simple thing to say: Ten years from now, people will still be spending billions of dollars making phone calls, except they'll be making them with companies like us, because the other guys are going to be too busy trying to figure out why the sexy new technologies didn't catch on.

So far, with only nine years to go, I'm sticking with my prediction.

Shortly after Geneva, the *New York Times* ran a front-page story in their business section describing how our little company was cutting international telephone rates by more than 50 percent worldwide. *Time, Newsweek, Forbes, Business Week, Der Spiegel,* the *Economist,* the London *Times,* and the *Wall Street Journal* soon jumped on the story. Suddenly telecommunications directors from the Fortune 500 were calling us back saying they had reconsidered and wanted to use our service. Firms from around the world did the same.

Suddenly we were in the telecommunications business—big-time! Often we reach turning points in our lives that are easily missed, and only years later do we recognize their importance. But this one came with banner headlines and I instantly recognized it as momentous. Only later did I have a chance to ponder the business lessons that I learned in Geneva.

First, every company needs to have a distinctive personality. We went into this business to be renegades who would take on the huge telecommunications carriers directly, and not be part of their old boy network. By sticking with this goal and always behaving accordingly, we eventually became the "outsiders" to turn to for lower prices. Along the way, we became the darlings of the international media and saved a lot of companies a lot of money. In this case the corporate personality fit neatly with my own. My corporate life has raised the stakes, but I'm still the same rebellious person that I always was.

Second, I realized that you have to select a single focus and stick to it. We had one aim: cutting international rates. There are many other uses for the technology we developed in both the cellular and data markets, but had we pursued them we would have lost all direction. By concentrating on a single killer application for our technology, we were able to wedge our way into what had been a completely closed industry.

I also learned this: Listen to your spouse. If it were up to me, I might have given up before Geneva. I was already shell-shocked from so much rejection, and I couldn't see that we were at the precipice of real success. Sometimes a spouse or a close advisor can appreciate the larger picture. So, if you're lucky enough to have people around you whom you can trust, listen to their advice when it's given.

Chapter Nine
Raising Money

❖

My grandmother, who was once a young, well-to-do widow, lost everything in the Depression. Her stocks collapsed, the bank foreclosed on her mortgage and took away her home, and she had to work for years in an unheated newspaper stand in order to earn enough money to support herself and her son, my father, her only child. Growing up with two pesky sisters, I spent most weekends sleeping over at my grandma's house on Bruckner Boulevard in the Bronx. She was my best friend, and she warned me against borrowing money, investing in stocks, and not preparing for a rainy day. I listened attentively. Although I'm a baby boomer, a large part of me has the values of someone who grew up in the Depression.

For this reason I have always been averse to borrowing, unnecessary risk-taking, or taking in investors. Thus, as soon as I was able to put together enough money, the first thing I did was pay off my mortgage. (Yes, I know it doesn't make much tax sense, but I'm sure my grandmother thought I was right.) And even as my business grew from a one-man operation to a million-dollar operation, I never secured a bank credit line or sold stock. It has always seemed to me that the best, most rational way to grow is out of profits. When you're spending your own money, you tend to make sounder decisions and take less foolish risks. You also sleep better at night.

Upon entering the highly capitalized telecommunications business, I continued my old policy. All our start-up product development sales and equipment acquisition expenses were paid for out of our publishing profits. Of course, the only equipment we needed in the beginning was one $500 callback device about the size of a pie box for each of our customers, and as I pointed out earlier, we didn't have too many customers.

To conserve money, our offices at that time were crowded into a small converted funeral parlor in the Bronx that we shared with my father's insurance brokerage. As there was absolutely no spare room in the office, when we finally got a couple of clients, we put their modems in the men's bathroom, sitting on top of the toilet bowl water tank. In those early days, whenever the callback rang, we would all race into the men's room to watch the little red lights that indicated the progress of the call. With each completed phone call we would all hug, embrace, give each other high fives, and then leave the men's room.

By the time we had eight boxes and a half dozen phone business employees, however, three things became clear. First, we couldn't all fit into the men's room. Second, if we got any more clients, all the boxes would tip and fall in the toilet, destroying our business. (These days, my constant concern that everything could go down the toilet is more euphemistic in nature.) Finally, as the business grew, new boxes were going to cost a lot of money.

My concern stemmed even more from the cost of keeping the boxes in operation than from purchasing them. Each box, you see, required two telephone lines in order to work. New York Telephone was charging us about $30 per line monthly. This came to $720 per year in line fees for each box we had in operation, far more than the actual cost of the units. It wasn't long, though, before we discovered that in New Jersey, home state of AT&T, local phone access lines only cost $12 per month. This meant we'd save over $400 per unit annually (roughly the actual cost of a box) by moving our callback units to

New Jersey. Of course, our savings would be reduced by the amount of any rent we'd have to pay in Jersey. Not wanting to have this savings reduced, I tried to see if there was a way we could get free rent.

Through my involvement with a charitable organization and the good agency of my dear friend Michael Becher, I had a passing acquaintance with David Steiner, the most prominent industrial office park developer in the United States, one of the largest property owners in New Jersey, who was also famous as a very generous philanthropist. Surely, I reasoned, this kind of man would give me a free storeroom in one of his many buildings to house my boxes. Through a close friend of mine who was one of Dave's codirectors in this organization I was able to secure an appointment with Mr. Steiner.

In life I have found that no good deed goes unrewarded. In my case, this has been so much the case that I actually find it troubling. In fact, the rabbinic sages say that no man has ever become impoverished from giving to charity. Moreover, they state that those who give to charity will reap a tenfold return on what they have given. In my case, this has definitely been true. But how is one to get any satisfaction from acts of self-sacrifice if, as an almost immediate result of these acts, you actually find yourself substantially better off? As evidence, my accountant, who really knows how incompetent I am, says that each year, after reviewing our books and business deals, he can attribute our success to nothing other than the disproportionately large percentage of our income that goes to charity. In other words, an act of G-d.

Dave Steiner, at sixty, was as kind and hospitable as I could have hoped. He didn't act at all like an important, busy man with many pressing responsibilities who was squeezing in an appointment he wanted to be quickly finished with as a favor to a friend. Rather, he treated me the same way he would have treated a fellow real estate mogul, or Fortune 500 CEO who wanted to discuss a new headquarters building. I was given the royal treatment: coffee, closed door, "no phone calls, please, for the next hour." I had it made.

Unfortunately for me, however, David Steiner and the IRS had the same policy on charitable donations. It was okay to give all you wanted to nonprofit causes, but business was business. Or, as Dave more succinctly put it, "Young man, I worked my way up from the bottom. Your business ideas sound great to me, and I like you. But there's nothing for nothing in this world. So tell me what you'll give me if I give you the space."

Well, I hadn't come all this way to pay rent, so I needed another idea. The word "nothing" gave it to me. By moving to New Jersey I would be bringing down our costs to operate my boxes to next to nothing. But the cost of buying hundreds, and perhaps thousands, of boxes was still potentially crippling. A light went on in my head. If I could get Dave to pay for the boxes, I'd really be off to the races. "Tell you what," I said. "If you give me the space, I'll let you pay for all my boxes, and I'll give you ten percent of the profit I make on each one."

"You, young man," he replied, "have *chutzpah,* but it sounds like it might be a good deal. Write it up. I'll review it with my partner and if this deal is as good as you say it is, we've got a bargain."

I could hardly wait to get back to my office. If this deal went through, everything seemed possible.

But what, you may ask, about my principles? What about never borrowing or taking in investors?

To begin, I didn't really consider this borrowing or taking in investors in the classic sense. At this point, David and his partner, Peter Sudler, had no equity in the company. I still owned IDT 100 percent free and clear, even if technically they owned some of our equipment. I also didn't consider this a loan. I was under no obligation to make any fixed repayment schedule. Therefore, if things did not go as well as I hoped, nobody would be in a position to foreclose on me.

True, in order to entice David and Peter into the deal, I had to throw in some other goodies, like the right to do all my future equipment financing on the same terms. I, however, controlled the amount that customers would be charged for our service. Therefore, I controlled the amount the "investors" would actually make. Ten percent seemed to me a pretty fair return, given the fact that this looked like it would become a pretty capital-intensive business.

The investor got one other large benefit in this deal, a huge tax write-off. Because the investors were the ones who were buying the equipment, they were entitled to depreciate it over a few years. Given their high tax bracket, this meant that each dollar they invested would actually cost them only fifty cents.

Although I came to this idea almost by accident, it has helped me to formulate some ideas on raising capital, particularly for relatively small operations that require tangible assets.

I strongly recommend that those trying to finance such a business look for some way to divide the entity up into its component parts and sell off those parts. This will result in your keeping full control of the business. It also means your investors get something tangible that they can keep even if you flop.

As an example, consider the opening of a restaurant. If your investor simply buys the actual building, land, and appliances, he could rent them to you for a fixed percentage of the sales for the first five years, and some flat rent plus percentage thereafter. You can even build in a fixed buyout price, if the investor lets you. Now you own 100 percent of the restaurant without partners, and you don't even have to worry about the rent if the business is bad in the beginning. Your investor, on the other hand, doesn't have to worry if you're an incompetent. In five years he'll own the building, which he can throw you out of, and in the meantime he's depreciating the property.

One of my favorite high-tech variations of this is to create a subsidiary company to develop a new technology. The investors in this company get a minority interest in the stock, entitling them to a fixed percentage of the licensing fees. The parent company pays the subsidiary for use of this technology. The amount of this payment is a fixed percentage of the sales from service that incorporates the new technology.

This winds up being a good deal for the business because you've got the money to develop the technology without diluting your ownership interest or taking on crushing debt. It's also not a bad deal for the investors because they know exactly what they're investing in, and if it works, their return is guaranteed, not plowed back into corporate expansion.

To get back to the story, though, David did tell me one other little thing: His partner had to do his due diligence. At the time, I had no idea what this meant. I thought perhaps it meant he had to diligently go to the bank and present a check to me, to whom it was due. What I learned is that "due diligence" means that prospective investors have the right to come in and thoroughly examine your books and all aspects of your operations. With some investors, due diligence is just a formality; with others, it is a virtual inquest. With Peter Sudler, it was definitely the latter.

Peter Sudler was at the time David's younger partner. He had once served as one of the lead U.S. attorneys to the Justice Department's Organized Crime Strike Force, and he approached due diligence with the zeal of the prosecuting attorney he once was. If there was excess waste or corporate expense account padding that his and David's money were really going to finance, Peter Sudler would find it out. But from the moment he pulled into the parking lot of our ramshackle headquarters building in the Bronx, he knew that this definitely wasn't the land of padded expense accounts.

Our books were so simple it took less than an hour for Peter to review them. We bought our phone time for X and sold for Y. Each client required one box, which served as their callback connection. They'd call in, the box would recognize their signal, and immediately call them back with an American dial tone. The average profit per client was quite high, and the list of companies waiting to sign up was quite long. In short, it didn't take much to see that this was a good deal.

As to expense accounts, we didn't have any. I didn't even take a salary. We didn't have a secretary. In fact, this was just the problem:

We were too efficient. We had no PBX, only old desks and chairs, no conference rooms or corporate cars, no media advertising budget. In short, we didn't seem like a company at all. We were more like a Boy Scout troop trying to earn an international telephone merit badge. Couldn't we spend just a little more money on basic amenities? Peter wanted to know. But he did make the investment.

In a way, Peter was right. He pushed us to get a first-rate, big-name accounting firm when I had previously used only a solo practitioner. He convinced me to buy the twenty-thousand-square-foot building in Hackensack we now hardly fit into, when I was happy with the twelve hundred square feet we had in the Bronx. He was even the one to convince me to do a public offering several years later, when I might have restricted our market share forever due to lack of capital.

The fact is, however, that for everything there is a season. Had we started out Peter's way, with fancy officers, big law and accounting firms, and other needless start-up expenses, we'd have gone broke before we ever got to the next stage. Today our law firm, accountants, and underwriters are all the largest and most prestigious in America. We did get bargain rates from them, though. Our desks are still secondhand, but, unlike most people in our business, we're profitable. You've got to set your priorities early.

I was so happy about my deal with Peter that I convinced Harvey Beker, another philanthropist I knew from Michael Becher (and the head of a large commodities trading firm), to also buy about $100,000 worth of equipment for me. I got around the problem of how I could sell the same boxes to two different people in an interesting way. We created what we called shadow boxes. Each box, we explained, needed a certain amount of marketing budget to see it was placed into service. The second investor could put up this money and receive another 10 percent of the generated revenues. Now I had money to pay my salespeople and their expenses, as well as the money to buy the boxes. And the best part was I still got to keep 80 percent of the revenues. High finance was really fun.

Unfortunately, though, the business went really well but expansion expenses came up that I hadn't anticipated. I had never run a phone company before, and so things like switches and cable and monitoring equipment were new to me. Maintaining the network required an around-the-clock crew. It seemed that every $1 in sales cost $2 in expenses. In less than a year, I had sold out all the boxes. The investors were getting a good return, but I was almost broke again. No problem, I thought; I'll just sell Dave, Peter, and Harvey some more equipment. This time it didn't work.

Dave and Peter sat me down and put it to me this way. "This business can really become significant if you start running it right. The days for individual modem boxes are passing and you need to develop some large-scale commercial switches. All the major business magazines have already written you up. You have tremendous potential. A chance like this comes only once in a lifetime. All you're missing is capital. We have it. We'll give you one million dollars for ten percent of the company. We don't want any more of your boxes or shadow boxes. Give us the equity, and together we'll make this a great company."

Naturally, I said no. Reluctantly. I really wanted that million dollars, but I wasn't going to give up my equity. I was sure I could convince them to do some kind of box deal again.

I couldn't. They only wanted equity. "Remember, we backed you when all you had was an idea." True, I thought. "You can be sure if we put this kind of money in, we'll do everything to see you make it and to protect our investment." Reasonable, I thought. "Either take this offer now or just go back to the Bronx and keep struggling to make it one box at a time and forget the big-time. Howard, a million dollars is a lot of money and we're willing to give it to you now. Be smart. Take the money."

They had me. I really wanted to go for the big-time. I needed the money. I'd done everything I could up to this point to hold on to all the equity. I took their offer.

Did I make the right decision? Even now I'm not sure. The fact is I could have squeezed the necessary cash from my personal savings and publishing business. Although at a later point this actually became necessary, I was unwilling early on because this was still a risky business. If I put my life's savings in and everything went kaput, my family would have been left with nothing. Today, when it looks like Dave and Peter will make a better than thirtyfold return on their investment, it's easy to say I should have mortgaged my house and done it myself. But I've made plenty of money as it is, and the truth is, I'm just not that big a risk-taker. They were probably right. Without taking the equity investment I might still be living hand to mouth, peddling boxes.

Not only that, but many times our investors have helped me to see the light when I refused. Insofar as I take a small salary and am some sort of an ascetic anyhow, I had a tendency not to care that much whether we showed profits or not. All I really wanted was to keep on hiring people and keep on growing. I've always been ready to reinvest the profits from any established part of our business into another part that shows long-run potential. The problem is, sometimes I don't know when to stop. Ultimately, if a business is justified, it has to be self-funding and profitable eventually. Aiming for profitability also forces the business to grow in the proper way. Our investors, who are many times more concerned with the bottom line than I, have more than once persuaded us to take drastic steps to put our new enterprises into the black. Before we went public, our outside investors never held more than 20 percent of our stock, so they had to persuade rather than force us to make these moves. I think this is the best kind of balance a company can have.

As we continued to grow, more capital was required. Eventually we sold another 10 percent of the company to various investors that our original core group brought in, until we finally reached the point that our own revenue was sufficient to fund all but our most outrageous ambitions. Along the way we've taken in some fascinating investors. Almost all are very rich men. I'm always afraid that if things go sour I don't want someone like my grandmother, who couldn't afford it, getting wiped out, just because she had faith in me.

One of the more interesting investors we've taken in has been Mario Gabelli and Gabelli Funds. I was introduced to Mario by Harvey Beker. In fact, I've met most of my investors through other investors. Once you get into those august circles, it seems that everyone knows each other. They invest in each other's funds as a kind of hedge.

Mario Gabelli, for those of you not familiar with Wall Street, is the country's leading telecommunications investor. The Gabelli Fund has over $12 billion under management. Presidents of countries and financial potentates use all sorts of stratagems to secure a meeting with this most powerful individual.

We were therefore thrilled when Mr. Gabelli agreed to visit our office. In our industry this is vaguely akin to a visit from G-d. Not that I felt we should act differently or put on special airs in deference to the visit. If Mario liked us the way we were, great. If not, then he was not the right partner for us.

On the day of the great man's visit, therefore, all our people were wearing jeans as usual. The ramshackle used desk and chairs were as tightly crowded together as usual. And the general chaotic frenzy of our office was undiminished.

I did, however, make one concession to this great man's visit. I ordered in a couple of pastrami sandwiches in case he was expecting lunch.

As we were eating our sandwiches and talking, Mr. Gabelli told me how impressed and refreshed he was by our no-nonsense approach.

"Where do you come from?" he asked me.

Rather than putting on airs and telling him I graduated from Harvard, I told him where I was really from. "The Bronx," I said.

"No kidding," he said. "I knew it. I'm from the Bronx too. We Bronx boys aren't impressed by all that corporate bullshit." Amazed, I asked him where in the Bronx he was from. "You wouldn't know the area," he told me. "It was called Bathgate Avenue."

"Bathgate Avenue," I responded. "I used to help my grandmother buy fruits and vegetables from the Italian sidewalk vendors on Bathgate Avenue."

"No shit," he said. "I used to help my uncle run one of those stands."

A real friendship was born that day.

There are two questions you might ask at this point. If I'm so against giving away equity, why have I put so much effort into getting investors? The answer is simple. I needed the money. Business is not a place for absolute principles. You have to be willing to compromise and alter tiny—and large—preconceived notions when the situation calls for it. This is not to say that principles are unimportant. They keep you rooted. Even while pursuing investors, I hated giving away equity and always looked to sell as little as I could for the fairest price I could obtain. Many times I walked away from deals others would have taken because it would have watered down our control. As a result, we still own a larger percentage of our own equity than any comparable firm in our industry. If you were to reply, yes, but selling this much equity isn't something your grandmother would have approved of, I'd have to say, true, but let's face it, Grandma mostly made potato pancakes. She wasn't in the capital-intensive telecommunications business.

Why, you might ask then, do we have such a variety of investors when any one could have funded all our capital needs? This is an interesting question, and I'd like to tell a short rabbinic tale to explain.

One of the great rabbis of nineteenth-century Europe was the Vilna Gaon. When he was newly graduated from rabbinic school with the highest honors, he went to apply for a job as the rabbi of his own small town. There, the selection committee of the synagogue turned him down. Eventually he became world famous as the chief rabbi of a much larger city. One day on a speaking tour he spotted a member of the original selection committee in the audience. "I always wondered why you turned me down for that first job," he prompted.

The man responded honestly. "Rabbi, today you're a great man, and when people see you, they see a great scholar. But we, who knew you when you were growing up, could see only a small boy in knickers."

So too with investors. Those investors who befriend you early when your company is very tiny can never really see you as the company you grow to be. Somehow, it is difficult for them to justify the ever higher evaluation of the worth of your stock. Like elderly folk who still find it hard to believe that it costs more than a dollar to get into the movies, they too are, to some extent, always rooted in the past. Thus, as your company progresses, you sometimes have to be prepared to include new partners who are willing to see you in a completely new light. Oftentimes, their more optimistic and up-to-date appraisal of your value is just what is needed to help older investors see the light, as well.

I should mention here one of my favorite investors and one of my most eccentric. Meyer Berman is perhaps the most famous short seller on Wall Street. In this capacity, it is his talent to pick out those companies everyone else thinks are great, but that in fact are in trouble. When the stock collapses, his clients profit. I suppose it's obvious why it's sort of a thrill to have this kind of a skeptic as one of our main backers. Meyer usually only makes money on other people's failures. With us, he believes in our success. As a professional contrarian, none of Meyer's views are fixed. He is always ready to accept that the company's growth validates ever higher valuations, and so he is someone we can do business with on an ongoing basis. He is also a true friend.

Recently I was looking to raise half a million dollars to develop a new technology in a subsidiary created for that purpose. I called Meyer on my car phone on the way home from work and asked if he could recommend any investors for this proposition.

"What's wrong? My money's not green enough for you?" he asked.

"No," I replied. "I just didn't want to hit you up again."

"Well, how much would you like me to put in?" he countered.

"I guess a hundred and fifty thousand would be okay," I said.

"Too much," he toyed with me. "I had a rough day in the market."

"Okay, Meyer," I replied, taking the bait. "How much do you want to put in?"

"Do you have a coin in your pocket?" he asked.

"Yes," I answered.

"Well, take it out and look at it." Trying to steer the car and examine the coin at the same time, I informed him I was looking at it. "Okay," he devilishly responded. "Now I want you to flip it. Heads, I'll give you a hundred thousand for one percent; tails, fifty thousand for half a percent."

"Meyer," I reasoned, "do you really expect me to tell you the truth?" I said.

"I know you won't lie to me," the sly fox told me.

"Okay, Meyer. Listen, how 'bout we just compromise?"

"Fine," he said. "I'll give you seventy-five thousand for three-quarters of a percent. Write it up, send it to me, and I'll get you the check."

"Meyer," I told him, "I don't know if I'd invest in me."

"Why not?" he asked.

"I've got no balls," I said, laughing.

"I'd rather do business with someone who sees the downside," he countered, and the phone clicked off. As I said, Meyer is one of a kind.

With any investor there is something the importance of which I can't stress enough. My first criteria is that there should be strong chemistry and commonality between us. An investment in a private company is usually long-term. A bad partnership, like a bad marriage, can ruin everyone's life and might even wind up in court. My own father once had a partner with whom he got along so poorly that the two did not speak for over five years in spite of working in the same office. My family thinks my father's angina and need for bypass surgery is directly attributable to this partnership. To this day, the ex-partner is never referred to in my parents' house by name, but simply as "the beast."

To me, it's a very personal thing. In fact, almost everything about business, from the people I hire, to my suppliers, to my investors, is a personal thing with me. If someone has something good or bad to say about IDT, I take it personally. That's the point of being a person in business rather than a robot.

Decisions made only by the numbers are dehumanizing. But if this is how your valuation is to be based, then why go to a private investor? You can always do better from the public markets, and when really big money is needed, that's where you belong. Until that time, if you're going to take a little less in cash, see that it's made up for in the value of the relationship.

As you have seen, many of the initial people who funded IDT were contacts I made through my involvement in charitable causes. Though getting to know these kinds of people is obviously its own reward, I'd like to tell you a little bit about why I feel it's so important for a businessman or anyone else to contribute generously, in both time and money, to good causes and to those less fortunate.

First, however, I need to confess a little bit about myself so you can understand where I'm coming from. To begin with, I am largely a media creation. The self-confident Howard Jonas you read about in magazines who fearlessly challenges large corporations and state monopolies is not me. Though I play up to my role like any good actor who's finally landed a successful part, I am anything but arrogantly self-confident. In reality, I am usually as scared as a person left alone in the wilderness, and I'm in a constant state of anxiety over what to do next. And while I can't deny I enjoy the image the press has given me of being a whirlwind boy genius who's taking the high-tech world by storm, this too is an extreme exaggeration. I'm neither the smartest person in my company nor even one of the youngest. In fact, I'm already over forty. Maybe I look younger than I really am. Appearance, I have found, is often more important than reality.

This said, there is a certain grain of truth in associating me with youth. I don't feel I've ever really grown up. As a child, I used to complain to my parents that I was an adult trapped in a child's body.

Now, ironically, I feel just the opposite. I'm just a young boy trapped in an adult's body. I think when you strip away all the pretension, many of us are still just our little boy (or girl) selves. You already know about my earliest business ventures and my high school and college careers, but let me tell you a bit about the young me so you can understand the old me better.

I grew up as one of the few white kids in a mostly black neighborhood, and then as the only Jewish kid in an Italian Catholic neighborhood. As a result, I was always an outsider. As I grew up, I almost never managed to have more than one good friend, if that, at any time. On top of this I was a bookworm and athletically uncoordinated in neighborhoods where sports were everything. This meant I got chosen last, if at all, for every team. Finally, I was a stubborn nonconformist who had to do everything my own way. This meant that even in school the teachers hated me and seemed to call in my parents at least weekly to complain that I wasn't living up to my potential and was perhaps in need of special ed.

To give you a few snapshots of my fifth-grade year, I can remember the hell that I got from my parents after my fifth-grade teacher in P.S. 32 called them in and demanded I be placed not in special ed, but in a mental institution for not behaving in class. (I mention, even now, in my defense that this behavior that made me the "worst one in the class" consisted of talking to the girl next to me. Fellow classmates who brought switchblades to school and used them to extort lunch money were considered by Mrs. Bright to be more socially acceptable.) This finally pushed my parents to move to another neighborhood (with, of course, a new school). Before leaving, however, I went around the class and asked each of my "friends" to sign my autograph book. Most simply wrote things like "drop dead" or "I hope you get hit by a car." One little girl, though, surprised me by composing a whole poem on my behalf. I remember it even now. "I wish I were a grapefruit and here's the reason why. Because when you come to eat me, I'd squirt you in the eye."

Upon moving to my new school, my first notable act was to strike out in a schoolwide softball game, thereby eliminating my class's team. After that, I became the key player in a new game. It was called "Let's Kill the New Kid on the Way Home from School." The way it was played was that every day after school about a dozen boys from my class would gather outside the door I was supposed to exit from in order to escort me to a vacant lot about a block from school and teach me a lesson. I, having no desire to learn whatever it was that they so badly wanted to teach me, would each day trick them by exiting from an unexpected door. Inevitably, within seconds someone would scream out, "There goes the new kid," and the game was on. I'd have to run five blocks home and slam the door before any of the boys, usually lagging half a block behind, could catch me. In spite of having flat feet, the motivation factor made me very fast and I usually got home safely. (To this day, like Forrest Gump, I still run; only now just for exercise.) Occasionally, though, they would catch me. At this point, I would appeal to the group's macho instincts and tell them I'd fight whichever one wanted to beat me up. In this one-on-one confrontation, I, the much more motivated fighter, inevitably beat up my tormentor, more than once breaking a nose in the process. This, however, only made things worse. The assailant's mother would usually come in to school, and I'd get in trouble for starting a fight. Then all the boys in the class would agree that now I really had to be taught a lesson and the cycle would begin again. The game only finally ended after several months when Kelvin Gibson, a very large black boy I had befriended in my former school, suddenly began being bused to my new school. He was immediately recognized as the school's finest athlete and thus became the main man in class. Only when he, in a gesture of friendship for which I am still grateful, declared the game at an end, and me under his personal protection, could I again walk home like a normal person.

Not that this ended my problem. My new teacher again called my parents in because I wasn't living up to my potential. At this point, my father took two new approaches. First, he informed her that I was, in fact, performing way above my potential. In fact, he assured her, I really did not have potential, but was gifted in making people think that I did. Second, he drove me down to the Bowery (the section of New York where drunken vagrants live on the street begging for coins from motorists) so I could see what I would amount to if I didn't start shaping up in school. The trip, however, had an unanticipated effect on me. I didn't at all see these men as worthless vagrants. Rather, I saw them as fellow nonconformists who had been beaten down by teachers, the boys in the fifth grade, the grapefruit girl, and all my other enemies who only wanted to marginalize people. These were my friends. Someday I would liberate them. For now, though, I demanded we stop the car so I could give them all the money I had.

None of these experiences, however, in any way broke my spirit. I simply refused to accept the values or judgments of the world around me. In order to keep any self-esteem, I had to retreat into my own fantasy world, where everything was good and everything was possible. I actually saw everybody's rejection and disapproval as some kind of necessary character-building I had to go through before I could achieve something great and show everyone they were wrong about me all along. I also became a person who never gave up. In my own mind I would glamorize every failure as some kind of valiant effort against all odds, laudable just for the attempt. ("The Impossible Dream" was my favorite song growing up, and Don Quixote I saw not as a sad lunatic but as a real hero.) I'd also romanticize every small success as a major step in my inevitable march to some kind of great glory. Thus, for close to ten years following college, when my main business consisted of driving around all night delivering brochures to hotel lobbies, worrying that my old van would conk out, thus killing the business, I imagined myself not as the truck driver I really was, but as an advertising mogul building a solid base for a future display advertising empire and beyond.

Of course, I realized I might always stay a deliveryman. Even worse, I knew I could even lose that. I might lose my brochure clients and then I'd be a complete zero. Even when things started to get better, I was always aware that just one misstep and it could all be over.

When you've been on the bottom for so long, it's hard to take success seriously. When people start calling you "Mr. Jonas" instead of "Howard," it's sort of surreal. When you see your picture on the front page of the *New York Times* or have people treat you with all kinds of respect because they read about you in *Business Week* or *Forbes*, it's hard to take it seriously after so many years. It's strange that people think you're unusual because you don't lock yourself away in a fancy corner office, still wear blue jeans to work, and answer your own phone. Really, nothing's changed from getting chased home from school, booed off the stage, or working as a deliveryman. But the breaks have gone my way, so the fantasies are becoming true. Still, I know only too well that it might not have gone that way and even now it could reverse. That's why I find it much easier to relate to those whom society calls "losers" rather than the "winners." Frankly, I think we have a lot more in common.

Sometimes, though, if you just keep on plugging, the world changes enough that those who were out of fashion or broke one day are suddenly in vogue and prosperous the next. By the end of high school, the political climate (and I) had both changed and I was elected student body president. Also, my little advertising business was starting to make what I felt (though largely in my fantasy world) was a good deal of money. The first thing I did on getting elected president was appoint all the kids nobody liked as committee chairmen. The first thing I wanted to do when I started making money was to give it all away to others who were still on the bottom of the heap. These were the people I really could identify with and wasn't going to forget now that things were a little better. Who knows, in the same position, maybe one of them would do the same for me. I started giving a lot to charity before I left high school.

I was reluctant, however, to give everything away. If I did, then how would I ever be able to save enough to invest and get really rich and really redress all the injustices in the world? But if I started to think like this, then maybe I'd just become selfish and out for myself and just like all the people I didn't want to be like. This dilemma really bothered me.

At just that time, though, I was starting to rediscover my Jewish roots. I was reading the Bible for the first time and it had a really great idea. It said all people should tithe their income. That is, give ten percent of everything they make to charity. The commentaries go on to say that people can give away up to 20 percent if they want to, but they're not allowed to give more. If they did, that would endanger their own financial standing, which would be bad for society as a whole. I therefore happily decided I'd try to always give around 20 percent of my earnings to charity. It's hard to even begin to tell how satisfying this has been.

First off, it's fueled my fantasies and my self-image in a way nothing else could. Imagine how rich you feel every week, no matter how much or how little you've made, when you can sit down, think about all those people who are truly needy in the world, decide which ones you want to help the most, and actually just send them a significant percentage of your earnings.

I can tell you from firsthand experience it makes you feel like a millionaire. It's impossible to feel needy when you're able to give away money you might otherwise waste on some luxury. It makes an accessory you don't have seem unimportant. And this is just as true if you're living hand to mouth as when you're living in clover.

Giving to those more needy also keeps your mind pointed in the right direction. Instead of making you envious and unhappy by concentrating on everybody who has more than you or is doing better, it makes you grateful and satisfied by concentrating your thoughts on all the hardships people less fortunate than you endure. And thinking about all this hardship is a good motivator for making you want to do even better.

When you think about it, doesn't it seem like an empty life to put all your creative powers and energy to work in order that you can drive a Lexus? To me, it seems nuts. If that's what life's really all about, maybe it would be better to stay home.

On the other hand, the people who are working so they can accomplish something noble wind up elevating their whole existence. Going to work every morning is no longer a mundane task. It's spiritually uplifting. You're doing it not only for yourself, but to help others and make the world a better place.

It's good to remember that nobody's immune to disasters that could ruin your whole life as you know it. And the line between success and failure is pretty thin, believe me. Just imagine yourself in the shoes of someone who might need your help and think how you'd feel about yourself if you helped, or if you didn't. It's important to help make the world a better place. Why, you may ask, can't G-d do this Himself? Why does He need us? For years this question troubled me from a religious perspective. I mean, how could G-d let awful things happen? Then one day an answer came to me. G-d really has no choice.

The way I see it, it's very important to G-d that people have free will. Exercising your free will is being like G-d. That's why the Bible says G-d made man in His image, and this is why freedom is so important. The only way we can "get credit" for doing the right things is if we do them of our own free will. If people only do good things because they're compelled to, because G-d is right in front of them threatening to punish them if they go wrong, then what's the merit in that? In this scenario, it's actually better for G-d if people are just a little unsure as to whether He exists or not. Because if His existence were 100 percent definite, only a lunatic wouldn't do the right thing all the time. If bad things didn't happen to good people, this doubt would cease to exist.

Let's take the worst-case scenario—a small innocent baby dies from some sickness. What injustice! What did the baby do to deserve this? Obviously, nothing. Is it the baby's parents who deserved punishment? I think not. What would happen, after all, if the children of the righteous never died? It would become immediately obvious that nature wasn't operating normally. Newspapers would headline stories showing that none of the millions of children of parents who either attended religious services or gave to the United Way ever became seriously ill—that in fact, even if one of the children were thrown in front of a speeding truck, he or she would always emerge unharmed. At this point people would lose their free will and just become robots, attending services and giving charity, not because it was right, but so that their kids wouldn't die (or perhaps so they'd get rich). So G-d has to let the basically good processes of nature operate. This even means He sometimes has to let evil people do wicked things. This is their free will. Also, human nature is just as much the working of nature as is gravity, cancer, or trees blooming.

This is not to say G-d doesn't want the universe to be good, or that G-d can't intervene or make it so. G-d does intervene, but usually only after He has allowed the natural process to take its course. Then if humankind is headed in the wrong direction, He takes corrective action to remedy the situation. Good people are born who take the place of other good people and fill their roles, or sometimes do even better. Tyrants and genocidal killers are defeated by the forces of light. Liberty and self-determination are almost miraculously restored to those who have been exiled and oppressed. Mankind slowly but surely is steered toward a just, kind, and perfect world.

It is as if all the people in the world are in a giant ship. Aboard the ship, free will reigns. The passengers may treat each other well and live in peace, or they may attack each other. Sometimes, if they get too raucous, they may even back into the wheel and knock the ship off course. At times this may cause the ship to rock so violently it may seem like it will capsize. Often this is enough to get the passengers to calm down. Then, unseen to everyone, G-d sees that the ship is off course and sends gentle currents to put it back on course. So too G-d steers human history to its predestined goal.

Of course, this does nothing for those passengers who were killed in the disturbance along the way or drowned in the storms. If these people feel G-d owes them, maybe they're right. I can only suppose that in some way (whether in "heaven," through reincarnation, or something beyond human imagination) these people eventually get to share in the happiness that comes through the world's gradual, eventual perfection. They contributed to it. And justice demands they share in it.

As an example of justice, I take the rebirth of the state of Israel after the Holocaust. Whether or not the time for the Jewish people's redemption from exile had come, I cannot say. I can say, however, that for the first time in history, when the Jews faced extinction, no nation on earth opened its door to them, not even America. What choice, then, did G-d have if He wished to preserve us, than to give us our own land and make us masters of our own destiny?

I also note that throughout history Jews have always lived on the edge of extinction, never knowing if there would be a tomorrow. Is it not ironic that some of the very Jews Hitler sought to kill, people no nation sought to save, were responsible for producing America's first atomic bomb? By doing so for the United States (and not for Germany), they not only guaranteed Hitler's defeat, but created a situation in which all the world's people have become "Jews." In the Atomic Age, none of us knows whether there will be a tomorrow.

Some nights, I lie in bed, after I've seen injustice or faced my own internal problems, and think of these things and take some solace. During the days, however, I've found more comfort in actually taking action to make things better. I think this is what G-d (who gave us free will) would want us to do.

In helping to change the world, there will always be some causes that are more appealing to you than others. Me, I'm big on self-reliance, so I especially like organizations that seek to improve people's lives by making it possible for them to get on their own feet, through educational and vocational rehabilitation. It's almost impossible for me not to give to them. For someone who's willing to try, it would be crushing not to be given a chance. I know this sounds corny, but I mean it. There's no force in this world more important, more powerful, or more unstoppable than a motivated human spirit determined to succeed. I think the thing I really like the best about how our company has grown is that now whenever I meet one of these people, I can just offer them a job and figure out exactly what it is they'll be doing later. (Usually, these "charity" cases turn out to be unbelievable assets and wind up making later growth possible.)

I'm also very big on causes that have to do with extending what I'll call basic human liberties to people who don't enjoy them. The best way I can think of to free the human spirit is to first remove political oppression. (More on this in the chapter about our creation of the Digital Freedom Network.)

But even just simply giving a poor person something to eat is very important. Years ago my wife and I used to go downtown at least one night a week and give away bags we made up with sandwiches, fruit, and a drink to poor people who lived in parks, train stations, or on the street. You couldn't believe how grateful and gentle these people were. I'm sort of ashamed that with our larger family and added responsibilities we haven't found the time to do this often enough anymore. Maybe writing this will get us started again. I certainly think it would be great for our kids too. Even without this, one of the things Debbie and I are proudest of is that our kids never pass a poor person by without giving them something. If we've taught them nothing else (and sometimes we feel we haven't), this would still be the most important thing to us. It's just basic human decency.

In any event, whatever charity you choose to give to, or with whatever charitable organizations you decide to involve yourself, you'll be improving not only the lives of those you're trying to help, but your own as well. Not only that, but you'll be a partner in bringing the world closer to perfection, and as I've said previously, I think that that's really why we're here in the first place.

One last thing. By getting involved in charitable organizations you'll meet great people. People with really good values whom you'll relate to and might become close friends with. Not only that, but some of the people will be really important and powerful, too. While these powerful people are usually inaccessible in a business setting, they're usually accessible here. Who knows? One of these people might even give you a million dollars someday so you can pursue your own dream. It happened to me. I'm not saying this is the reason you should get involved in these organizations. The only reason to do this is because you honestly believe in, and want to help with, the cause. But if the contacts you make doing the right thing help you in other ways as well, I think that's just great.

Chapter Ten

1-800-SCREW-AT&T

❖

As we worked the knots out of the callback business, it began to seem that we were really on to something big. We were going to make it as a phone company. The big guys, the world's phone monopolies, were really in trouble now. We were on a roll and we were sticking it to them but good. For close to a century they charged as much as they felt like. Now, with the money I'd raised from investors, we were able to compete with them all over the world. Our roster of clients went from dozens, to hundreds, to thousands. Suddenly, all over the world, from the capitals of Europe, to the jungles of Africa, to the rain forest of Peru—IDT reps were knocking on doors offering to undercut the local monopoly's phone rate by two-thirds or more. Few prospective customers could turn down that kind of savings.

The world's press had dubbed this a "David versus Goliath" struggle, one in which they felt David would soon be wiped out by foreign regulations. It wasn't working out that way, though. We were now handling millions of calls. We had people working all night just to keep filling the fax machines with paper as new orders poured in twenty-four hours a day. Far from being wiped out, David was kicking butt. Maybe even feeling a little smug. That was when Goliath attacked.

AT&T's petition to the Federal Communications Commission de-

manded that our service be declared illegal and turned off immediately. The FCC, it demanded, needed to stop our theft of service from
AT&T before we harmed them irreparably. They claimed that every
call that dialed in to signal a callback request and hung up without
being answered utilized their network without paying them. This was
theft of service, plain and simple.

Wait a minute, we responded. Nobody told AT&T and their foreign partner they couldn't charge for uncompleted calls. This was
their own decision in order to encourage more calling. We were
just taking advantage of their own rules. Not only that, but every
incoming nonrevenue-producing "signal call" triggered a revenue-
producing callback. What were they complaining about? This was
only a legal trick to maintain the high rates from overseas, which the
foreign monopolies shared through a complex system called settlement fees with AT&T. Now AT&T and their foreign monopoly partners were using the theft-of-services argument to keep competition
out of the marketplace.

There was only one problem. The FCC didn't see it that way. According to our sources in the FCC, the ruling against us would come
out at the end of the month, following which all of our lines would be
turned off. All American phone companies would be prohibited from
doing business with us. And AT&T would be free to sue us up the
wazoo for damages.

This was a bad situation. We'd been tried and convicted without
even getting to testify. When no one at the FCC would even take my
calls, I went into near panic. How could everyone in a large federal
agency have been unavailable? Was there a kangaroo convention in
town?

If this ruling quietly went through, we'd be destroyed. Everything
I'd spent years building would be destroyed in an instant and no one
would even know. Our lines would just go dead, and our customers
would just shrug, think it was too good to last, and go back to using
the high-priced monopoly. Good-bye IDT. Sayonara Howard Jonas.

Next time, don't go where you don't belong and save everyone a lot of aggravation.

But I wasn't going to go down quietly. No freaking way. If AT&T and the FCC were going to try to eliminate me, they were going to pay for it. If there's one thing a rat or a government bureaucrat is afraid of, it's a shining light. Sure, in the dark they'll tear you to pieces. But have someone enter a room with a flashlight and suddenly they disappear. The press, I realized, was the searchlight I needed to stop any quick back-door deal. Once the press got into the act, we'd have to get a fair hearing. And a fair hearing I knew we'd win.

I called every important reporter who'd ever done a story about us or anything related to telecommunications, trying to convince them that AT&T's petition to the FCC was big news. Most said it would be big news when the FCC ruled against us. For now, it was just a government filing. Don't worry, they told me, when the FCC rules against you, we'll do a really big story with photos and everything. Oh, great, I thought, we've made it. The *New York Times* is going to put our obituary on Page 1. What more could you ask for? Eternal fame? We didn't care about eternal fame; we wanted to live. Better a story now in the back of the paper about the fight than a front-page story when it's too late.

I kept looking for a way to make the story interesting. My only hope was the David versus Goliath theme. The poor struggling company versus the global behemoth. I invited reporters to our ramshackle offices just to see what a mismatch the fight was. If nothing else, I told them, it'll give you a jump on your competitors for the big obit piece.

A reporter from *Forbes* took the bait and came to visit. The two-page *Forbes* story about the back-room deal came out a week before the ruling was to be issued. And guess what? No ruling. The commissioners, on reconsideration, decided to hear arguments from both sides before deciding. We'd dodged the first bullet.

Now it would be a fair fight. Both sides would get to fairly present their case. Well, sort of. Actually, it was over a hundred AT&T lawyers and lobbyists filing tons of documents against me and a solo practitioner lawyer. The lawyer told me things weren't looking good. But if I lost, he'd give me a discount off the bill. Is this guy nuts? I thought. If we lost, there wasn't going to be any money to pay anyone's bills, least of all his.

I needed help from higher up. I needed someone who could counteract the pressure the AT&T lobbyists were putting on the FCC. I visited every congressional chairman and staffer in Washington. They were all sympathetic, but I wasn't a big contributor and this issue wasn't going to get them any votes. On the contrary, it might get AT&T pissed off.

It seemed like the only way the FCC wouldn't rule against us was if the President of the United States personally told them to save IDT. Great. I'm sure that's just what the President wants to do when he gets up in the morning. Forget about the military situation, taxation, homelessness, and health care. Just go down to the FCC and lobby for us.

On the other hand, what's to lose? Half the prisoners in the country write directly to the Supreme Court to have their convictions overturned. Why shouldn't I go directly to the President?

I also had one big advantage all the prisoners lacked. I had Jim Courter as my friend. Jim, who eventually became IDT's president, was a former congressional colleague and friend of both President Bush and Vice President Quayle and, unbeknownst to him at that time, he would soon be asked to take a Cabinet-level position in the administration. Could he, I asked, possibly get me in to see President Bush so I could tell him how important my new industry was to America's competitive position in the world and what a disaster it would be if the FCC killed us?

After making inquiries, Jim determined that the President would be away till after the ruling would be issued. "Then I guess we're finished," I said.

"Not exactly," Jim said with a grin. "The Vice President wanted to know if he'd be good enough for you."

All right! I high-fived him. The Vice President! We're in business!

The whole thing was like a dream. Jim and I showed up for the appointment at the old executive office building on the White House grounds, went through the metal detector (the Secret Service had done a background check on me in advance of the meeting), took the elevator, and suddenly there we were. Cabinet secretaries' names on the doors. Young, well-groomed aides purposefully striding down the halls. And suddenly—this couldn't be real—Vice President Quayle waved the Secret Service guards away as we approached his office and started hugging Jim.

"How's Marilyn?"

"Just back from taking the kids to college. I'll tell her you're here; maybe she'll come by. And this is the young entrepreneur. Well, I've been looking forward to meeting you. Please tell me your problem, and also tell it to Dan McIntosh here. He's the head of the Competitiveness Council. We're really interested in this issue."

An hour later they were still interested. They were so in favor of IDT, I could have sold them an equity interest in the company—if they weren't running the country. "Don't worry," Dan told me. "If everything you've told us checks out, I'll speak to the FCC." They did this not to placate me or any lobbyists either. They heard my arguments in favor of competition, and agreed with me. That made it even sweeter.

I was so wrapped up with the issue I'd temporarily almost forgotten where I was. Now, suddenly, with the meeting drawing to a close and the objective secured, the full unbelievability of where I was and what was happening fully hit me. I was in the White House with the Vice President. He was talking to me. Nobody would believe this. I wanted to savor the moment. I wanted a memento, some proof I was really here. I gave the Vice President my business card and asked if he'd give me an autographed one of his own in return.

"I'm sorry," he said, "I don't have any business cards."

"You don't?" I blurted out. "Well, what do you give other vice presidents when you meet with them?"

"That's funny," he laughed. "I guess no one ever considered that."

"Well," I asked him, "would you mind just autographing the back of my business card?" "Of course," he graciously assented. I'd probably gone from being a world-class entrepreneur to a starstruck kid, in his eyes. But what the hell? I wouldn't have been the real me if I didn't ask.

The lobbyists from AT&T would probably never have asked for the autograph. Too bad for them. Had they asked, at least they would've come out of the fight with something. Instead they got nada. Nothing. The big zero.

When the ruling came out a week later, to everyone's surprise, the FCC came out for IDT and competition. AT&T's petition was not only denied, but the commission issued a policy statement in favor of the new callback industry.

Newspapers around the world wrote up the story. Many of the would-be obituary writers called for interviews. Sure, I'd give them an interview, but not until I gave the first exclusive to *Forbes*. I owed them, after all. The *Forbes* reporter didn't disappoint me. I liked seeing my picture in the magazine, but I liked the headline above it even better. DAVID 1, GOLIATH 0.

Years later, when we started advertising our low-cost Internet phone service in the States, I wanted a catchy number, so I got 1-800-SCREW-ATT to use on the Howard Stern show. The shock-jock was afraid to use the number on the air, and after I called him a chicken-shit in *New York* magazine, I believe he came close to starting a listener boycott of our firm. Stern's radio station, I was told, was scared of what AT&T's reaction to the number would be. Wasn't I also afraid of AT&T? the radio station's sales staff wanted to know. Not in the least, I told them.

Want proof? Put down this book for a minute and dial 1-800-SCREW-ATT. See who answers. And don't forget to ask about our special discounts when you take more than one service from us.

Chapter Eleven
Free the Internet!

❖

After our victory over AT&T, IDT was ready for a new challenge. Little did I suspect that the challenge would almost bankrupt us a year later.

In the early spring of 1993, I had never heard of the Internet. I certainly could never have imagined that less than three years after that we would be the fastest-growing Internet provider in the world and one of Wall Street's most eagerly anticipated Initial Public Offerings.

The Internet story began with a letter that was sent to my home. This letter did not come from a businessman. The return address was a dormitory at Georgetown University in Washington, D.C. This piqued my interest, and I opened the envelope.

The student, it turned out, had read an article in *Forbes* about my fight with AT&T and had some technological suggestions about how I might circumvent their objections. The letter mentioned that the sender owned his own student business installing computer networks. It was signed Maximillian Robbins. Frankly, the suggestions in the letter didn't really interest me, but meeting a young man with a technical background who was ambitious enough to send it did. So I invited the author to New York for dinner.

I liked Max right away, and so did my kids. Max was a six-foot-two weightlifter who loved kids, and seemed to be joking all the time.

This made him an excellent wrestling companion for my three oldest sons. He was good-looking and red-haired, like a Ken doll. My then four-year-old daughter developed her first crush.

Instead of taking Max to a restaurant alone so we could talk, we had a family barbecue in the backyard. Midway through dinner, I offered Max a job. Over hamburgers, he told me he still needed another year to finish college. As we were putting up more hot dogs on the grill, I told him what a waste college had been for me and what a great opportunity it would be for him to work in a real high-tech start-up company like ours. He said he would think it over. Apparently the hot dogs helped the thinking process. Over watermelon he told me he had decided to take a year's leave from school and join IDT at the end of the spring semester. We shook hands, opened the marshmallows, and Max was hired. Little did I know it then, but IDT would never be the same.

As you know by now, I have become something of a fanatic on the subject of youth. Perhaps because I started young in business myself, I've always believed that young people have much more intelligence and management ability than they are generally given credit for. They also tend to be much more energetic, hardworking, and motivated than people who have been around long enough to have developed a "thank G-d it's Friday so we can get home to our gardening" attitude. Come in to IDT any night after ten o'clock, or on a Sunday afternoon, and these eager beavers are busy working. Sure, the place is covered with soda cans and potato chip bags, and an occasional stray Nerf football may bop you on the head, but that's just the point. For these people, working and having responsibility is fun, just like the football team or the college newspaper. When night comes, the fun is just beginning. IDT's young staff is not big on gardening or mowing the lawn, but they're big on winning.

Not that there is a lack of gray hair at IDT. For many positions, there is just no substitute for experience, and recently we have even hired some retirees. Although this part of our staff may be older chronologically, in terms of their attitude they are just as energetic and spirited as the recent college graduates, sometimes even more so. Partially that's because these are the only kind of people we hire. More than that, I believe working in such a youthful environment just brings out the spirited kid in everyone, the same kid that corporate culture usually works so hard to suppress. I know IDT has had that effect on me. I feel more adventurous, driven, and playful now than I did five years ago. I haven't changed my diet, so I can only conclude that it must be from working with these kids. Many times at work I actually feel more like I'm a head counselor at a day camp than the head of a legitimate business. I don't fight the feeling; I just try to keep the campers' spirits high.

But back to Max. In his first few weeks at IDT, Max was turning out to be a fine addition to our engineering department. He was obsessed, however, by one thing. From his very first day at work, he kept asking me, "Where's my Internet connection?"

"What's the Internet?" I asked him.

Thus began the next phase in my continuing education. Max explained to me that the Internet was originally a computer network set up by the federal government to link important national defense institutions. Its great advantage was that because data flowed across it in a "packetized" format, if any piece of the network were to be knocked out by an enemy attack, the rest of the network would continue to function and effectively replace the section that had been knocked out.

Before Internet technology was developed, if a computer user wished to send a message to another user via a modem, he had to establish a direct telephone link between the two computers. If this link were to be knocked out, no communication would be possible. It was also extremely inefficient, because no other data could travel these wires other than that from the two participating users. If a third party were added to the lines, total confusion would result.

The Internet approached communication in a completely different way. On the Net, each message that I want to send to a particular individual is broken down to its component parts. Thus, the message "I need you," would be broken down into eight parts, as follows, I/N/E/E/D/Y/O/U. The first part, *I,* is assigned the number 1, and the last part, *U,* is assigned the number 8. Each part is then given the address of the recipient to whom it is being sent. If I wanted to send a message to Max, as an example, the order number of the message, and Max's name, together with the actual content being sent, would constitute the package. Thus, the first packet would be *I* number 1 to Max. The final packet would be *U* number 8 to Max. With this new system, you need only a single wire to hook together hundreds of computer users. As thousands of messages flow by Max's computer, his computer, in effect, puts out a paddle to receive. Only those messages that are labeled "Max" would adhere to his paddle. The computer then arranges the packets in sequential order, as they were sent. A million people can share one fiber-optic cable, and every space on the line can be filled with messages, and still nobody gets anyone else's stuff. That's what makes the Internet so unique, and so efficient. Now, what actually happens is that the packet is also coded to include the name of the sender and the time the packet is being sent. You can therefore receive messages from dozens of senders, and your computer will read each of them separately. This, in a nutshell, is how E-mail works.

Because the Internet was cheaper, more efficient, and more reliable than any other form of computer communication, universities that were doing defense research wanted to be added to the burgeoning network. Slowly, every major university the world over was also added. Soon professors in Argentina discovered that they could communicate with colleagues in London at virtually no cost over the Internet. It wasn't long before students came on too. Now that these students, accustomed as they were to the advantages of the Internet, were graduating from college and going to work for large companies, they would be pushing their new employers to go on line, just as Max was pushing me. Not only that, but these former students would want a commercial service to replace the free Internet accounts that they had gotten used to in college. Max assured me that the Internet was going to be the biggest thing ever. I thought it was just a fad.

I did authorize him, however, to get our office hooked to the Internet just to shut him up. Pretty soon everybody in my company was going Net crazy. They were sending messages to friends in Hong Kong, downloading computer games, checking out stocks, and making travel arrangements. And if I wasn't mistaken, it seemed to me that I occasionally noticed pictures of unclad women suddenly vanishing from computer screens every time I happened to stroll through the office. Max had awakened a monster. The Internet was more than a fad, it was an obsession, and I was sure that before long half the country would be addicted to it.

I knew one other thing for sure: If the Internet was going to be as big as it seemed, I wanted to get in on the ground floor. Once an industry becomes established, it's almost impossible for a newcomer to become a dominant player. Sure, you can compete by sniping at the giants from the bushes, or you can go after small market niches that the giants are unable or unwilling to defend. But to actually take their primary market from them? Not likely. I tell everyone that IDT is after AT&T and that we're going to be bigger than they are. It's certainly a worthy goal, and it keeps everyone excited and motivated. But hundreds of companies, some with multibillion-dollar budgets, have tried everything they can think of to take AT&T's business away from them, and AT&T just keeps on getting bigger and bigger. Today they do more than $80 billion in sales and command more than 70 percent of the U.S. market. Does IDT really want to pass them? Of course we do. Do I really believe that my company can pass $80 billion in annual sales in my lifetime? Not a chance. Well, maybe just a little chance.

The fact is that once an industry becomes established, the major players have almost insurmountable advantages over the new guys.

To begin with, they have brand loyalty and customer relationships. They know about, and have solved, the hidden technological issues that only experience can unearth. They have developed the production and distribution systems that newcomers can only replicate through trial and error. They even know where the new business is likely to come from and how exactly to capture it. They have positive cash flow and deep pockets. Most important, they are reliable. There are no surprises when you patronize them. Because they have already developed proven systems, customers are unwilling to leave them.

In almost any stable industry, the giants of yesterday are still the giants of today. Remember the big soda brands when you were growing up—Coke and Pepsi? Remember the big U.S. car companies—General Motors, Ford, and Chrysler? How about breakfast cereals—Kellogg's and Post? Oil companies—Mobil, Texaco, and Esso? (Okay, so they changed their name to Exxon.) How about the dominant TV networks—NBC, CBS, and ABC? They're all the same today. Does this mean that no smart, promising newcomers have entered any of these fields in the last thirty years? Of course not. It's just that the advantages of already being established are almost impossible to overcome.

The exceptions, of course, are those companies that have totally changed the nature of things. Apple and Compaq computers are important companies today because the mainframe business that IBM dominated has all but ceased to exist. In fact, the PC business is practically a new industry altogether. It's as similar to mainframes as credit card terminals are to cash registers.

The fact that computers allowed for a new industrial revolution should not have been all that surprising to anyone who knows about youth. New things most often start with young people. They are the most willing to experiment, and they have the fewest bad habits to break. Jogging, yoga, computers, and the Net—they all began with young people. It's not so strange that little stores that prospered near the Harvard campus when I was a student have gone on to become national chains.

What all this means is that if a person or a company, young or old, aspires to true greatness, he or she had better set off on a whole new path. The people in seventeenth-century Europe who were able to rise to true greatness were those who jumped on a boat to try their fortune in the New World. Even in the New World, those who were poor and aspired to more jumped on a wagon train and headed west. Today there are no more unexplored continents and few open frontiers. Occasionally, however, there are new industries being born, and this is the place to go for those with dreams that being a niche player will leave unsatisfied. For me, I had seen the new frontier, and it was the Internet. This was where I was going to stake our claim. There was only one big problem: Some other guys had gotten there first.

These other guys had names like PSI, UU Net, and Netcom, and they were already national in scope. There were also hundreds of little local Internet providers, many with their own big dreams. Finally, there were big on-line services such as CompuServe, Prodigy, and America Online who were getting ready to move in. Pretty soon this market would be totally dominated by others. At that moment, however, these companies were still getting their acts together. Customer loyalty hadn't jelled yet. Their systems were still being developed, and the kinks were still being ironed out. Not only that, but more potential new clients were being identified monthly than the entire industry had served just a few months earlier. In short, there was still time to become a major player, but time was running out. We had to do something dramatic immediately if we wanted to get in the game.

The press seemed like the obvious answer. The press had made us in the callback business, and I knew how to work with reporters. Not only that, but the press just couldn't get enough Internet stories. Major publications were appointing reporters and editors to cover the Internet exclusively. They were creating entire sections to deal only with this new phenomenon. Internet news was becoming almost as big an industry as the Internet itself.

This created a problem. In this game, unlike in the callback business, everybody was playing well. Reporters were being overwhelmed by the big providers with tales of their exciting new services and the thousands of new clients who were signing on. It seemed like everybody who knew how to turn on a computer had a press agent touting their technological prowess. Just being a nice guy in an exciting industry wasn't going to make headlines here. Like a Hollywood press agent, if we wanted a really big story, we were going to have to come up with an incredible hook to hang it on.

Suddenly it came to me. What if we offered everyone in America free Internet service? Yeah, what if we formed a nonprofit association so no one would suspect our motives, and actually offered free Internet access to the whole country? This would mean that the Internet was no longer the plaything of the well-to-do, but everyone, regardless of income, could benefit from coming on line. Later on we would figure out some way to make money by offering the users some enhanced service, or selling them telephone time, or something else. For now, what did it matter? We had a big story, and we were going to be famous. We would be national heroes, and we would come to totally dominate the industry. I incorporated the International Internet Association, sent out press releases, and waited.

I didn't have to wait long. Within two weeks a thousand people had requested free accounts, and within a month three thousand. The only fly in the ointment was that we didn't have a clue about how to run a commercial Internet service. No problem, my telecommunications gurus from Bellcore, the telephone industry's leading research and standards organization, assured me. We have half a dozen modems ready to go, and if that's not enough, we'll get up as many more as you want as fast as you need. Our six modems could only accommodate a few dozen users, and we were talking thousands. I told my telephone gurus once again to increase capacity to several hundred units. They said no problem. They lied. Apparently, Internet technology was much different than telephone switching. Telephone switching is precise and reliable, while Internet technology is unstable and always changing. Our Bellcore Ph.D.s were the best that money could buy, but this was out of their league and they just couldn't seem to get it right.

Still the requests for free lines continued to pour in—ten thousand, twenty thousand, thirty thousand—it just wouldn't stop. We couldn't keep up with the demand, and I couldn't keep up with the bills from the Bellcore team either. I had already sunk close to a half a million dollars into the technology, and it wasn't up to snuff.

I know this sounds unlikely, but orders were pouring in so fast, we didn't even care that nobody was paying anything. With this kind of volume, we'd sign everybody now, and make money later. The International Internet Association (IIA) was becoming a nationally recognized group for their free Internet service, and Max, the association's executive director, was being heralded in the media as a national hero for putting poor people up on the Net. This kind of publicity had to be worth millions. It had better be, because by the time the Ph.D.s finished with us, that's just what it would cost. The better things got, the worse they got, and unfortunately, things kept getting better. Forty thousand, fifty thousand applicants, the system still wasn't working right, and still no one was paying us a dime.

In desperation, I called a staff meeting before we went nuts and I went broke. There were essentially two big problems, as I saw it. First, we had put ourselves in the hands of technology gurus who just weren't Internet people. The obvious solution was to hire people who had the experience to make an Internet service of the magnitude that we were operating run smoothly. The second problem was to figure out a way to make some profit from all the "free" service the IIA was providing. Max agreed to handle the technical problem and I decided to tackle the financial one.

Left to his own devices, Max solved his end of things in no time. University computer freaks, he realized, were the ones who built and ran the Internet, not phone company people. Soon all the Ph.D.s were fired. They were replaced by a ragtag assortment of hippies and nerds who, until they received the call from IDT, were sleeping under tables in university computer centers in South Carolina or were wired to consoles at the University of Illinois at Urbana. Max put out the call over the Net, and from across America these strange people came.

Some were shoeless. Some didn't bathe. Some only grunted when they were spoken to. Many of the guys had ponytails and earrings. They had nicknames like "Pig," "Countess," and "the Black Knight." These were not the kind of people I was used to. In fact, these people were scary. There were two things that persuaded me to give them a chance, however. First of all, they worked dirt cheap, and second of all, I had no alternative. Within a month, Pig and his friends had the whole system working perfectly. I was so grateful that I built him his own shower in the basement. Pig had grown to feel so much a part of our team that he actually used it. No one could stop us now. We were lean and mean. Our systems worked. We had tens of thousands of clients, and we even smelled good. No doubt about it, if we could only come up with some way to charge somebody for something, this Internet business was going to be a great success. But that was one big *if*, and it was left to me to find some way of getting people to pay for something that they were already getting for free. I couldn't just do the obvious, and charge a small fee, because that would destroy the IIA from a public relations angle, not to mention the fact that it would compromise our nonprofit status.

Instead, I zeroed in on the telephone bills that the users incurred. There are really two expenses that users incur every time they use the Internet. The first is the fee that they pay to their Internet provider for allowing them to log on to their systems. The second expense is the money that must be paid to the telephone company for dialing in to the Internet provider's modem. The IIA had already agreed to waive fees for the actual Internet connection, but that didn't mean we couldn't try to get a piece of the telephone charge for IDT.

In this embryonic period of commercial Internet, especially before the advent of the World Wide Web, most users logged on for only a few minutes a day. The myriad of interesting services that are available today were, for the most part, yet to be developed. Therefore it really didn't matter to most of our users that they would have to make a long-distance call to New Jersey in order to access our system; they were simply not on line long enough for the phone bill to really matter to them. But it did matter to us. According to our clients, AT&T was charging our typical client about 25¢ per minute during the day to make an interstate call. Through our arrangements with large wholesale phone carriers, we were able to offer our clients a long-distance rate of 15¢ per minute during the day, and still make a 20 percent profit for ourselves. We got such a favorable rate because of the business we generated from callback, and I was sure that the 40 percent savings we were offering would be irresistible, especially coming from people who had been nice enough to provide them with free Internet access.

I was wrong. Like MCI, I had underestimated the unwavering loyalty that people have to the AT&T brand name. People simply could not believe that anyone other than AT&T could actually make their calls go through. It didn't matter that AT&T was charging them higher rates, and it didn't matter that our network was as reliable as, and in most cases identical to, AT&T's. It especially didn't seem to matter that we were nice guys. People were not going to switch, and we were not going to make anything.

I have come to realize over time that our position as the nice guys actually worked to our detriment. People, it seems, expect charities to give them things for free and lose money. People will willingly pay top dollar for gourmet cookies or antique bric-a-brac, but let a Girl Scout troop start charging premium prices for their cookies, or a church or synagogue bazaar demand market prices for antique collectibles, and people will just refuse to pay. It's not that people are inherently rotten, but they have certain fixed notions about "value." AT&T is allowed to overcharge, but the Girl Scouts aren't.

I was still naive and unaware of this quirk in human nature. Perhaps, I reasoned, people don't want to switch from AT&T because that would mean that IDT would be carrying all of their calls. Perhaps people felt that it was only fair for IDT to carry those calls which are going to the IIA's Internet service. In some way, there was a strange logic to this, and so I unknowingly embarked on a course of action that almost destroyed the IIA and our Internet aspirations along with it.

What I did was arrange a system whereby people could reach the IIA's modems over toll-free lines rather than by making a conventional long-distance call, if they so desired. Those choosing the toll-free option would be charged 15¢ per minute directly on their credit card, or they could continue using AT&T.

I even went one step further. Every time clients logged on or off, I had the computer tell them how much money they were wasting if they had reached us over AT&T or some other overpriced service provider, and how much they would have saved on IDT's toll-free connection. I also made a policy decision that all of our clients would have to keep valid credit card numbers on file with us, in the event that they saw the light and began to use our cheaper toll-free lines. Thus, users would be more apt to switch to IDT if they'd already gotten past the obstacle of credit card registration. Nothing had changed. We were still offering free Internet service to anyone who wanted it, only now it looked as if we might actually make some money, as the number of billable minutes on our toll-free lines soared daily. A lot of people, however, didn't see it my way.

The IIA had made a lot of friends, but it had made enemies as well. The large Internet providers, for instance, hated us. How were they going to continue charging large monthly and hourly fees to use the Net if we were giving it away for free? Many computer industry magazines hated us too. Who was going to shell out big advertising dollars to push expensive on-line access with us around? Finally, there were what I call the "Internet vigilantes." These were people whose goal it was to see that no commercial activities infiltrated the Net. From the start they suspected the IIA, because they felt that no one would give away so much for nothing without wanting something in return. Now they felt our evil side had been exposed, and they were ready to move in for the kill.

First, they had to overcome the tremendous goodwill that we could count on from our thousands of satisfied free users, and from large parts of the media, which still saw us as a quixotic organization struggling to do good against established interests.

The battle appropriately began on the Internet. Overnight, dozens of messages began appearing on popular Internet bulletin boards across the country warning that the IIA and IDT were engaged in a secret program of large-scale credit card fraud. This was, of course, ridiculous, and I decided to ignore it. But it was only the tip of the iceberg.

Soon messages were posted on the Net claiming that we were in business to carry E-mail for the Colombian drug cartels. Still other postings said that we had plans to introduce a computer virus into the system of any user who wouldn't use our toll-free lines. We hadn't yet been accused of kidnapping or murder, but who knew what they'd come up with next?

We were like the O.J. trial, only for computer nerds. No detail about our company was too small to escape the attention of someone or other. One lunatic went so far as to go to the home of an IDT employee who maintained an Internet link and report on all the comings and goings there. This included a detailed description of the employee's wife and kids, along with his home address, so that any nut in Net land could just show up there. This was too much; we had to respond.

Many IIA users had already been responding to these vicious postings to tell of their own good experiences with us. But they didn't have all the facts that we did. We pointed out that more than 80 percent of our usage still came in as regular long-distance calls, for which we received no money. Moreover, we let people know that the toll-free and regular dial-up lines all fed into the same modems, so that there was no priority given to paying accounts. Furthermore, we documented just how much the typical user actually saved when we did bill their credit cards. We even described our revenue stream and profit centers just so people would know that we were not a front for others. Slowly but surely, the tide of postings began to shift, first a little, and then overwhelmingly, in our favor. The libelous postings stopped, and we seemed to have won the battle. But our good name had been dragged through the mud, and I was disillusioned. I had seen the Internet's dark side.

I was particularly troubled by this, because I have always held freedom of speech as one of the highest ideals known to humankind. Sure, I'd often heard and read that freedom needs to go hand in hand with responsibility, and I've even repeated the thought myself. But now I understood firsthand how important this concept really is.

The American media, and people in general, had until now, in my experience, been very responsible about making public pronouncements. Group libel and character assassination are very rare in the American media. Perhaps it is the fear of lawsuits that buttresses this responsibility, or perhaps the press is aware of the important responsibility it has been given in our society, and acts accordingly. Even the Joseph McCarthy era seemed to me to have been an aberration that passed quickly and was fortunately behind us.

Unfortunately, however, I can now see that this was not entirely the case. Armed with the anonymity of a personal computer network, many people felt free to engage in every kind of possible character assassination. What's worse, some of these groups and individuals felt that their intellectual and technical prowess in being able to master the Net made their opinions more worthwhile than those of people who might disagree. They felt they had the right to disparage and destroy their "adversaries" in every imaginable way over the Net.

I am no stranger to these intellectual elitist practices. At Harvard I couldn't help but notice that much of the faculty was politically left-wing. Those who were not complete socialists in their hearts were, at

the very least, ardent advocates for the welfare state. Few and far between were the champions of individualism or laissez-faire capitalism.
Sure, the buildings may have been named after great capitalists and
chairs were endowed in their names, but it would be a cold day in
July before you'd hear any of the occupants of these chairs say a good
word about the values of the benefactors who were paying their
salaries. Frankly, it occurred to me that what was at work here was
simple guilt and envy. The professors felt guilty that rather than con-
tributing anything productive to society, they were sitting in the university, living on someone else's largesse, someone they held in
intellectual contempt.

The only time and place in history that the intellectual elite was not
sequestered away in a university, or a church, or as a vassal of some
aristocratic patron, was in America around the time of the Revolution. And the true intellectual giants, men like Jefferson, Adams, and
Hancock, were also successful businessmen. They operated farms, invented things, engaged in commerce, did import-export, and the like.
They dirtied their hands. They competed. Sometimes they failed, but
more often they succeeded. They participated in economic life, and
didn't just study it. Is it any wonder that the quintessential documents
of liberty were drafted by this generation?

Computer society and the Internet are, like it or not, outgrowths
of the universities. As such, they embraces many of the universities'
values. As more and more businesspeople log on to the Net, these values are becoming somewhat moderated. But they still exist because it
is as difficult to remove the founding values from an institution as it is
to take the values a child is brought up with and try to change them
as an adult.

I am not comfortable with intellectual elitists. I just don't like or
agree with them. They think the whole world exists only in the minds
of those who share their values. Computer people often exhibit the
worst traits of this elite. Many of them honestly believe that the whole
world exists only on the Internet. What's on the Net is what matters,

and what's not just doesn't. I don't want to become estranged from the real world outside of computers. That's one of the reasons I don't use a computer, not at home and not at work. Never. Even this book was written in longhand. A lot of industry bigwigs are disturbed by the fact that I don't use a computer and don't even have an E-mail address on my business cards. You'll never be a Bill Gates with this attitude, they tell me. Frankly, that's fine with me. I'd rather read a book than play on a computer anyway. Thomas Jefferson is my hero.

I would be the first one to agree that computers are an important part of the world, but they are only a part. Perversely, some might argue, this perspective has helped to make us successful in the computer business. We don't only publicize our new developments on the Net, but we try to get into the real, regular media as well. And let's face it, a hundred Internets wouldn't have the power of the *New York Times*. We don't only advertise in computer magazines and computer shows, but we try to reach people in any way we can.

That's why we were able to ignore the scandalous rumors about us on the Net for so long. We recognized that only a small, obsessed subgroup was logging on to these discussion groups, but then something alarming began to happen. Real reporters from legitimate media started to follow all the furor surrounding the IIA that was going on all over the Net. To their credit, they did not just irresponsibly republish all the garbage, but started asking a lot of questions. This was serious; it wasn't just the lunatic fringe anymore.

The questions all revolved around one central issue: Was the IIA out to give everyone free Internet access, or was it only going to provide service to those who paid? We had better convince everyone that it was the former, or else there would be no IIA.

At just this time, one of the industry's most important conferences, COMNET in Washington, D.C., was approaching. This prestigious event is attended by the press, as well as thousands of key people in the computer and Internet industries. The IIA was scheduled to have its own auditorium at this event to present lectures and demonstrations about the Internet.

The auditorium we were given was large enough to hold several hundred people. We decided to confront all the questions about the IIA directly by holding a press conference in our auditorium, right in the middle of this event. We sent out press notices, posted notice on the Internet, and informed all the reporters who were calling. A typical press conference at COMNET attracts between eight and twelve reporters, but this one was going to be different. Within three days we had so many reservations that we needed to order more chairs. Every reporter at COMNET was coming. This was big news, and nobody wanted to miss the fireworks. We knew we had one shot and we'd better make it good.

The whole idea was to do everything possible to bolster the credibility of the IIA. We approached this along several different tracks. To show that the IIA was charitably minded and really benefited the user community, we invited a dozen or so longtime users from the Washington area to speak about their experiences with the IIA on the Net. Of course, we selected those users who seemed to be particularly articulate and Internet-savvy, based on the E-mail we regularly received from them. We also chose users who had been eloquent and outspoken in their defense of the IIA in the various discussion groups we monitored on the Net.

We went one step further to ensure that our good works would not go unnoticed. We contacted a school for underprivileged children from the Bronx where we had donated computer equipment and set up an Internet training program, and asked if we could bring one of the students down to speak at the convention. The school was so excited that they sent the whole class, at our expense. What did it matter? we thought. These kids were so cute, everybody was going to just love them.

To establish our intellectual, cutting-edge credentials, we decided to bring down a leading expert on telecommunications technology and regulation to speak on recent trends and developments in the industry. We chose a highly regarded individual in this field, Professor Eli Noam from Columbia University, who ran a telecommunications institute. I visited him and met with his staff. I invited him to tour our facilities, and some members of our team even attended his seminars. By the time I finished, Professor Noam not only liked our organization, but also was willing to speak at our presentation. More importantly, we had become friends. This friendship later resulted in the formation of the Digital Freedom Network, which works with human rights groups around the world to fight against press censorship and governmental repression.

Finally, we took a secret step that we held in reserve until just before the conference: We abolished the credit card requirement. This involved tremendous manpower and equipment costs, because it involved creating two parallel Internet systems. One would handle only regular dial-up users, while the other would only service credit card users. Any user with a valid ID could pass through the dial-up lines, but only those who were credit-card-validated could gain toll-free access. Though this solution seems simple, it actually took months of around-the-clock programming to have it functional in time for COMNET. But now we were ready.

Or should I say, they were ready. Our management group had decided at the last moment that I was a liability. I was, after all, a businessman. I owned IDT. I was out to make a profit, and in this context, profit was a dirty word. Furthermore, if the IIA was going to portray itself as an independent organization, it should only be represented by its own staff and executive director, not by its benefactors or service providers. The management group also told me that they were afraid to have me answering questions because I was a loose cannon, prone to say whatever came into my head, whether it was politically correct or not. I didn't argue, because I knew they were right. This was their show.

Just how much it was their show became apparent to me as soon as I took my seat in the back row of the IIA auditorium. It wasn't just that I had to wear someone else's name badge, which irked me, nor was it the fact that I couldn't be up on stage horsing around with my buddies. No, what drove me up the wall was that these lunatics had ordered platters of fruit, cakes, and cookies, along with coffee service provided by the convention's caterer. These kinds of amenities are as expensive as having fresh blueberries flown in from Australia during the winter for your breakfast cereal. This was costing a fortune. Sure, it added to our credibility, but who did they think was paying for these cookies? I didn't know whether to count cookies or reporters. Soon the answer was obvious. As the room filled to overflowing, there were far too many reporters to count. I gave one of them my seat and moved near the catering display. From here I could get a better view of the proceedings and also get my money's worth by eating the fruit before the vultures descended.

The show was so good that pretty soon the cookies hardly mattered to me. The presentation by Max and the rest of the IIA team was virtuoso. They looked like such nice guys, you just couldn't help liking them, in their foolish IIA T-shirts, jeans, and sneakers. The school kids looked great, and having Dr. Eli Noam as a speaker really impressed everyone. When it was time to take questions, however, nobody wanted to hear from the Bronx kids or the big-name professor. People only wanted to hear about the relationship between IDT and the IIA, and whether the service was completely free or not. Max and his crew were definitely winning the day, but I could see a strange division emerging from the reporters. The mainstream press was becoming more and more sympathetic to the IIA guys as the afternoon wore on, and the questions they were asking were more and more like cotton candy, the kind you love to get. On the other hand, the fringe press, which consisted mostly of a few Internet specialty publishers, many of whom had ownership interests in competing services, was becoming more and more abusive and reckless in their questioning. Max handled each of their attacks with good-natured equanimity, and neutralized them completely. I bristled, but said nothing, although several of these questions were actually slanderous attacks on me personally. I also acted with good-natured equanimity. I gnashed fruit between my teeth instead of jumping on the backs of these phony reporters and beating them savagely about the head and face with one of my expensive pineapples.

Then something unexpected happened. One of the reporters referred to our invited IIA users as stooges. The "stooges" became incensed and turned on the reporter. Several young professionals we had never seen before jumped up and declared that they were also IIA users, loved the IIA, and resented being labeled. It had become a revival meeting, as each one stood up and demanded to share with the audience his or her own personal, glowing experiences with the IIA. I was loving every minute of it. People were standing up just to tell Max what a great job he was doing and to keep up the good work. I think one young girl in blue jeans actually ran up on stage and kissed him. You could not have orchestrated such a performance if you'd tried. Two hours later, almost all of the press had filed out, and I was exultant. I say almost all of the press because a full three hours after the press conference had ended, I still couldn't approach Max and Steve to tell them how proud I was of them. One Internet "reporter" was still engaged in an argument with Max and five users of the IIA service, and it seemed he wasn't going home or giving up, ever. I flew home and figured I'd congratulate them in the office tomorrow.

The next day we really had something to crow about. The *Washington Post* had written an article about how great the IIA was and how everyone should use it. They went on to write a long piece that detailed the dangers of having innocent people or groups disgraced on the Internet. The example of what had happened to the IIA was explained in depth, and the reporter pointed out the unfairness of the attack and exonerated us completely. We didn't hear from the Internet vigilantes again.

Alas, sometimes you can win every battle and still lose the war. It would have seemed that the road to riches and industry leadership lay wide open before us and we had nothing left to do but collect the prize. Unfortunately for us, while this whole fight was going on, something had happened in the industry that made the whole victory pointless. The Internet was growing up. The number of services had increased tenfold, and people were no longer spending a few minutes a day on the Net, they were spending hours. Now the cost of telephone time really mattered. Users were unwilling to pay us 15¢ a minute anymore, because this amounted to $600 per month for someone who used the Net three hours a day. Of course, nobody would pay AT&T 25¢ a minute either for long-distance access, but this was small satisfaction to us. What people really wanted was local access in their own area codes. We weren't offering this, and slowly but surely, our billable minutes began to fall. Soon we were losing money again, and I had had enough. I needed to refocus and save the business that was still profitable, and so I decided to cut out our Internet service.

But life is not so simple. I had responsibilities to all the people I'd sold on our Internet dream. I told them I'd find places for everyone in the phone company and that they'd be able to fulfill new dreams there. You can't tell people what to dream, though. These people were Internet dreamers, and that's all they wanted to do. "If people want local access, let's sell them that," they demanded.

"But the IIA doesn't sell anything. We give things away," I reminded them.

"Then to hell with the IIA Let's have IDT sell the local access that our users are demanding," they said.

I couldn't believe my ears. "Are you nuts?" I said. "After everything we went through to build the IIA, and now you want to throw it away and start a commercial service?"

Their answer came back, "Why not?" The only "why not" I could think of is what if people wouldn't buy.

A month after COMNET we informed all the New Jersey users that in thirty days the IIA was turning off its service unless the users were willing to pay something for it. Eventually Max and his users agreed that $15 per month for unlimited local access would be so low a price that most people would be able to live with it, but it was still enough for us to make a profit, if we did a high volume.

"Very high volume," I protested, but my protests fell on deaf ears.

Sometimes when people join you with dreams of their own, you have to run quickly to make sure you're in front leading them to where they're already going anyway. "Okay, there's nobody better at creating tremendous volume than we are, so let's get started."

The day we offered $15 unlimited Internet access to all of our New Jersey users in place of their formerly free access, to our surprise and delight, more than 60 percent of the users took us up on the offer. That still wasn't many people, but it was a start. We were in the Internet business . . . again.

The truth was, though, that we were now more than a year behind our competitors, a whole year since I'd cooked up my IIA free Internet brainstorm, and I had no one to blame but myself.

I had lost sight of the first cardinal principle of business: A business exists to make money. Once a business is making money, it can do many fine and noble things. It can give people jobs, explore new technologies, and undertake altruistic endeavors. But the important thing to remember is that these things are only side benefits of running a business that is oriented toward profit. Any other type of business can't do these things, because in a competitive environment, no other kind of business can succeed.

In the end it comes down to the fact that you simply can't serve two masters. Each of the thousands of decisions that must be made in running a successful business must, in the end, be governed by one overriding criteria—which course of action will maximize the ultimate profitability of the undertaking. This is similar to war. All of the decisions must ultimately be judged in light of which course is most likely to result in victory.

Whenever decisions are made for secondary motivation, the war is lost. The Nazi decision to utilize valuable resources to keep operating the concentration camps when those resources were needed to thwart the Allied invasion helped ensure Hitler's defeat. Similarly, the decision to attack Russia because of Hitler's racial hatred of Slavic peoples was self-defeating and insane. For purposes of this discussion, however, it was incorrect because it was made for reasons other than actually winning the war. The American decision not to blockade North Vietnam or invade and destroy their military strongholds early in the war doomed us to years of pointless carnage. Once the decisions of battle were made with an eye on domestic and global politics and power relationships, rather than with an eye on winning, we would have been much better off to pack up our men and go home.

This is not a recent phenomenon. The British decision to spend the winter of 1777 in Philadelphia rather than out in the field in pursuit of the colonists sealed their fate, and it was motivated not by military genius but by the leadership's preference for the diversions of Philadelphia society.

In business this is even more true, because the competition is usually more numerous, more motivated, and smarter than you are. It's hard enough to field an army of draftees against career military people even when you are focused. Good businesspeople are single-minded in their pursuit of excellence and profit. Japan's rise is not the result of superior intellect or capital base. It is, rather, the result of highly focused action, with a simple goal: the long-term profitability and global dominance of their companies. They were hungry and dangerous competition for former leaders of the American automotive industry, who may have been focused on corporate politics, stock option plans, or skiing in Aspen. Those in Tokyo were working day and night for the profitability of their ventures. Just look at the result.

I would like to disabuse people of one of the most ridiculous myths that has been nurtured and promulgated by the American business press. Often you'll see the head of some company that makes skis or surfboards posing on the slopes in full regalia or in bathing trunks on the beach, surfboard in hand. The captions and the stories in our great business magazines go on to tell how the founder wasn't really interested in business. He was just a good ol' boy who loved to ski or surf or whatever, but his equipment just wasn't working right, so he designed something better. Soon all of his surf or ski bum friends wanted him to make one for them too, and they even pitched in to help the reluctant entrepreneur. Next thing you know—poof!—they're the hottest athletic goods manufacturer in the world. Even better, they're all zillionaires, but they still spend most of their days just skiing or surfing and living the life of Riley. The subtle point of these stories is that the key to success is not the single-minded, obsessive pursuit of excellence and fanatic attention to the bottom line, it's just that if you do what you enjoy the most, success will come to you. Bullshit.

These same magazines have all done stories on me and taken my picture too. They love to play up the human and quirky side of our business. No one wants to write about the fact that I, and almost everyone who works for me, am obsessed. Obsessed with making IDT as profitable as it can possibly be. Believe me, when the other guys were out in the surf with the California girls, the founder was sitting in his office for days on end trying to get his distributor to push a few more container loads of surfboards, or getting a little better terms on fiberglass. If he lost sight of this, he'd still be on the beach, but somebody else's name would be on the board.

For my part, I screwed up. By turning our Internet business into a nonprofit entity, I warped our priorities. Rather than doing what made the most sense for us and for our customers, I did what would make us seem most like heroes in the press. I became concerned not primarily with the consumers' purchasing of our service, but with the press's reception of our company. As a result, I almost missed the boat, and didn't begin selling local Internet access until the window of opportunity had almost closed. Only the fact that this was a brand-new industry, and all of our competitors were making their own strategic mistakes, saved us from oblivion.

One might point out, of course, that the whole IIA fiasco did involve us in the Internet and developed both our technical and business ability to master it. Well, maybe, but I'm just not sure. It seems to me that once we got our feet wet in the Internet, we'd have had to be dead not to realize that it could be a gold mine. We would have been a year ahead of the game if we'd tried to sell it cheap rather than giving it away, but I'm finished crying over spilled milk.

In a way, the IIA was similar to my college experience. For me, Harvard was a prison, and I hated virtually every minute of it. I found it intellectually sterile, arrogant, closed-minded, and unfriendly. People tell me that surely I must be mistaken, that perhaps I gained something from being in the heady atmosphere of the place. Perhaps, they say, it made you more polished, or more erudite. I always answer the same way. You can't spend three or four years of your life in any environment, having a set of new experiences, and not come out with new knowledge or perspective. The only thing is, I'm sure I would have gained just as much if I'd spent three years as a zookeeper's assistant or as an actual prison inmate.

The IIA, I'm sorry to say, is pretty much the same story. Sure, we learned a lot, but what a wasteful way to have done it. I suppose, though, that I did take one genuinely valuable lesson away from the experience. I'm much less concerned with what the press thinks, and I do many fewer interviews now than I used to. I'd rather see my advertisements for customers in publications than read articles about what an "aw, shucks," kind of guy I am. I've also become much more focused on market share and profitability than I am in exploring every new opportunity for its own sake. In the short run, this sometimes makes life less interesting, but in the long run it opens up much greater vistas.

I'm tempted at this point to tell a little story. It seems that in days of old, people were very prone to idol worship, and this was very disturbing to the righteous people. So the righteous prayed to G-d that the desire for idol worship should disappear. G-d warned these righteous men that He would comply with their request, but He wanted them to know that as a result, religious fervor in the world would be diminished. The righteous felt that the cost was worth it, and the Lord complied. Afterward, the righteous felt that things had been improved.

They then prayed to G-d to remove all selfishness and love of gain from the world. G-d again warned them that this was dangerous, but they insisted. G-d agreed, but said He'd give it a three-day trial, and only make it permanent if the righteous still wanted it then. After three days, no farmer had milked his cow, no builder had raised a hammer, no carriage driver had harnessed his horses to a wagon. Everyone was just sitting at home, lazy, unmotivated, unhappy, and hungry. After three days, the righteous people realized their mistake and begged the Lord to relent.

The profit may not seem pretty, but like the old joke goes, we need the eggs!

Chapter Twelve
It Could Always Be Worse

❖

We offered unlimited Internet access in the hope that people would buy it, and buy it they did. Soon we were selling so many unlimited $15 dial-up accounts in New York that we could barely order the phone lines and the modems fast enough. My own enthusiasm made matters both better and worse. Sensing that we could repeat our New York area success on a nationwide basis, we installed Internet sites in Los Angeles, Washington, D.C., Philadelphia, and Phoenix, and started advertising in these areas as well. Business started to pour in from all over. But by now our finances were really being strained by all this expansion, and though we were growing unbelievably, we just couldn't afford to put up additional sites in any more cities.

This was a tremendous problem, because I could see we were riding the crest of a tidal wave of a whole new industry. If we didn't manage to stay out front, we would be washed away as one of the market leaders and others would take our place. Being number one was not just a question of ego. You see, the Internet business has unusual economics of scale. It costs so much to set up a network and put in switches all over the country that you need a huge volume to make it pay. That's why so many little Internet providers have been swallowed by the big guys. Even CompuServe, the second-biggest provider, was eventually gobbled up by America Online. Now was the time we had to expand nationally, but we just didn't have the financial or, for that matter, the engineering resources. At moments like this all you can do is pray for a good idea.

For some reason, this reminds me of a story I like to tell people. In the play *How to Succeed in Business Without Really Trying*, Morty the window washer rises from the mailroom to become vice president of advertising of the enormous World Wide Wicket Company, just by following the careful brown-nosing instructions laid out in a paperback success manual that he studies. The manual congratulates him on doing such a fine job and rising so high. The book says, "Now you're a Vice President, and you can just rest on your laurels. You can enjoy the executive washroom and country club and relax. Unless," it cautions, "you're the Vice President of Advertising. In this case, you're in big trouble. You need to come up with a new great idea every day." This, I tell people, is what it's like to run a large Internet company. You may seem to be on top, but you're in big trouble if you don't have a new idea every day.

Fortunately, at just this moment, I did have a great idea: Why not go to all the small local Internet providers around the country and offer to make them our local partners? We'd form a kind of alliance with them. We'd do the sales, advertising, customer support, and collections. They'd support the all-important local dial-in modem access and Internet processing resources. As far as any of the accounts would know, they were signing on with IDT, the large, powerful national Internet provider that advertised on network TV, radio, and print media. Behind the scenes, though, dozens of local businesses would actually be doing a large share of the work. In exchange we'd give the local provider $10 per month per account, or about 40 percent of what we actually took in from our average client. Our policy of always pushing premium service enabled us to actually take in much more than the industry average per account, and had given us much bigger margins to work with than our competitors. I was sure if we explained to the local provider that much larger competitors like

AT&T, AOL, and their local phone companies would soon be coming into the market, slashing prices, and promoting like crazy, the small providers would see the benefit of coming under our protective marketing umbrella in order to withstand the coming onslaught.

Many people, both within and especially outside IDT, questioned the merits of this idea. On the one hand, they argued, the little companies would never go along with it, and if they did, it would only be for a while so that they could steal all the accounts. On the other hand, they argued, the little guys were incompetent. They'd never be able to handle the volumes I was planning on generating. We'd never be able to coordinate the orders. Within weeks of starting this process, they argued, we'd be finished.

The program, of course, succeeded beyond our wildest expectations. Within months we were selling and provisioning over a thousand new accounts a day. We were one of only three national providers (the other two being public companies who could afford to burn money), and the only one to be offering totally flat-rate service. Finally, we were on the map and Wall Street started to beat a path to our door. Why was I right and all the pundits wrong? Simple. Having been a small businessman for over twenty years, I realized just how creative and competent entrepreneurial businesses actually are. My father, himself an entrepreneur, once told me, "Never underestimate anyone who's managed to stay in business for a few years. He has to be a genius to overcome all the many crises which keep cropping up all the time." I've never forgotten this advice. I'm sure there are many guys running shoe stores, restaurants, and small trade magazines who could much more competently manage some of America's industrial giants than they're currently being managed. After all, these people have had to steer their ship of dreams into unfriendly seas and navigate them profitably against all odds. The ones who succeed are heroes. Not only heroes, but often creative geniuses as well. Many of the people who run large corporations, on the other hand, have never done anything more dramatic than kowtow to their superiors. Is there any doubt in an even fight as to who would prevail? The fact that almost all employment growth in the last twenty years has been from these smaller companies bears out what I'm saying. The only way for big business to really succeed is to incorporate the dynamism of these entrepreneurial personalities within their fold.

Not only, I realized, would our small alliance partners recognize the merit of our new relationship and service all our accounts honestly and well, but they'd bring their dozens of creative ideas and improvements to our company. In a fast-growing industry this would give us an invaluable advantage over our corporate-think competitors. In fact, as things evolved after we went public, most of our premier alliance partners actually folded their businesses into ours and their former owners have become some of our managers. Part of this was no doubt due to the extremely hostile, competitive, and financial situations in which most independent local providers have found themselves. An equally large part, I think, is that having dealt with us for a long period of time, these entrepreneurs know that in coming to work for us they won't have to sacrifice their independence and put their dreams on hold. Rather, they know they'll just have more resources at their disposal so they can get the job done.

The alliance partnership program only temporarily relieved our financial problem. True, we didn't have to buy more equipment, but we now had to pay for national advertising that would cover more than a hundred cities. Signing on Internet accounts was pretty profitable, but it took months till those profits covered the cost of sales and advertising. Ironically, the more accounts we sold in any given month, the bigger our financial problems. And, as before with the IIA, things were going so well that soon we'd be broke.

At this point we needed another great idea. Before telling you what we did, let me ask a question: What exactly is a great idea? Simply a way of reorganizing the assets you already have so you can accomplish something new. Praying or hoping that someone from any planet or someone you never met from the other side of the world will just appear and save you isn't a great idea. It's wishful thinking. This is what the Wizard of Oz was trying to tell Dorothy and her friends. The answer to your problem is in your own hands or, in Dorothy's case, on your own feet. I call this my "ruby-red slippers theory of business": The answer almost always lies within your own control. You just have to concentrate on how to refocus your resources.

In our case the answer was as obvious as the nose on your face. It was profitable to sign up Internet accounts. The problem was it took too long to collect the money from new sign-ups to pay the account acquisition costs. We were looking around for someone to underwrite our acquisition costs in the belief that our clients really wanted the service and were willing to keep paying for it. The industry was too new, however, for leaders to have any experience on which to justify that belief. Wherever we turned, every leading institution said no.

Then we realized there *was* one group of people who really knew that our subscribers wanted our Internet service, and they were willing to keep paying for it. That group was composed of the subscribers themselves. Why not have them underwrite our growth by paying for their first year of service up front? We figured all we had to do was offer the clients a meaningful discount and they'd be glad to pay up front. We eventually determined that by offering prospective clients three months free, a motivated sales force could get just under 20 percent to pay for the year up front. This wound up almost tripling the amount we'd bring in from new clients in the first months, and it allowed us to keep expanding when everyone but our public rivals were beginning to run dry.

Getting a motivated sales force together large enough to handle the new volume was another challenge. Fortunately, once again, the ruby-red slippers saved the day. We did, as it turned out, already have a fantastic sales force in place. They were busy selling thousands of businesses our domestic long-distance service bundled with free Internet access. This division was definitely profitable, but as long-distance service was such a competitive field, we were only able to sign up a few hundred new accounts per week.

So one day I called a big meeting and explained to all the domestic telecom sales managers that starting immediately, they were an Internet sales force. Of course, we kept on a skeletal crew to keep telecom going because I have a rule: You never give up a profitable business, and you never abandon a market niche, even if your foot is barely in the door.

Running a business, I've discovered, is much like fighting a war. If you want to be a great manager, you need to act like a great general. For instance, you have to be willing to deploy your resources into those areas where they can result in a big victory for you. You can't win with an attitude that says, "this unit is specially trained in desert warfare, so I won't use them to complete the encircling of an enemy battalion trapped in the jungle."

To win a war you have to be willing to use your force in new and unexpected ways as the situation calls for it, though I don't make such moves frivolously. I am often willing to move a talented executive from one division of the company to a totally different one, if I see that his or her unique skills can benefit us elsewhere. Occasionally, as in the case of going for the Internet opportunity, I'm even willing to move the whole division.

This is at variance with the way things work at large companies. There, executives and division heads stake out their own areas and become very territorial and possessive about their responsibilities, budgets, and personnel. Corporate politics make it almost impossible to redeploy people or resources out of one area and into another. The largeness of the company starts to become its own weakness. Even if one division starts to do great, it was the burden of carrying the whole company and its corporate infrastructure along with it.

This is why, although I am a great believer in giving people independence and fostering their entrepreneurial impulses, I see that they need a strong leader to guide the process if they hope to succeed big. An army must have a commanding general; you just can't fight a war by committee. Corporate politics inherently creates CEOs who aren't true visionary leaders. Visionary leaders do not micromanage and take over their managers' jobs. What they do is let everyone know that the company has a clear direction and see that it moves that way. This frees up everyone else to really do the job of running the company.

In those few instances where a small firm somehow crashes through the many natural obstacles that exist and, still led by its founder, becomes an industry leader, the firm will usually go on to totally dominate its field. Such is clearly the case with Microsoft. This company is virtually unstoppable, and it's not just because it has a lock on computer operating systems. It's because Bill Gates has a clear vision of where the industry is going and how he plans to master it, and there's no uncertainty about which goals are going to be pursued. I hope we're on the road to being such a firm.

A general and an army, no matter how formidable, are nothing without supplies and ammunition. History has taught repeatedly that the side that can keep providing the most on the home front wins. In reality, Rommel and the Nazi army were probably superior to Eisenhower and the Allies as far as military strategy goes. It is ultimately the productive capacity of the United States, "the arsenal of democracy," and not the genius of our generals, that turned the tide of battle and won the war. In business this ammunition is called money, and you better have plenty of it if you're going up against the giants. Nowadays, the only way to initially raise the kind of money we're talking about is to go public.

Going public, though, is not as easy as it sounds. We had made moves several times over the years to start the process of going public, only to get shut down before we even started.

The story was always the same. We were too small or our business was too inherently risky. We didn't have the proper business systems in place. If only we had just a little longer operating history. Not only this, but we were told going public would be a long and arduous process, so why not try to get "quick money" privately?

Finally, however, we looked around and said, hey, a lot of companies who are going public are no bigger than us. In fact, a lot of them are in the same exact business we're in. The only difference is they now have tens of millions of dollars to grow with and we don't. If we're going to be a great company, we can't keep living hand-to-mouth. We need some real capital to play in the big leagues. Our investors were thrilled, and so my partner Howie Balter and I decided we were going to do whatever we had to in order to go public. And that was that.

Deciding to go public is sort of like deciding to get married. You can't do it alone. You need to have an underwriter to go public with. The underwriter is a large Wall Street investment firm with a sales force and a research team that can help you to sell an equity interest—stock—in your company. And just like there are all kinds of potential spouses out there, there are all kinds of underwriters as well. There are desirable ones who will help you get huge market valuations and support your stock price for years to come, and there are undesirable ones who will do everything in a small-time way and dump you as soon as the transactions are over. With the good underwriter you wind up being worth hundreds of millions and your stock trades on the NASDAQ big board; with the crummy underwriter you're a penny stock trading on the pink sheets.

Surprisingly, much as with marriage, it sometimes is almost random as to what kind of underwriter a company winds up with. Some great promising companies never get anywhere because they just couldn't get the right stock market firms behind them. And occasionally some really lousy company makes the big-time because one of the big-name firms decides to throw their weight behind them. And, it's often some inexplicable chemistry that plays a role in drawing companies and underwriters together as much as basic business fundamentals. And just as in marriage, where people often meet through introductions and usually don't marry people from the other side of the tracks, often the main thing that matters is that the company and the underwriters are part of the same sort of privileged club which generally pairs up with other members of the club.

Thus, many successful new companies are, in actuality, just break-offs of old companies. The prime example of this is Lucent Technologies, one of the hottest "new" companies in recent years, which is really a spinoff of AT&T's research division. They have been predestined to be readmitted to the big money club in their own name as soon as they come of age. This can also happen when the top technical people or managers of a public company join with well-known venture capitalists to start up their own competing firm. It's just a matter of time till these companies go public. The venture capitalists are bringing deals to the underwriters all the time. They depend on each other. The big firms know that the VCs wouldn't put their money into the firm if they didn't think it would succeed. Not only that, but because VCs wind up usually controlling the firms they invest in, they almost always install a management team with a good track record managing other public companies. Thus, the underwriters wind up dealing with people they already know are dependable. The whole system is very safe and very insular.

The same people keep dealing with the same people and make money off each other. Not only that, but everybody uses the same big six accounting firms to check the books, and the same dozen or so big law firms to draft the documents and deal with the SEC. The point is, almost nobody new is allowed into the club unless they're sponsored, usually by a big VC who bought a big part of the company at a tiny fraction of its soon-to-be-public valuation.

Our problem was that I didn't come out of a big company with a stellar track record and I never was willing to sell a big piece of *my* company cheap to some parasitic venture capitalist.

As the doors of Wall Street's big names refused to open for us, I could see I was being punished for being the quintessential outsider. Some of the larger firms even came straight out and told me that we had a great company and if we'd only go out and even now sell a big piece of it cheap to a prestigious venture capitalist, they'd be happy to be part of our underwriting team. If not, we could go to the penny stock brokers and forget about it. This, I reminded myself, was going on despite the fact that we were leading players in the Internet business, which was, at the time, the biggest phenomenon Wall Street had ever seen.

The one day a strange thing happened. Someone took us into the club. A friend of mine, who had formerly worked at Skadden Arps, one of the world's most prestigious law firms, suggested that if we were going public, I should consider engaging Ira Greenstein, a senior securities lawyer with the firm, as my attorney. I called Ira on the phone. Something clicked, and he agreed to come out and visit us in New Jersey.

He came out to visit, and it was love at first sight. Here was the lawyer I'd been looking for all my life. In one of his previous assignments, Skadden had lent him out to Tower Airlines to serve as their general counsel. The year of actually working in a hangar at Kennedy Airport had apparently removed any of the uppitiness you'd expect to find in a big corporate attorney. He was prepared for our stripped-down blue jeans style of doing business. When I told him we couldn't possibly afford to pay Skadden Arps' bills, he told me not to worry, he'd see that we could manage it, and we could pay when we had the money. Like I said, Ira was the miracle we were waiting for.

It's difficult to pinpoint exactly what clicked between us. My late father-in-law, Irv Yatzkan, used to say, "When the rocks in his head fit the holes in hers, it's a perfect match." Perhaps that is as good an explanation as any. All I know is that as a business we owe everything to Ira. We simply couldn't have gone on without going public, and we couldn't have gone public without him.

It wasn't so much that Skadden did our legal work. It was that they became our ambassadors. They went back to every firm on Wall Street and told them they wanted them to meet with us about taking IDT public. Skadden told these underwriters that IDT was a great firm and *Skadden* wanted them taken public. Skadden Arps does the securities work for many of the nation's largest firms. As such, they are in a position to direct billions of dollars worth of business to those securities firms whom they favor. The firms know this. Skadden is definitely a member of the club. Anyone who Skadden wants in will get more than a fair hearing.

All of a sudden, prestigious underwriters started to show interest and send out teams to see us. They started bringing custom-printed booklets explaining why IDT should consider using them.

In the investment banking business, at least as far as high tech is concerned, there are basically three tiers of firms. The first tier consists of the dozen or so giants led by Goldman Sachs, Morgan Stanley, and Merrill Lynch, who specialize in handling the investments and banking needs of Fortune 500 firms and government.

The second tier are the five large high-tech "boutique" firms—Cowen, Alex Brown, Robertson Stevens, Hambrecht & Quist, and Montgomery—who specialize in taking promising smaller firms public and helping them grow. Then there is the third tier—the hundreds of smaller, less specialized or regional firms who would also like to get a piece of the action.

Though we got many nibbles from the giants, it soon became clear that our deal was too small for them and the talks they were having with us were more to facilitate future business dealings than to help us now when we needed it. On the other hand, we were already too large for the third-tier players and going with one of them would just discredit us in the eyes of the financial community. I did think, however, that it might be prudent to take one of these smaller firms on to our team. We were running out of money and couldn't afford to have our offering delayed. From what I was hearing, it was not uncommon for the larger player to pull out of the deal at the first sign of trouble or even at the last minute. The firms who got pulled out on went from riches to rags overnight. Often, all their activities were so geared toward a successful Initial Public Offering (IPO) that when it didn't go off on schedule, they actually went bankrupt. A smaller firm, I reasoned, to whom the fees from such an IPO would be a fortune and whose industry position would be much enhanced by pulling it off, would be almost sure to take the IPO all the way. They might not raise as much money, but they'd raise some. Taking on one of them would be like applying to a safe school (one you know you'll get into) when submitting college applications.

The small firm I selected as our "safe firm" was First Albany. They'd done some slightly smaller deals on their own. They'd been "on the covers" with the larger guys before. Their research was top-notch. And most importantly, their lead banker, Charley Manuel, was dying to do the deal. I really liked Charley. He was the kind of guy I just knew I could trust.

Traditionally three underwriters take a small promising company public. Since I'd already selected First Albany as our "insurance policy," this left room to select only two of the five boutique firms. We met an analyst at Alex Brown and knew right away that we wouldn't work well together. We agreed on nothing from a business perspective, and I, who have always felt the analyst is more important than the bankers, wanted nothing more to do with him.

We all fell in love (in a professional sense) with Maria Lewis, the senior analyst at Cowen. Thousands of analysts across America are ranked every year by their colleagues and the twenty or so best are featured as the All-American analysts by *Institutional Investor* magazine. These are the people whose opinions move markets, the ones whose say-so is enough to make investment managers invest. Maria has been an All-American several years running. She could work at whatever giant firm she wanted and be paid almost any amount. But she liked being a partner at Cowen. Not only that, she loved us, our style, our business plan, and she loved how we were executing it.

Wow! If we could have her, we thought, our problems would be over. Everyone would buy our stock with her as the analyst.

We were therefore thrilled when Maria invited me to speak about IDT at Cowen's technology conference in Boston. My speech at the conference went well and that night we were invited to a small private reception to be held at Harvard University's Fogg Art Museum.

It had been twenty years since I'd started at Harvard, and now I was going to go back—although in my three years in Cambridge I never went into the Fogg. For the first time in twenty years I had a warm feeling about my alma mater. The Fogg was definitely where I wanted to be. No blue jeans tonight. Tonight a new suit, a new tie, and we were on our best well-mannered behaviors.

There was a small problem, though, when Howie Balter and I arrived at the museum. Appetizers and drinks were being served, and people were standing around eating them and making polite conversation. The appetizers, however, were not kosher, and so we couldn't partake. On the other hand, if we just kept turning them down, this would also draw attention to us and make us seem not to fit in. Discretion being the better part of valor, I suggested to my colleague that we walk around the museum and pretend to look at the art until dinner (at which kosher meals had been specially ordered for us) was served.

The museum actually had an unbelievable collection and I became lost in a reverie trying to figure out how much the many Monets, Rembrandts, Degas, and Picassos added to Harvard's endowment. I was also trying to figure out how much my stock would have to be worth to have enough to invest in this kind of extravagance.

As we stood in the third gallery filled with various crucifixions and other scenes of religious bloodletting, who should come walking through but Maria Lewis accompanied by Lisa Powell, our investment banker at the firm. "Why, Howard," Maria said, "I didn't know you were an art connoisseur. Joe Cohen, the head of our firm, would be so pleased to know that. He's quite an avid private collector, you know.

"But, actually, Lisa and I were just talking about what an impressive presentation you made this morning, and I was wondering about some of the numbers in your projections."

"Excuse me," I interrupted, staring around at the ominous artwork on the wall. "Could we move to the next room? I think I like the artwork much better there, and I can see we're going to be talking a while."

"My, you are a connoisseur," she said. And so we moved on to a room containing "gentler," more auspicious art, without the crucifixions.

There, among the Old Masters, the four of us gathered as if in a football huddle, expressing our comradeship and discussing strategy and the anticipated game plan for going public.

Suddenly, as if on cue, who should enter the gallery but Joseph Cohen, chairman of Cowen and Company and for over twenty years one of the luminaries of American finance.

In business, as elsewhere in life, there are people who have the title, and then there are people who are really in charge. The Queen of England does nothing; the Prime Minister is the boss. Similarly, most chairmen of huge companies decide little more than which color to wear when having their photos taken with the color-coordinated chairmen of other large entities. In Joe Cohen's case, however, as I'd been told by almost everyone at Cowen, this was not the case. Joe Cohen was the boss. What he said went. And apparently on all major decisions, like whom to take public, he had something to say. As the Cowen people were falling over themselves introducing their chairman and trying to say nice things about us in the process, I was determined to make a good impression and seal the deal.

Now, there are two ways in life to make an impression. The first is to conform to the appropriate norms of a given situation: Dress like everyone else, speak deferentially, and show you belong. The second is in some way to break with conformity and establish yourself as a unique individual. This is the more risky path. The trick is to let people know you're an honest and uniquely independent person who can probably do unusual things and who has to be treated as an equal. At the same time, you have to be earnest, charming, and self-deprecating enough that people's reaction is to be charmed by your folksiness rather than put on the defensive by your nonconformity. As I said, this is the more risky path. It's the one I almost always follow and tonight it was going to backfire big-time.

Since I figured that, judging from his name, Joe Cohen was one of the few Jews to actually chair a major Wall Street firm, I decided to try to put him at ease and confront the issue of my own obvious religiosity head-on.

Noting that his name was Cohen and the firm's name was Cowen, could it be, I suggested, that the name of the firm had been changed to make it more acceptable? "No," he replied, without smiling. The firm was named after its original founders and had been so called for close to a century. He was unrelated to the founders in any way. As I looked at this perfectly tailored and manicured poster person for American finance, I could tell I had made a major faux pas by playing the ethnic card. In a situation like this a normal person's reaction would be to politely end this line of conversation and change the topic quickly before he buries himself for good. I clearly have a screw loose, however, and decided to plunge headlong into the abyss I'd just created by telling the most inappropriate ethnic joke one could come up with under the circumstances.

"Well, Mr. Cohen," I went on. "Your firm's name reminds me of an old story. A poor Jew in London was, for many years, the *shamass* [caretaker] of an old synagogue. Every day he'd dutifully fold the *tallesim* [prayer shawls], put away the *siddurim* [prayerbooks], and otherwise clean up and look after the place. One day, however, an educated young rabbi determined to reinvigorate the aging congregation with a new 'modern' approach, took over from his aging predecessor who had held the position for over half a century. On the job for less than three days, he asked the old *shamass* to put the books in the library in alphabetical order. On learning that the *shamass* could not do this because he was illiterate, the young rabbi, ignoring the *shamass*'s long tenure, fired him on the spot.

"Broken, the *shamass* went out into the dark misty afternoon to the bus stop to go home and break the news to his old wife. Nerves, though, created in him an overwhelming need to have a smoke first. Nowhere in the vicinity of the bus stop could a tobacco shop be found. Well, thought the old former *shamass,* I'll open a tobacco and sweets shop here on this bus stop to try to scrape by. More than scrape by, though, the stand prospered. So much so that with his excess profits the former *shamass* was able, over the years, to open more and more stands at other bus stops. As these stands too thrived, the business slowly became an empire and the old Jew needed a barrister to tend to his legal needs.

"Wandering the streets near his old stand, he surveyed the various brass plaques on the buildings before selecting a barrister he felt appropriate for him.

"The senior partner of the selected firm was gratified to receive such a large and prestigious account, all the more so since the principal had only just walked into his office like a common client. 'What was it,' he inquired, 'that made you choose me?'

" 'Well,' the old former *shamass* replied, 'I chose you because you were Jewish.'

" 'Jewish?' the old coifed barrister sputtered.

" 'Sure,' said the former *shamass*. 'I saw your name on the plaque downstairs, Cohen & Company.'

" 'Cowen & Company,' the barrister hastened to correct. 'That's not Cohen & Co., it's Cowen & Co. I'm not Cohen, I'm Cowen. And I'm not,' he continued with proper diction, 'Jewish. I'm Anglican. I'm Anglican,' he repeated. 'My father is Anglican and my grandfather Alav HaShalom [Hebrew for may his soul rest in peace] was Anglican.' "

This joke usually brings hearty guffaws when told to ethnic Jews who know what *siddur, talis, shamass,* and most importantly *Alav HaShalom* mean. It gets an even better response when told to Jews who know the lingo but are "making it" in big professional firms in the gentile world.

Joe Cohen, however, just stood there icily. He clearly wasn't familiar with the lingo, which I now (digging my grave that much deeper) was trying to explain. I had now not only told him a dumb joke he didn't understand and assumed an ethnic familiarity he did not reciprocate, but I was insulting him as well by saying I thought everyone knew the expressions with which he was clearly unfamiliar. At this point I was sort of hoping the ground would swallow me up. I could forget about going public. In fact, it would soon be *me* out on the bus stop. In my mind's eye, I was peddling hot dogs again rather than tobacco.

Joe Cohen just stood there for a moment, ashen (this word is overused, but, believe me, here it was appropriate). And in that moment, I kid you not, the other three people in our circle were so appalled, they literally froze in midsentence. I know this sounds like poetic license, but I assure you it was true. Everyone was shocked, and there was nothing anyone could say to extricate themselves or their respective companies from the debacle.

At this moment, Joe Cohen turned to me and, apparently looking for my one redeeming virtue, or one area of common ground, said, "Come with me. I'd like to show you a picture on the other side of the far wall." As we left to go see the picture, the remaining three stood there looking at each other in suspended animation waiting for the next calamity to blow them all away.

"Well, son," Cohen said, looking at me and then turning to gesture at an old painting, "I see you're interested in artwork and the Old Testament" (he didn't add, "and tasteless jokes"), "so I wanted to show you this Orazio Gentileschi. Gentileschi, you know, is one of my favorite painters of biblical scenes."

For a moment I just looked at what was to me a pretty mediocre piece of wall covering and wondered what to reply. I knew enough to now that art has its own lingo. If I could only find the proper cultivated observation to make, I could perhaps dispel the illusion that I was a worthless Neanderthal. I would have to find something more appropriate to say about the painting than that I liked it or that the colors were pretty. Describing it as a home run, a grand slam, or a great touchdown for Gentileschi was also out. I thought to say something about the texture, but I didn't know what to say about it.

I decided my only hope was to steer the conversation away from art and on to the Bible, where I could display some erudition. "My," I improvised, "Gentileschi really has captured the spirit of David's anguish at being betrayed. Whenever I read this story I always imagine the scene in my mind. It's just unbelievable how well Gentileschi has captured it. He must have been a great biblical student to have been able to capture the moment so well."

"Yes," Cohen averred. "The emotion of Gentileschi's strokes has always moved me."

Now we're getting somewhere, I thought. Just remember: Talk Bible, not Art. "I'm so glad you showed me this," I continued. "Tell me, which other scenes was Gentileschi able to capture on this level? I'd really like to see them as well."

"Well," Cohen replied, smiling for the first time, "many people think his greatest work is *Joseph Fleeing Potiphar's Wife*. Gentileschi actually painted two versions of this scene. The one most people are familiar with hangs in the Louvre in Paris. That one, though, is damaged. The undamaged version is actually in my private collection at home. I was able to obtain it from a dealer some years ago before Gentileschi was so popular."

This guy is really loaded, I thought. "That's unbelievable," I said.

What could I say next? In life, occasionally there are moments that can only be characterized as sublime, serendipitous. Moments when you say or do absolutely the right thing. Like when Babe Ruth, with two strikes on him, pointed to the stands beyond the outfield and batted the next pitch there for baseball's most unforgettable home run, or when Churchill, answering an obese woman who had just called him a drunkard, responded, "Madam, you are fat, and I am indeed inebriated, but tomorrow I shall be sober." In these situations, where great men do absolutely the right thing at the right moment, you have to call that sublime.

There are times, however, when complete idiots, against all odds, and in contradiction to all previous history, deliver in the same spectacular way. Like when the fat kid who struck out all year hits a grand slam homer in the bottom of the ninth to win the series, or when the klutz in left field not only gets a near and sure home run ball, but actually catches it and holds on despite crashing into the fence and being knocked almost unconscious. These moments are not just sublime, they're miraculous. Your life is sometimes irrevocably altered once you experience one. I was about to experience exactly such an unlikely moment.

I, of course, had never seen or heard of Gentileschi's *Joseph Fleeing Potiphar's Wife*. Norman Rockwell and the *Mona Lisa* were all I knew about art. (In fact, I'm not even sure who it was who painted the *Mona Lisa*, though I'm fairly sure it wasn't Rockwell.) I did love my grandmother, however. I loved her company, her cooking, her house—everything about her. In fact, as a kid, I spent so much time in her apartment I knew every inch of the place: where the cans were stored, where the washboard was kept, what chairs were worn out in the arms under the seat covers. I not only knew where things were, I knew everything about them because I asked questions incessantly. Thus, I knew how my grandfather had bought my grandmother her bureau, how to do the wash on a scrub board, why you got more vitamins if you squeezed the oranges fresh on Aunt Anna's glass squeeze from California, and other such trivia.

The material centerpiece of my grandmother's home was a huge glass-covered tapestry that hung over the living room couch that a long-dead cousin had given to my grandmother as thanks for her hospitality when my grandmother took in her family during the Depression.

If you guess that this tapestry depicted Joseph fleeing Potiphar's wife, you would be correct. If you also guess that I'd spent hours staring at it growing up so that it was undoubtedly the only piece of art in the world I could easily re-create from memory, you'd be right again. It was, of course, extremely unlikely that this tapestry had anything whatsoever to do with Gentileschi, but it just might. Insanely, I decided to risk it all and bring the conversation back to art.

"That's not the painting where Potiphar's wife is clinging to Joseph's scarlet cloak as he is fleeing the bed?" I asked.

Cohen turned to me, a look of total shock on his face. "You know the painting?" he asked almost reverently.

"Know it?" I said, seizing my advantage. "It's my favorite painting in all the world, though I've only seen it in reproductions. I thought it was so magnificent, I actually had a tapestry made of it."

"You don't say," he replied, dumbfounded, but also electrified at finding a fellow fanatic aficionado of the three-centuries-dead Gentileschi. "You'll have to come to my house, then, to see the original."

His house? Did my ears deceive me? Forget about Bible, *talk art.* Go for it, you lunatic! a voice inside me started to scream. You're in the Twilight Zone anyway.

"You know," I went on, "I can't believe how fortunate I am that you pointed this Gentileschi out to me. The great works here always brought me a lot of comfort during my college years." (This was somewhat true. My off-campus college apartment was only two blocks away, and during a rash of burglaries in the late seventies, our apartment building was one of the few that went untouched due to the plethora of security agents stationed at the Fogg.) "And though I always appreciated the Reniors, Monets, van Goghs, and Rembrandts, I never realized that there was actually a Gentileschi right here. I mean, every great museum has their Rembrandts, but to find a Gentileschi, that's a real discovery."

"I'm so glad you feel that way." Cohen beamed. "My wife and I just have to have you over for dinner. Don't worry, we've heard about those kosher rules, so we'll prepare something you can eat." (At this moment I would have gladly eaten the carpet at his house if this was what was being served. I figured I could work out the details later.)

"Well," he said, "it seems like we both made a great discovery tonight. You discovered Gentileschi, and I discovered you."

It was as if a benign heavenly light had seared through the roof and upper floor of the Fogg and was now focused exclusively on me. As we approached the original group from whom we had departed a full ten minutes before, this supernatural feeling was reinforced by the fact that they all seemed to have been frozen in exactly the same position we had left them in. Their total mortification at the previous

chain of events had left them no graceful way to depart, but no graceful way to continue relating either. The spell was broken when Joe put
his arm around my shoulder and said, "You folks don't know what a
treasure you have here. Why, this boy could give you a tour of this
museum. He's an absolute expert. Lisa," he continued, "as soon as
you get back to New York, I want you to arrange for Mr. Jonas and
his wife to join my wife and me for dinner and drinks at my apartment. I'm so pleased you introduced us. I'm just so pleased. I'm sure
our firms will be doing a lot of business together." And with that, he
went on to greet his other guests.

There was a well-known television commercial where El Exigente,
the coffee taster for a major premium coffee, arrives in a small
Colombian coffee-growing town once a year to sample the coffee. If
he approves the single test cup, the entire town will enjoy prosperity
for a full year. Everyone in the commercial waits in anxious anticipation as El Exigente sips his coffee. When he smiles and nods his head,
whistles blow, church bells ring, guns are discharged, people begin to
embrace wildly, and the announcers tell us in the background that
"the people are happy."

The commercial never tells us what would happen if El Exigente
said no, but one can surmise that misery far surpassing that which
gripped Mudville after Mighty Casey struck out would ensue. Imagine, then, if El Exigente didn't just dislike the coffee. Imagine if it was
so bad it actually killed him. Imagine him lying there as the mayor
and town dignitaries, in shock, contemplate actual suicide. Imagine
the ineffable joy that would follow if El Exigente then rose from the
apparent dead and said, "Wow, that's the strongest cup of coffee I
ever had; it nearly killed me! I'll pay you triple for your beans so we
can use it in our new super-strong espresso." The town would go absolutely wild.

Polite investment bankers and the top executives of prospective
companies do not ring bells, dance jigs, or discharge firearms to cele-
brate great milestones, especially not in the Fogg. But from the mutual

handshakes, adulatory comments, and almost uncontrollable laughter that began to follow even the lamest jokes, it was clear that a celebration was going on here that would rival any coffee taster's resurrection in even the rowdiest of South American villages.

My side, of course, was stunned. They never knew I was an art expert. They were in awe. When I told them the whole story, they were even more in awe. Before the story I was just an art expert. Now I was sort of a mythical character in an Aesop's fable who, at the moment he is to be eaten by the lion, is saved when the lion recognizes him as the grown-up little boy who'd removed a thorn from his paw so many years before.

The rest of the night passed in a blur. We were introduced to first this and then that important personage. And as each introduction grew more lavish, the enormity and inevitability of what had occurred and what was to follow became apparent.

As we walked back to our car, for the first time I felt like a "son of Harvard." For the first time Harvard Yard seemed romantic and beautiful to me. For the first time it felt like it was truly mine. Only twice before in my life, when my wife agreed to go out with me for the first time and when our first child was born, did I actually go someplace and have the feeling that I was walking on air. I find it sort of embarrassing that the prospect of great wealth and power would put me in that same frame of mind. But there is no denying the truth. That night I was walking on air.

By the time, several weeks later, that my wife and I actually did visit the Cohen house, everything was more or less settled. Cowen would be our lead underwriter.

It turned out that my wife had attended the same school as one of the Cohen boys. Our pedigrees established, I acted as deferential as possible, stayed on my best behavior, and avoided any more jokes. Joe Cohen gave me his personal commitment that evening that Cowen would lead our IPO. I accepted the offer gladly. Now all I had to do was select the number two firm.

Montgomery Securities and Hambrecht & Quist, both from San

Francisco, seemed so anxious to do business with us that I never even contacted Robertson Stevens, the last firm, which was also from the Bay area.

H&Q invited us to their investment conference at the Pierre Hotel. Their analysts and bankers came to visit us and told us they were enthused. Dan Case, the chairman (and brother of AOL's Chairman Steve Case), took time out from his conference to meet with us at a conference room at the Pierre. They gave us a H&Q briefcase and coffee cups. Things certainly looked good here. We felt important.

I didn't drink from their coffee cup, though. Nor did I drink from any of the dozens of other coffee cups various firms had given me. To me, coffee is something personal. If you drink from a cup with someone's name on it, it's like you're married. This isn't something to be taken lightly. You better be sure.

Sure, Case had seen us, but he hadn't come out to our office. He hadn't invited us to dinner. And the analyst—well, he liked us, but he didn't seem to know much about us. He hadn't really asked the hard questions. He'd only spent a couple of hours with us and just said he was satisfied. This wasn't necessarily real love; it might just be infatuation. Like a nervous suitor reading meaning into every action, looking for any innuendo, we wanted reassurance that we were wanted before we committed ourselves.

As time went on, it started to look better and better. More guys from Montgomery came. They started calling Cowen to lobby them. They just tried harder than H&Q. I was ready to choose Montgomery, but one thing was bothering me. Tom Weisel, the legendary founder and chairman of Montgomery Securities, still hadn't asked me to lunch. I needed more reassurance; I needed to be fed. Then came the invitation. A catered lunch in our honor with the entire senior executive corps of Montgomery at their offices atop the Transamerica building in San Franciso. That settled it. Montgomery would be our second underwriter. It was now time to get down to the real work of preparing for a public offering.

Due diligence went smoothly enough. There were some questions about our database's ability to keep up with our swelling customer base, but this was solved by hiring the chief database guy from a big Fortune 500 firm. Under the watchful eye of Maria and Skadden Arps, things were going like clockwork. And then weird stuff began to happen.

First, Cowen came to me and said that they were working on another deal taking Vocal Tec public. Vocal Tec was like us, a pioneer in the field of Internet telephony. Their products, however, were designed to connect two people already on the Internet with each other. You just paid for the Vocal Tec software and the call was free. Our system connected someone on the Internet to someone on a real phone. The software was free, but you'd have to pay us for the call. We didn't see any conflict. Neither did Cowen. Vocal Tec did, though. Cowen either had to drop their lead deal with us or lose their secondary position on a much higher profile Vocal Tec deal to Lehman Brothers.

I was sure Cowen was telling us this as a preliminary to leaving. No, they said, they just wanted us to know what was happening. If Vocal Tec wouldn't relent, they could do the deal without Cowen. Joe, Maria, and Lisa (the banker on the deal) were proving a lot more loyal than I'd hoped. (Vocal Tec didn't relent, despite hours of my pleading with Vocal Tec's chairman not to hurt Cowen just out of spite. In the end, they replaced Cowen with Lehman Brothers, did the deal, and shortly after, their stock collapsed.)

Shortly after this, Cowen and First Albany's commitment committees passed the deals, unanimously clearing the last hurdle for an offering. Montgomery had only to pass the deal on Friday and we were ready. Sure enough, Friday afternoon the call came from Montgomery. They were out.

Out! Not in. Now what was I going to do? I called the analyst. Yeah, he still loved the company. He just didn't know till now what the problem was with the banker. But you can't do a deal without a banker. I called Tom Weisel. I told him to talk to the analyst. He called me back later and told me to talk to his head of investment banking. I called the head of investment banking. He wanted to do the deal, but needed a banker. I called Tom. Our investor, the best friend of the vice chairman, called. The vice chairman called the head banker. The head banker called Tom. The analyst called me. Soon everyone was calling everyone. Eventually the head of investment banking promoted a junior associate on the deal to banker just to get it done.

The newly promoted banker came out to check things on his own, liked what he saw (surprise, surprise), and went back to the commitment committee.

This time the call came from the head of investment banking himself. "Tom just wants you to know we're in. Great effort on your part. Thanks for sticking with us."

Skadden told us, "This is the first time in a decade we've ever seen a commitment committee reverse itself. You guys are unbelievable."

Of course, we knew if Montgomery dropped, Cowen would follow. "Bet you were pretty nervous," I kidded Maria.

"Not at all," she replied. "Joe was ready and able to do this deal on our own without them. But we're glad you got them back nevertheless. The extra research coverage will be good for the stock."

Were they really this loyal or was this just bravado after the fact? We'd find out sooner than we thought.

A week later the red herrings, the preliminary offering books, were ready after a forty-eight-hour marathon involving bankers, accountants, and lawyers at the printer's offices. (For this reason financial printers' offices, usually in lower Manhattan, are like well-appointed hotels, complete with large-screen TV, billiards, Ping-Pong, showers, twenty-four-hour hot and cold buffet—anything you could want, even complimentary cosmetic and personal hygiene kits. No one should go through life without spending at least one night there.)

As a routine gesture, our lawyer called Cowen, Montgomery, and First Albany to tell them the books were going into circulation. No! Wait! came the reply from Montgomery. There's a problem here. The analyst just quit. We can't do this deal without an analyst. We need some time to figure out what we're doing. We'll pay to reprint the books in the meantime.

Would Cowen quit now? Joe said, "Print the books with just two names on the cover for now." They'd add back Montgomery's name on the final S1 book, the final offering to go out next month after they got their analyst, which Tom had assured him would be done quickly.

Three weeks later, more bad news came. Montgomery had gotten an analyst. A well-known one. One they had hired from another firm. From Alex Brown, in fact.

"Oh, no!" I exclaimed, "Not that one. Not the one I almost threw out of the office."

"Yes," they replied, "that one. And guess what? He still hates your firm. Sorry."

When Cowen heard Montgomery was really out, they held everything up. "It's not good to go out with just one firm doing research," they said, completely ignoring First Albany. "We've got to bring someone else in, in the next two weeks. If not, we'll do it on our own, but it won't be best for you."

Oh, great, I thought. They'll never do it. I knew it. They're outa here. We're dead. How are we gonna get a big-name firm to do this in two weeks when it took Cowen and Montgomery six months to get up to speed? Still, we had no choice but to try.

There were only two possibilities (Vocal Tec had ruled out H&Q): DLJ or Dean Witter. Both these firms were giants, both had experience in our industry, and both had been making overtures to us. Cowen preferred DLJ. They became our number one priority. All the senior management at the firm was summoned, and they all showed up to meet us, either in person or via teleconference, at a hastily called meeting at Skadden.

They loved the story. They were really looking for a way into this sector. This was highly unusual for them; they usually moved more slowly. But this was an unusual circumstance and opportunity. Plus Cowen had okayed everything, and Cowen was as conservative as they come. And Skadden was behind it. You could trust Skadden. They'd do it. It was nuts, but they'd do it. They just needed to get their analyst to look it over.

The analyst, it turned out, was a nice young man—not too knowledgeable, in my opinion, but a nice, very scared young man who'd never done a deal before. When the commitment committee asked him if he was willing to stake his reputation on this deal, he wavered. He'd only had a few days to check it out; he didn't know the industry yet. It seemed good, wasn't that enough?

"Not good enough," said the committee. "Are you ready to stake your reputation on this?"

"No," came the reply. So much for DLJ.

Cowen was also disappointed. "Let's see what Dean Witter does," they said, as I pushed them to do the deal alone.

Dean Witter looked like a sure thing. The banker loved the deal. The analyst loved the deal. The analyst's boss, the head of research, loved the deal. The banker's boss, who was the head of investment banking and ran the commitment committee, loved the deal. "Forget about DLJ," they told us. "This is a shoo-in. You can depend on the Dean."

So what do you know? It seemed like someone up there liked us after all. It usually took months to find an underwriter, and here, in under two weeks (okay, true, we met on Sundays too), we'd apparently locked up one of the biggest ones in the country. If Dean came in, then Cowen would be reassured and our offering would be back on.

Prior to Dean, I'd begun to despair of Cowen's ever going forward with the deal and had started talking to First Albany about doing it on their own. Charley told me that friends said of him, if ever they were stuck in a foxhole under fire, he'd be the one they wanted with them. He now proved as good as his word, telling me First Albany was ready to print the books and do the offering on their own. I was ready to do just that.

But Skadden told me to wait. "You'll never get as good a valuation," they advised, "*if* First Albany is able to pull this off alone. And that's a big *if*. Let's see what happens with Dean first. Anyway, Cowen's still telling us they're behind this deal and we believe they'll do this with or without Dean."

Well, that made one of us. But to wait just a little longer seemed the right thing to do. Tomorrow, my patience would be rewarded. The Dean Witter commitment committee was scheduled to rubber-stamp the deal and we'd be in the money.

I went to sleep early, confident finally that this time we were going to win. I slept soundly and well.

So soundly, in fact, that I didn't even notice when the snow began to fall. Didn't notice as it started to pile higher and higher on my roof, completely covering and then burying the skylight, through which the morning sunshine usually shines on my bed, waking me in time to prepare for the day and help get the kids up and ready for school.

Without my solar alarm, though, it was the kids who wound up waking us, and they were jubilant. They bounced from bed to bed, telling us the good news. School had been called off for the day! The boys were going sledding; the girls were going to build snowmen with their friends. It was still snowing, wasn't this great? Maybe there'd be no school tomorrow too.

"And don't worry, Dad. You just rest in bed. We'll shovel out the house for you. No point going to work. Nobody'll be there anyway; the roads are all blocked!"

Turned out if someone up there liked us, He had a funny way of showing it. There wasn't just no school the next day, there was no school for a week! This wasn't just a snowstorm; it was a blizzard, the highest snowfall in the history of New York City. Obviously, the commitment committee wasn't going to meet today. I'd have to stay on pins and needles till the next scheduled meeting, next week.

I have an expression I always use that people sometimes have a strange reaction to. They ask me how I'm doing and I say, "Well, I could be worse." At that moment I thought the worst thing in the world was that the commitment committee meeting was being put off.

But if you use your imagination, you can always imagine how things could indeed be worse.

What would happen, for instance, if all the little guys on the committee, the ones we never talked to, the real conservative ones who lived in apartments in the city, showed up? What if this patchwork committee, none of whom knew the first thing about IDT or the enthusiasm of Dean's snowbound management, met and decided to give us the thumbs-down? What if they couldn't take the risk? What if these were the kind of guys who'd never risk their careers committing to an IPO that no one at the firm had ever heard of two weeks ago? What if these guys wanted to impress the firm by showing up no matter what the weather? What if they actually came in by subway, in the middle of the worst blizzard in New York history, and turned down our offering while their superiors—bankers, analysts, heads of research and investment banking—sat home, snowbound in their spacious homes in Westchester, Connecticut, and Long Island, unable to even communicate by phone due to downed utility lines? Now, that would be a lot worse. In fact, it would probably really embarrass all the top guys at Dean who had told me not to worry.

To their credit, our backers at Dean were embarrassed. They all called personally to apologize. Not that they could change anything. The committee was the committee, even if only a few stragglers had been there to vote. My worst "what if" nightmare had come true. The rules were the rules, though. And the rule was that the committee's decision was final. Better luck next time.

You know how sometimes it's obvious you're just doomed? How thing after thing goes wrong until you're just wiped out? How like Icarus, the feathers are just meant to melt away? Well, this is how I felt when I called Lisa at Cowen to tell her what happened at Dean.

"Oh," she said, offering no reassurance. "I'll have to tell Joe." Yeah, I figured that.

My job now was to wait around and get myself ready. Sort of find a comfortable kneeling position and get the basket adjusted just right under my head and wait. This way I wouldn't have to even get up and listen while Joe mumbled some insincere platitude about how sorry he was to have to be the executioner. He could just pull the lever, let the guillotine go, and fate would be satisfied without any more lies.

But an unbelievable thing happened while I was kneeling there playing with the basket. (Okay, okay, so I was on my cellular phone with First Albany. But why ruin the whole scenario?) Joe didn't pull the lever. He didn't give me a lot of B.S. platitudes. He just called and said we'd made a good effort. He was sorry for all our sakes it didn't work out, but he had a lot of faith in me, he had a lot of faith in the firm, and his word was his word. He was directing Cowen to *print the books on their own with just First Albany*. Now we'd better start preparing for the Road Show (a three-week traveling marathon during which you are taken to meet all the world's principal money managers in order to sell the offering). And that was it.

THAT WAS IT! I couldn't believe it. The mounties had arrived at the last minute. Superman had swooped down and saved the heroine, just in the nick of time! The Allies had landed!

Joe had kept his word at a crucial moment when I had nowhere else to turn. Now you can understand my personal attachment to Joe, Maria, and Cowen. This was something deep and personal to me.

Yeah, I was going to do the Road Show. I was going to raise the money. We'd all get rich. But first there was something I had to do, a conversation I had to have with myself. Why was I so paranoid that this offering wouldn't come off? Why was I so certain the big investment banker would abandon me? That is a very good question and deserves very careful answers.

Despite everything you may read, society is basically divided into classes. You're either from the right side of the tracks or the wrong side of the tracks.

People are very careful to associate only with people on their own level or higher. These levels are determined by different things: education, family, breeding, ability, and, most importantly, money.

In order to maintain this hierarchical structure that keeps people from lower levels out, society employs gatekeepers.

You've all seen these gatekeepers. Often they are just that, gate-keepers. They stand at the gates of exclusive private country clubs in their ornate uniforms and only let dues-paying members in. They can also be found at the front doors of fancy mansions or apartment buildings. But this is only the most obvious form of gatekeeper. There are many other gatekeepers in society besides the maître d's at fancy restaurants or the doormen. They just lack a uniform. They are on college admissions committees, they are executive directors of muse-ums and charities, they run industry trade groups and standards com-mittees of government regulators. All of them work to perpetuate the established order and prevent newcomers from joining the club and annoying or perhaps displacing established members.

We had already shaken up a lot of the telecommunications indus-try. We'd ruffled a lot of feathers. AT&T had gone to the government to shut us down. For that matter, whole countries were passing laws against us and trying to close us down. We'd also offended moralists against pornography on the Net, phone companies fighting against unlimited flat-rate Internet access, long-distance providers scared of Internet telephony. The powerful entrenched interests were all against us. We were getting way too big for our britches. A nasty innuendo here, a well-placed confidential badmouthing phone call there, and we'd be finished. I couldn't stop trying, but I wouldn't be terribly sur-prised when the ax fell either.

Now, I'm not saying that there's no fluidity between the classes or that people born poor and unconnected don't get rich and rise to the top. It happens all the time, and much more often in America than anywhere else. But it's not that simple.

There are two main reasons people are able to move up through class lines. The first is that ambitious, talented young people simply can't be kept down. The aspirations of everyone not born to privilege to move up creates such pressure that if society wouldn't allow hard-working talented individuals upward mobility, society would explode. In America particularly, upward mobility is one of the basic beliefs on which our society is built. The reality of this mobility is the main glue that, in fact, holds society together. Better to get rich than get the rich, so to speak.

The second reason for upward mobility is that the upper class needs to be periodically enriched by the creativity and talent of the rest of society if they hope to stay on top. This is true both on the personal and economic levels. The upper classes need the most educated and talented people to enrich their gene pool, just as they need new entrepreneurial businesses and business approaches to reinvigorate the economy and make it more competitive.

These rationales for class mobility create different mechanisms for this mobility. First there are large parts of the economy that are understood by all classes to be sort of free for all zones. Places where established wealth has no inherent advantage and all that matters is hard work, guts, and ability. These are industries like real estate development, filmmaking, retailing, and the high-class restaurant business. These businesses are a reflection of the creative personality and drive of the entrepreneur behind it.

This winds up being good for everybody. Steven Spielberg movies and Donald Trump buildings help the economy to boom and create new wealth. This wealth is used to buy more from the establishment part of the economy. Not only that, but the notion that anyone can make it is reinforced, preventing class hatred from tearing society apart and providing an outlet for the talents of those not born rich.

Another way talented strivers can succeed without threatening the established order is to invent a whole new field of enterprises where none existed before. Obviously, if there were no competing enterprises there before, no one is threatened. Just invent automobiles, word processing, or in-line skates and you're an instant mogul. A new branch of the established order overnight. Again, this is good for everyone. Other strivers will take heart from your success, the establishment will supply you with many of your production needs, the whole economy will boom, and everyone will get richer.

A different way the economy is able to deal with talented newcomers is to actually absorb them into the established order and let them become part of the upper class. You see, the established classes need the new vitality that the best of the aspiring class has to offer, but they want it only if they can harness it to their advantage in order to perpetuate their own dominance over society and the economy.

The real-life club is sort of like a country club. You have to be sponsored by a current member to get in, and your entry can't be threatening to other club members who might vote against, or blackball, your admission.

In order for a current member to sponsor you, you need to be talented and you need to be doing something for him. Sometimes, if all you want to do is get into an exclusive university, all you need to be is talented. Even more importantly, though, the upper-class companies, whose grants support the university, need talented managers, engineers, and the like to stay in business. They need a pool of talent from which to draw their new leadership. That's why they support the university in the first place. It's in their own self-interest.

The trick is that once the students are educated, the upper classes don't want them to emigrate or open fancy restaurants. They want them to join corporate America and contribute to reinvigorating or building the establishment.

The established club members need newcomers to accept the values and morals of the establishment until they come to embody it. Young lawyers aren't just given partnerships in big firms. They're exploited until they can think of nothing but the firm. For years the junior associates are forced to work eighty-hour weeks. They give up nights and weekends to brown-nose every partner with whom they come in contact. Ninety percent of these associates will wind up getting nothing but a paycheck for these efforts. (And just to be selected to compete in this manner, they had to be in the top 5 percent of law graduates.) The lucky few who finally are selected, though, get Nirvana—a huge partner's salary at a big law firm. And so the best of the aspiring class becomes the established class.

But what of the true innovators, the entrepreneurs who build their own enterprises? How do they fit into the picture? Very well, thank you. Most fledgling businesses, you see, will require capital to get started. This capital doesn't come cheap. The capital comes from the establishment as it is dispersed by the venture capitalists, who take huge, often controlling interests, in the new companies in exchange. In this way the establishment hedges their bets. They own not only the current means of production but have an interest in any new methods that might come to threaten them. As time goes on and the new company succeeds, it will need financing. Again, this time, through insurance companies and pension fund portfolios, the established interest increases its controlling stake. If the new company really wants to grow and do a joint venture with an established company, shares of the ownership in the new company must often be given to the establishment company, as part of the deal.

By the time the new company is ready to go public, "professional managers" (read, "establishment executives") must be hired and given big option packages in order to provide the necessary experience and "give the market confidence." These options also represent more of the ownership percentage going over to the establishment.

By the time the firm finally goes public, the original entrepreneur's stake is down to almost nothing. The ownership of the firm is almost entirely in the hands of the old established order. Like the Chinese, they've absorbed the barbarians and made them Chinese. Not that the original entrepreneur's small stake doesn't make him rich. It does, feeding the notion that anyone can get rich and persuading more people to try.

The original entrepreneur is now one more new member of the establishment. He can use his experience to select the right young companies to finance and control. The story has now come full circle. The entrepreneur has become one of the gatekeepers. What a racket!

The ultimate and final gatekeepers in this process, though, are the big investment banking firms. They're the ones who determine who's really going to cash in big. Not get seed money, but get real money and become a cornerstone firm in the economy. Part of the real establishment.

Investment bankers are basically little more than gatekeepers at the country club or the bouncers at the club. All they do is check your credentials and make sure mutual funds and other investors will find you an attractive prospect. But they're worshiped because the gate they control is the one the money's behind, and that's what the whole thing is really about.

The power all gatekeepers have to determine individuals' or firms' places in society inevitably goes to their heads. They are not only worshiped but well-paid to boot, in a class above mere mortals. So they've come up with a new moniker. They call themselves Masters of the Universe. I kid you not: Masters of the Universe. No earthly limit to the powers of these guys. They control the really big money. The whole universe, they believe deep down, needs to answer to them.

But in spite of all this planning, in spite of all these gatekeepers, in spite of everything the establishment does to see they control the game, what happens if a firm actually slips through and gets to the IPO stage and nobody in the establishment owns even the least little piece of that firm? What if the founder still owns the vast majority of the stock and he doesn't want to give any to the old establishment club?

What if not only that, but he's put himself on a collision course with AT&T and the whole telecommunications industry? How's the investment banker going to behave while this is going on? They're the gatekeepers, after all. They're supposed to keep this from happening. How are they going to act when all the venture capitalists, financing guys, and establishment managers they're used to dealing with aren't around? Is due diligence on this firm going to just be a routine matter? Are any small problems that come up just going to be routinely glossed over? Is handling an underwriting like this a low-risk job for which there are no possible consequences for the firm?

The answers of course are no, no, and no. The amazing thing, therefore, to me was not that Cowen might have dropped out, especially when it became clear that no other establishment underwriter was willing to share the risk (even for a couple million dollars' fee for which no work was required), but that Cowen had come as far as they had with us.

That they were willing to do it at all was the result of four factors: Joe Cohen, Maria Lewis, Skadden Arps, and prayer. Having the country's leading law firm in our corner no doubt helped calm down Cowen every time a new problem came up. As to prayer, each person has to make his or her own judgment.

Maria and Joe were the crucial players, though. Cowen is known as a research firm. Their industry position is due largely to the prominence of their analysts. Obviously, Cowen can't afford to pay its analysts what Goldman Sachs does, any more than the Milwaukee Brewers can afford to pay a freelance pitcher what George Steinbrenner can. They can, however, offer the analysts an independence of decision making, status, and position within the firm that the big guys couldn't match. The handful of ranked analysts who accepted this in lieu of higher monetary compensation elsewhere were, in my opinion, Cowen's crown jewels. They had to be coddled and handled with respect.

Once Maria took the position that we were a great firm that should be underwritten, this decision was not easily reversible. When she went further and personally went to bat for us, there were few in the firm who could oppose her without consequence. Not only that, but Joe Cohen's pledge proved to be unshakable.

Some people stick by their commitments no matter what. I had no way of knowing it at the time, but Joe is such a rare individual. All the theories in the world about gatekeepers are fine, but in a world of men, sometimes one or two determined individuals in the right position can create an exception to any rule. (Take Gorbachev, for instance. In independently acting differently from anything that was to be expected of a Politburo member, he probably is among the ten people who've had the greatest impact on the history of our world.) Fortunately for us, Joe and Maria were exceptions and so, much to my delight and surprise, the offering actually came off.

Clearly, not everyone at Cowen saw things the way Maria did. She told us on the Road Show just to be ourselves. People would love us. The banker, though, insisted I hire an elocution coach to polish my rough edges and make me seem more corporate. I agreed to keep peace till I found out that this female Henry Higgins was going to charge me $2,000 per day to turn me from a street urchin into a proper gentleman. At $2,000 per day! "Are you nuts?" I asked the banker. Instead, I hired my own coach, someone well known for coaching Fortune 500 CEOs. She was willing to coach me for $1,000 a day, and I thought maybe I'd like her better.

On the first day of the elocution lesson, though, I could see things weren't going well. She didn't like the way I walked or stood. "Carry yourself more like a CEO," she whined. She didn't like my jokes. "Try to be more serious, like a CEO." She didn't like my honesty. "Don't tell people you're not sure about the future. Be assertive and pretend you are like a real CEO." That was it! That did it!

"Okay, you want me to be assertive like a real CEO?" I fumed. "I'm starting now. This lesson is over. I've got more important CEO things to do all day than just keep repeating this speech. I'll pay you for today and tomorrow because that's what we agreed, but please leave now! Is that CEO enough for you?"

She understood I was a CEO just fine. Everybody on the Road Show seemed to know it too. I just walked the way I walked. Told jokes. Told them when I wasn't sure and they were so refreshed they bought our stock. Maria was right. All this corporate nonsense was just that. The trick was to be ourselves.

As it turned out, investors got to see how I acted as a CEO under fire rather than just having to judge from a canned presentation. This occurred when, only two days into our Road Show, AT&T announced they were going into the Internet business. Not only were they going into it, but they were offering free Internet service for up to ten hours per month to all their millions of clients, and matching our price to any of their clients who wanted unlimited service.

The market immediately went into a panic. The value of the other Internet provider stocks went into free fall. Some fund managers started canceling appointments to even see us. Market pundits in front-page stories around the world began to hail this as the start of the great phone giant's total domination of the Internet business (and the probable death of our offering). Even the team of Cowen personnel with whom we were traveling, along with the people back at the main office, went into a panic.

Everyone wanted to know whether I was also panicking and ready to give up and, if not, how I was planning to sell stock that it seemed nobody really wanted. Surprisingly, even to myself, I was not panicking at all. I had a feeling that, having come so far against all rational expectations, we were no longer subject to normal laws. Rather, like the '69 Jets under Joe Namath, we had become a team of destiny. Nobody had expected us to win even a game, but there was a spirit within us that kept us coming back again and again, so many times against all odds. Soon everybody, including me, began to feel that in some almost metaphysical way we just could not be stopped.

The whole situation was so surreal that I had ceased feeling like a participant and had become a sort of audience watching disconnectedly in fascination. I was playing my leading role in the unlikely drama that had become my life. From this perspective I thought the AT&T announcement was actually a great dramatic opportunity. Great leaders, after all, only get to be great when they rise to the challenge of adversity. Without the American Revolution, the Civil War, and World War II, no one would have ever heard of, much less seen, the greatness of Washington, Lincoln, or Churchill. Here was my opportunity to show leadership. Everyone, even fund managers, wants to go with a hero, so all I had to do was overcome AT&T's challenge and the offering was secured. To me, it was fourth down and long yardage in the Super Bowl. I was Joe Namath, and my team had the ball. All I needed was a great play.

As I mentioned previously, it's usually careful preparation that makes for the greatest "impromptu" victory. And for this challenge we were prepared. It came as no surprise to me that AT&T was entering the Internet business. If they didn't, they would be laughingstocks on their way to becoming communications has-beens.

I was, in truth, not even surprised that they'd picked the beginning of our Road Show to make this announcement. As you've already read, we'd been a longtime nemesis of the communication giants. Anecdotal evidence I'd been hearing from former AT&T staffers indicated we'd become a sort of personal bogeyman to upper management. If they didn't kill us off now, the company they'd considered their most serious upstart rival would have the necessary financing to eventually take them on as an equal. (I think this is more than wishful thinking on our part. As future events and newspaper headlines would clearly show, AT&T was totally unprepared to enter the Internet business at this time and could in no way handle even limited customer demand. No other major rivals were about to upstage their entry. In fact, their premature entry into the business wound up being a great debacle, and AT&T is still feeling the effects.)

What did surprise me was that they had gone with an unlimited pricing plan. AT&T, highly conscious of their profit margins (and dividend checks), usually prices everything on a per-unit basis. Not only that, but to cover their high overhead, this unit pricing always winds up being the highest in the industry. Low, unlimited pricing, if successful, would actually bankrupt them. And that's when I saw their Achilles' heel. Instead of panicking, I'd run the ball right through what everyone thought was the strongest point of their defense.

The plan they laid out was not really to sell Internet access. It was a Trojan horse designed to get people to keep paying their overpriced phone rates in order to get the Internet. Attack the phone rates and they couldn't fight back. Their profit margin wouldn't let them.

As we drove from a large investment banking house in London to Heathrow, I formulated my 20/20 perfect vision plan. Bring us your Internet and phone business and we promise to cut anyone's rates (including, of course, AT&T's) by 20 percent on *both* services. As an efficient phone company it cost us only 5¢ to route the same calls AT&T charges up to 20¢ for. That made it easy for us to undercut them by 20 percent and still have more than enough margin left over to cut our Internet rates by 20 percent as well. In fact, it was much more profitable than the old way. AT&T, with only an 8 percent profit margin, could not match us. Our Internet rivals, with no phone capabilities, were equally hopeless. The plan was a great winner. As a member of my own audience, I cheered wildly. This was fun. Before arriving at Heathrow I called the Cowen analyst in Boston with the plan. She loved it. The market would eat it up.

In the car from Orly to Paris I got on the phone to New York with our advertising, PR, and operations people. The next day our response to the AT&T challenge was carried in *Investor Business Daily* and other major papers. Within two days the ads starting appearing around the country and, of course, in our Road Show presentations. Fund managers hostile to us when we walked in were won over. AT&T's gambit had gained them nothing.

By the time we reached New York our show had become more a bandwagon than an attempt to pry investment dollars from wary fund managers. People were throwing money at us, and the offering was already sold out several times over, in spite of AT&T's assault. The guys at Cowen and our family and friends were ecstatic. For our presentation at the Waldorf, Cowen had to secure a larger banquet room, not only to hold all the eager investors, but all the well-wishers who wanted to attend. Even Joe Cohen, Cowen's chairman, showed up for the lunch.

I was really on that day. I told the crowd how thrilled I was to actually have come in the front door of the Waldorf as an honored guest after so many years of coming in the rear door to deliver brochures.

Then I launched into probably the best presentation of the IDT story I ever gave. People laughed at the jokes. They gasped at the charts. They sat riveted during the stories. I was really on. I mean, how couldn't I be? My wife, my mother, my father—everybody I knew was there that day. This was *our* luncheon, and the room was packed with New York's financial elite.

Partway through the speech the crowd started nodding and smiling, the way people do when they're really with you. Soon they were starting to whisper to the Cowen brokers in the room, and the Cowen brokers were taking out their pads and writing. And then they were smiling too and giving the thumbs-up. They were getting orders and the presentation wasn't even over yet. No one had ever seen anything like this! It was as if the financial presentation had turned into a revival meeting.

I was so happy. I was so grateful Cowen had really done it for me. My speech was just about finished, and suddenly I felt I had to say something else. I just had to.

I told people it wasn't just us who had come so far. We couldn't have done it without our underwriters. I told them about the coffee cup, about Maria, about Joe. I said, "A lot of guys get big, and they forget about who made them. They leave the H&Qs and Cowens of the world and go to the Morgans and Merrills—the M&M guys. Well, not us. We're different. We're gonna become as big as AT&T someday, but we won't forget who brought us here. Someday we'll be back making a presentation to thousands of you, I hope in the Grand Ballroom, just like AT&T. But unlike the other guys, we won't be one of the M&M-size club. They can be part of the deal, of course. But only if Cowen is our lead."

At that moment, I looked over at Joe, afraid he might be crying. He wasn't. He was beaming from ear to ear. No one, people told me, had ever, ever said anything like this about an underwriter on a Road Show. "Well, I meant it," I said later. "I'm glad I put it on record."

I was also glad a few weeks later when Cowen sent us a check for the $40 million they'd raised in the IPO. With this money we'd really be able to grow. AT&T was gonna have a real competitor now, one with money.

By late 1996, six months after going public, our company was really on fire and the stock started to skyrocket. It was unbelievable enough to me that, after going public, I was personally worth over $100 million on paper. Soon I'd be Rockefeller. This was unbelievable!

We were, of course, still losing money, as we'd been doing for six months in order to achieve a growth rate that would satisfy the underwriters and investors, but what did it matter? We'd abandoned every rule my grandmother ever taught me. Wall Street had told us not to worry about the bottom line. We were a big-time corporation now, playing in the major leagues, not running a hot dog stand where you could calculate how much you made on every dog and soda sold at the end of the day. The trick was to keep growing at all costs. We were rapidly working our way through our $40 million nest egg, growing wildly, out of control. The nation's largest stock underwriters were lining up to do a secondary and raise us "some real money." (I'm talking nine figures.) Then, all of a sudden, it crashed. Every underwriter abandoned us, and it seemed we were finished.

Chapter Thirteen
Secrets of the Street

In a modern business, without the backing of the financial community, you're finished. This is because business has changed, particularly high-tech and communications businesses that have come on the market in the past fifteen years.

The whole world, in fact, has changed. Even change has changed. It used to be that change was gradual; it happened over many years. Even over decades, retailing, banking, and service businesses didn't change very much. This gave the little guys a chance to grow big on their own. Take any business—shipping, for instance. Someone would buy a ship and begin carrying goods between New York and London. He might even skipper the ship himself. Over time, if the business was run well, he'd buy a second, then a third ship. He'd hire captains and stay behind in the office, lining up more importers and exporters to use his service. Slowly, bank financing would become available. The fleet would grow to massive proportions. By the end of a forty-year career, he'd have an empire to pass on to his son. The whole business, though, wouldn't be that fundamentally different from when he had only one ship. And, in fact, even as he passed the business to his son, other solo captains with one ship would already be well on their way to building their own fleet and competing with the established company.

How different from today! Say a young man has an idea to go into the shipping business. His angle is to get the packages there overnight. After doing some initial start-up work he goes to a Wall Street underwriter and shows them his business plan. The underwriter brings the offering to eager mutual fund investors, who pour many millions of dollars into the new company. Suddenly the young man is able to lease large jets, fleets of trucks, airport and warehouse facilities across the country. He's able to hire a sales force and do a national advertising campaign. Federal Express is born.

With all this, on the first day and for many days after that, only a few dozen packages are handled. The firm is losing a ton of money. More than the captain made in his whole career. Losses big enough to crush not only his fleet, but a whole navy. Not to worry. Wall Street funds the deficit. Soon, surely enough, people start to use the service, and a new industry is born.

Forget about getting one van and starting to compete with FedEx. They're all over. There is no way to bootstrap yourself up to that level. Only Airborne Express or UPS, with Wall Street backing of their own, can hope to compete.

It just happens all too fast nowadays for the lone wolf to have a chance. Netscape's public offering creates a stock with a billion-dollar value overnight. This value is used to hire hundreds of top programmers, acquire complementary firms, hire salespeople and customer service reps across the country. Of course, the company's losing a fortune. They have no sales, because up till now all they've done is give away their product. Yet, as the Internet looms even larger, what start-up has even a chance to compete in the browser market against mighty Netscape? The industry is less than two years old and already market domination has been determined. Only mighty Microsoft, with an even greater capital base, is left to compete.

Simply stated, as computer, communications, and shipping technologies have speeded the pace and scale of change, massive financial support has become indispensable. This is because customer bases are now created and market position achieved long before the new business has any chance of being profitable. Whereas once capital was invested with those who showed profit, now it is those who attract the capital that get the opportunity to profit.

This may not be an altogether bad thing. A few years ago America seemed to be going under economically in a big way. Suddenly, now America is on top again. Sure, a lot of this is due to the fact that as the society that most prizes individualism, we are the one with the most innovation. And the only one best able to adapt to a faster-changing world. A lot of credit, though, must surely go to the fact that we have the most efficient capital markets. Years ago I thought it was a shame that so many of our best and brightest were going to Wall Street rather than into the "productive sector." Now I'm not so sure. Where, after all, would I be without them?

On the other hand, I am somewhat of an anachronism. For close to twenty-five years, starting with a hot dog stand, long before I ever dreamed of going into telecommunications, I had run a business with no outside financing. Like the sea captain, every year I turned a larger profit, put aside savings, and reinvested into growing the business. (I had no idea just how important this would turn out to be in the days ahead.) I still had old-fashioned values and taking losses didn't come naturally. In fact, taking money and giving control to others didn't come naturally either. So much so, that at one point along the road to going public I insisted on retaining at least three votes per share as opposed to a single vote for those in public hands. I didn't know how important this would prove to be.

By the early autumn of 1996, I was ready to put aside my old-fashioned values and turn, once again, to Wall Street to raise us more money in a secondary offering. The timing seemed perfect. Our stock had almost doubled since the IPO. Our sales had tripled. We were the fastest-growing Internet provider in the country. We were emerging as the world's leading international competitive telecom carrier. We had developed a new (and still unrivaled) technology for running normal telephone calls along the Net. Plus, we desperately needed the money. In spite of all our growth (or maybe because of it) we were going through tons of money on a monthly basis. If we didn't get a big infusion, soon our growth would stop. In fact, if we didn't get some kind of infusion, soon we'd be out of business.

It wasn't going out of business, though, that concerned me. The tremendous growth and high stock market valuation had gone to my head. We weren't ordinary people; we were supermen. We really were going to overtake AT&T. Superman didn't just raise $30 million or $40 million like we did in our IPO; he raised $100 million or more. To raise this kind of money people didn't go to Cowen. Sure, they were a good firm. Sure, they got us started. Sure, we owed them loyalty. But I'm talking $100 million here. Only a half dozen or so giant underwriters in the world could raise that kind of dough for our business. Giant underwriters, the kind who dealt with supermen.

These were the guys we ought to be talking with now, right?

A small voice inside me called out, No, Howard, this is just hubris. Remember your values. Remember what Cowen did for you. You don't really need $100 million. It's not healthy to be losing money this way. Start turning the business around now. Grow a little slower, but be profitable. Stand on your own two feet. Just be loyal. Stick with Cowen. Raise another $40 million or so and become profitable.

Hubris had gotten the better of me, though. Who's got time to listen to some small voice when you're Superman? When there are locomotives to outrace, tall skyscrapers to bound over, when there is a stock market to impress?

Howie, Jim, and I met and decided that we were ready to do a secondary stock offering, perhaps combined with a bond offering. If we were backed by one or two of Wall Street's largest investment bankers, we could have $100 million—even $200 million—to play with. We were so hot, we felt that raising money was like taking candy from a baby. With a cushion like that, who cared that IDT was still losing money, hemorrhaging in the cash flow department?

We'd squash our competitors and eat them for lunch. We were on a roll.

Underwriters, it seemed, were there for the taking. Unlike our Initial Public Offering, which we'd pulled off by the skin of our teeth with only Cowen and First Albany behind us, this time we had our pick. I magnanimously included Cowen in the secondary offering, although I let it be known that I was doing this out of loyalty, not good business sense. I had become so arrogant that I cringe to remember it. Some big firms didn't want to be bothered with Cowen and pulled out of the offering. But the rest were so eager to be part of our deal that they were willing to accept anything.

It wasn't easy telling Joe and Maria we were going to get a new lead underwriter, but we had destiny to answer to.

We engaged one of the largest and most prestigious of these underwriters to raise $100 million for us. (This meant that we were willing to issue more stock to raise additional capital.) Of course, this dilutes or lowers the ownership percentage of those already owning stock, but in theory positions the company for even greater growth by acquiring expansion capital. Usually stock sold in secondary offerings costs much more than that sold originally, since the company has already "proven" itself. The underwriters spent the next few months, from September to November 1996, doing due diligence, examining every aspect of the company's operations. They were thrilled with our prospects. A successful secondary offering seemed all but assured. The underwriters, however, did one more thing before signing off on the offering. They hired one of the country's premier private investigation firms to see that the firm and its principles were "completely clean." This, they assured me, was merely routine, pro forma.

Private investigators, I know, summon up images of seedy Humphrey Bogart types down on their luck working out of beat-up offices over pool halls. Just hire one of them and for fifty bucks they'll bribe the desk clerk, open the motel room door, and burst in taking photos as unfaithful spouses grab up the bedspread and scramble for their clothes.

Forget about your preconceived notion! Today, big PI firms do most of their work for the financial industry. They're accountants, lawyers, and former FBI agents looking to uncover financial wrong-doing, stock manipulation, and embezzlement. They're supposed to be beyond reproach. Their very names on a report throw fear into the biggest tycoons.

But based on my experience, the central casting smutmonger fits them better. In fact, I think it's too good for them. As far as I'm concerned, the whole PI industry is nothing but a heap of excrement irresponsibly ruining people's lives. Before you pass judgment one way or another, let me continue.

Our written report came back fine. It mentioned we were negotiating a settlement with some state attorneys general. We had agreed to refund money to some Internet customers who were unhappy with what they were getting. This was standard for our industry, though, and the negotiations with the state, the underwriter already knew, were just about amicably concluded. The report mentioned a handful of unpaid parking ticket collection disputes and lawsuits in which I'd been involved in over twenty years in the publishing business, but these had all long since been taken care of or were too trivial to be of substance. And it mentioned some ongoing IDT litigations that our attorney assured them were minor in nature. Everything seemed okay. They even gave us a copy of the report to keep.

At one point, one of the bankers asked Jim and I if we knew of any pending federal investigations of our company.

"No," I said. "That's ridiculous. If any investigator told you that, they're just looking to make business for themselves by coming up with dumb leads to follow up on. Don't you think if we were under investigation we would have heard about it?"

"Listen," Jim told the underwriter. "I've been at the highest levels of government for over twenty years. I have friends in high places.

They all knew I was leaving my law partnership to become president here. I assure you, if there was any investigation going on of IDT, they would have called me to give me a heads-up. And no one called. So there is no investigation. Do you understand?"

"Well, that's good enough for me," said the underwriter. We'd cleared the last hurdle. We were home free.

To our surprise, though, a week later the underwriter suddenly pulled out. The report was bothering them and they had some "other conflicts" they couldn't work out right now. Maybe in a few months.

At the time, we believed the "other conflicts" line. What did it matter? True, the stock had started to slide, but a lot of other underwriters were knocking on our door trying to displace our current choice. They were also big. They'd get the job done right away. With their backing, IDT stock would gain the few points it had lost and then some. We needed more money desperately, to hedge our bet. We started due diligence with another large firm right away, and this time it was completed in a week. Finally we were going to really make it. We'd get the money we needed. We'd ensure our market position and we'd be really rich. Then, unexpectedly, they also pulled out. Seems the PI report, of which they'd gotten a copy, was bothering them too, or so they said. Now we were in real trouble. And the stock really started to slide.

We pored and pored over that written report. There didn't seem to be anything bad or unexplainable. Jim brought it to a friend who had run the largest brokerage house on Wall Street.

"Perfectly normal, don't see any problem," he said.

Joe Cohen, the chairman of Cowen, also asked to see the report and said we looked fine to him. He'd talk to the heads of the other investment banks and try to determine what the problem was. Why hadn't we just stayed with Cowen? I thought. That was my mistake. My fat head. My abandonment of old friends. Now I was being punished, but good!

I waited to hear from Joe, but didn't get a response. Not right away, anyhow. He was always in meetings. He was always waiting to hear back from someone else. He was talking to Maria about it. He was on top of the problem. He wasn't on the phone, though.

And I was running out of money. And the stock was dropping. And I had nowhere to turn, and no one to talk to, so I talked to everybody.

Everyone I met, from top to bottom, any underwriter we'd ever dealt with, got a call from me. All were encouraging. They all told me what a great company I had. How they were sure we'd be doing business soon. How they were sure everything would be worked out.

How *what* would be worked out? *What? What? What?* There was nothing to be worked out. Just get us the money, take your cut, and everything'll work out just fine. The stock'll go up, the company won't go under, the investors will be happy. What's to be worked out? There was some kind of conspiracy going on around that report. Something someone wasn't telling us.

I kept calling, trying to cash in old chips, willing to issue new ones. Finally, a low-level due diligence guy at one of the large underwriters gave us our big break. Like Deep Throat of Watergate fame, he gave us the crucial missing clue.

"It's not what's in the written report," he said. "That's just a diversion. The problem's in the oral report. The one the great PI firm can't put down on paper for fear of litigation."

"Well," I demanded to know, "what does this oral report say?"

"No one's ever going to know where this came from?" he inquired one more time. "You know, they'd hang me for this."

"Look," I guaranteed him, "a deal's a deal. No one, I promise, no one will ever know this came from you."

"Okay, okay," he said. "The report says the feds are investigating you. Seriously investigating you, if you know what I mean."

I didn't know what he meant. How could we be under investigation and I not know about it? This couldn't be true. Maybe Deep Throat was lying. But come to think of it, hadn't the guy from the first big underwriter asked us about this? Hadn't he mentioned a federal investigation and just dropped it after Jim was so taken aback even by the suggestion? Sure, and right after that they dropped us. No, Deep Throat was no liar. I needed more facts.

"Tell me," I implored, "which federal agency is investigating us? I've got to know so I can clear this up."

"Look, I already said enough. You know what can happen to me if anyone knows I told you this? I've got a family to look out for."

"Please, please, you gotta tell me. I've got a right to know."

"Look," he said, "I don't know. I only know one more thing, but if I tell you, you gotta promise never to call me again."

"Fine, I promise, I promise. Who's after us?"

"I don't know who's after you. But it all starts in the New Jersey attorney general's office. That's where the PI firm got the info from." And then Deep Throat clicked off.

I kept my promise. I never called him again or let anyone know of his identity.

So now I knew. No wonder no one would deal with us. Everyone thought we were all going to the slammer. With this information, however, maybe we could set it all straight. But first I had to make sure it was true.

This was much easier than I thought. It seems the various underwriters were actually dying to share this information with us. They'd spent long periods of time with us. Many liked us personally. Plus there'd be no underwriting fees for them if we didn't get this cleared up.

The PI firm was apparently all-powerful on Wall Street, though. When you received their oral report, it was, by agreement, under the strictest confidentiality. If you were the one who leaked it, there'd be hell to pay. And not only in the courts. Leaking it would mean you were no longer a member of the club. You'd given away the secret handshake, the members' passwords. You'd violated your blood oath. You couldn't be trusted anymore. The PI firm couldn't let you know what was really going on anymore. The other members of the brotherhood couldn't share information with you either. You were a rat, a squealer, a turncoat. You were, in a word, out. No one would risk the ire of the PI firm and face suspension from the club. Not for any size underwriting. That's why no one told us anything.

Once we knew, though, then that was a different story. Once we knew and demanded confirmation, they couldn't very well deny it. I mean, just refusing to answer would sort of be admitting the fact. Plus, if we knew enough to ask, then someone else had already told us, so it wasn't a secret anymore. If it wasn't a secret, then they'd have no responsibility for telling a secret. They might, however, have some liability with us if they lied.

"Yes, yes," all the underwriters sooner or later admitted. "The secret oral report does say you're under investigation."

"By whom?"

"Well, if you don't know by whom, we can't tell you. But surely you can figure that out on your own."

It turned out the question of legal liability was a big one to the underwriters. Once the PI firm had told them even confidentially that we were under investigation, it made it impossible for them to do any kind of underwriting for us. The underwriters, you see, are legally bound by securities laws to inform the investing public of all the risk factors of which they are aware concerning any offering they might sponsor. This is why most company prospectuses, which are theoretically trying to sell the company's stock, are in actuality mostly taken up with enumerating various risk factors. The underwriter could be held completely liable if they knew of a risk factor, didn't report it, and the risk came to fruition, making the investment less valuable. This degree of liability would be enough to collapse almost any Wall Street firm, and so failing to report the rumor would be impossible.

On the other hand, the rumor was only that: a rumor. The PI firm couldn't prove it, so they couldn't tell us a thing. Had to protect their sources. They were not even willing to put it into writing. They were not even willing to let the investment bank tell anyone they knew of it. So the bankers couldn't report it. If they did and the stock collapsed and the rumor was untrue, all the current investors could sue them from here to kingdom come. Even if the rumor were true, they could get sued anyway. After all, hadn't they agreed in writing with the PI firm to keep it secret? It was a perfect catch-22. You couldn't say we were under investigation and you couldn't say we weren't. Only the PI firm could clear us, and they wouldn't even admit they'd said anything.

We had no idea who was behind this, and to this day I'm not sure. Of course, there are many potential suspects, although I have no reason to suspect one more than another. Competitors, for example, might well have wanted to ruin us. It's a lot of fun to watch your enemy crash and burn. Perhaps short-sellers had started the rumor that we'd committed some major federal crime. Our stock started at 10, rose to 17, and plummeted to 4 before this whole nightmare was over. A short-seller who knew that our value was collapsing could have made a fortune, a sure thing. Could there have been a renegade attorney general in some far-off state with an ax to grind against us? I racked my brains for an answer, but never could get the whole story. Could the PI firm itself have invented the rumor out of whole cloth just so they could show they'd earned their fee? I may never know. The bottom line was that nobody would underwrite us as long as this rumor was out. We were screwed. Big-time.

I called Maria. Maria knew everything about the company. The numbers, the prospects, the monthly cash burn.

"What am I going to do now?" I asked. "What options are available to me?"

Maria was my friend. She was always looking out for our best interest. Whatever story I told her, she was always figuring out how to put a positive spin on it. Like a good doctor who treats athletes or actors, she was always working to see that we appeared our best in front of the crowd, which in our case was Wall Street. But like a trusted family member, she was the one you knew would always give you the lowdown when everyone else was pussyfooting around.

Today, the doctor was somber. "I don't see you have any choice but to sell the company."

That was it. Sell the company. Doctor says we're finished. Inoperable cancer. No chance for recovery. Just try to sell off your possessions before you go so there'll be something left for the kids.

Sell the company? No way! So many years. So many dreams. So many people. All still working. All coming to work optimistic, signing accounts, providing service, unaware of the prognosis. Looking completely healthy. Must be the doctor's wrong.

I was in a panic. I consulted secretly with Howie and Jim. "We gotta get to the heart of this rumor quick, and disprove it."

If I had to go down shooting like Butch Cassidy and the Sundance Kid, there was no team I'd want around more me than the one I had now. And there was probably nobody in a better position to help than Jim. But first the two of us had to talk.

"Jim," I began, "look, I understand completely if you want out now. The stock has collapsed and your options are worthless. Maria thinks it's hopeless. And now we're really going to get dragged through the mud. We might go bankrupt. Maybe it'll turn out we did do something wrong. There's no upside for you. The main thing you've got is your reputation. Why give up something it took a lifetime to build? You could go back to law and lobbying and be respected and make millions. Nobody'll ever hold it against you that you mistakenly joined a firm that was already having problems. But if you stick with us, whatever happens to us is gonna happen to you. So, if I were you, I'd resign now."

"No way," Jim said. "When I signed on as president, I meant it. This is my company. This is my life. This is just a huge injustice, and we can't let it happen. I'm with you guys. We can fight this. Whatever happens, it happens to all of us together."

They say you never know who your friends are till the going gets tough. Well, I might not have had the greatest prospects, but I had some unbelievable friends. Howie wasn't giving up. Jim wasn't giving up. In time, all our top people would decide to stay and fight.

This was another visit from my imaginary monster the Meligoth. He stands for all evil, and for some reason, he's made it his personal obsession to go out after me. Every day he tries different ploys. Sometimes he makes me run out of gas, other times he makes major clients quit; now he was starting devastating rumors. Naturally, the Meligoth always thinks that with all his power, he's finally beaten me once and for all. And then, just when he's celebrating, I pull myself together, kick him in the head, start to beat his brains in, and the whole thing starts again. Every morning when I go to work, my wife sends me off by saying, "Go slay the Meligoth."

I don't have that many great attributes, but I am unbelievably resilient. That's why the Meligoth chose me as his earthly sparring partner. The Meligoth must surely have thought at this point that he'd finally won. He'd isolated me completely and was about to finish me off. Instead, he now found out he was up against Jim, Howie, me, and all of IDT, and we weren't going gently into the good night. Ah, if only he could get the pay-per-view rights on this fight, he could just retire and let some junior Meligoth take over.

Jim began with the New Jersey attorney general's office, where he had some influence. Prior to the Republicans taking control of the state government, Jim was their last unsuccessful candidate for governor. To Republicans, he was like a founding father, and the Republicans now ran the attorney general's office. Not only that, but a felony had been committed. All investigations were supposed to be strictly confidential. If someone in the attorney general's office was passing confidential information to an outside PI agency, well, that was a crime. I mean, if the attorney general's office had turned crooked, then there was no rule of law.

A week later the attorney general came back with good news. The office had investigated everyone and they were sure no one had talked. Not only that, but there was nothing to talk about. The matter with the states was being concluded, and there was no federal involvement. They were sure of it. The feds had not contacted them on this matter.

Excited, we raced back to tell the underwriter, sure they'd relent.

"Well, there's still the report," they said. "If the PI takes back the report, fine. If not, what can we do?"

A lot of answers were going through my head, but what I said was, "We just want justice. We'll even pay you to investigate your own report and either confirm it or dispel it, with no liability to you."

"But how can we do that when we won't acknowledge there's any report to begin with?"

The calendar said 1997, but these guys were in an Orwellian 1984 and wouldn't come out.

By this point, Jim, along with Admiral Elmo Zumwalt (a member of our board, former senior officer on the Joint Chiefs of Staff, former commander of all U.S. naval forces during the Vietnam War, and a great military hero) was visiting the chief guys at the investment banks.

I also offered Admiral Zumwalt the opportunity to resign. "Are you crazy?" he said. "I'm a soldier. I don't run under fire, and I don't allow bullies to push good people around. Don't worry about my reputation; I've been around a long time. I have a long list of friends and a long list of enemies, and I'm equally proud of both lists."

The bankers were now being confronted by a former congressman, presidential officer, and head of the U.S. Navy.

"This is a great company being run by great guys," they told the bankers, putting their professional prestige on the line. "They're being railroaded. It's up to you to stop this injustice by forcing the PI firm to prove its allegations or take them back."

"We'll work on it," the bankers equivocated. "We know it's a great company, and we trust the management. We just need time."

The bankers weren't giving in. They couldn't, but they were beginning to waver.

"Tell me," I demanded. "Who did the firm say is investigating us? Exactly who?"

"I can't tell," the senior banker protested.

"Well, don't tell me who they said is investigating. Just tell me which agencies you'd like to know aren't investigating before you'd be ready to sign off on the deal."

"Just one," came the reply. "The FBI."

The FBI. J. Edgar Hoover, John Dillinger, Efrem Zimbalist Jr., the Ten Most Wanted. Did he say the FBI? We were in the phone business. We didn't peddle drugs, kidnap children, or rob mail trucks. The SEC, the FCC, the FTC—okay, maybe. But the FBI? In a way, we were relieved. This was too ridiculous to be real. Time for Jim to check it out.

It's not easy getting to meet with one of the chiefs of the FBI about a possible ongoing investigation. I know it was well beyond me or my lawyer. On the other hand, after someone has spent decades in Washington, he does acquire powerful friends. And, for friends, the unlikely is sometimes possible.

"So," the senior FBI official said to Jim, "you want to know if you're under investigation? Well, I can tell you your 'Freedom of Information' form notes no investigation. It usually takes a year to process, but I can get it for you in a week. True, it wouldn't tell you if there was an ongoing investigation. I suppose you want to know that too. But, of course, I can't tell you that. I mean, if we did, every mobster would be asking us to confirm no investigation was going on, and if we couldn't, then they'd know they were being investigated."

"But we're not mobsters," Jim said. "We're running a public company and somebody is using your agency's name to ruin us. I think you owe it to us to say whether this is true or if someone is telling lies about what your agency is doing."

"Look, I just can't answer that," the FBI guy, now in a dilemma, protested. "But I'll tell you what. I can tell you that if we were investigating you, I'd want to talk to you about it."

"Yes?" Jim asked.

"You hear what I'm saying? If we were investigating you, I'd be talking to you now."

"And?" Jim asked again.

"And"—the FBI guy smiled—"I have nothing to talk to you about. Do I make myself clear?"

"Would you repeat that to the head of a big investment bank?" Jim asked.

"Depends on who, and only in private. Now, I'm way over the line, but using our name like that? Outrageous! Just outrageous!"

That was enough. Once the FBI itself nixed the rumor, the whole thing started to unravel. Another PI firm the underwriter had hired actually confirmed, in writing, there were no investigations. The states finished their settlement with us without even a fine. Just less than 5K in refunds and a $50,000 donation to the various states' Internet education funds. We were in the clear, just like that.

Soon we started getting invited to big investor conferences again. The bankers and analysts started to visit again. Everyone was willing to do business. There was just one problem. Nobody wanted our stock anymore.

Wall Street, you see, is like a romance. Full of mystery, hope, anticipation. New stocks are like meeting a new and pretty girl. You think maybe this is the one. Oh, for sure this is the one. You just know it. She may not love you or be earning money just yet, but look at those prospects. Other fellows can tell too. They're all swarming around taking positions. Better not get left on the floor. Better buy some and ask her for a dance now.

On the other hand, what about the girl who has been around the block, after she's tired and worn out, when none of the guys even want to ask her to dance anymore—when her stock has lost most of its value and the only place it seems to be going is further downhill? Well, who wants to get involved with her then? Not Wall Street, that's for sure.

This was where we were now. The blush was off the rose. Our once-rising stock price had sagged below the IPO level and was still falling. All Internet-related stocks had collapsed. Some small telephone companies like us were still doing okay in the market but with our banker out of the picture for so long, the market decided to take the worst view of things and see us as another failed Internet company. We were losing money, running out of cash, had no backing. What a mistake our original buyers had made to buy into us. The stock would probably fall further, but they had no one to sell it to.

We'd won the battle but lost the war. Now that the bankers had finally ended the blacklisting, nobody wanted anything to do with us again. Again came the hated suggestion: Sell the company, if you can still find anyone to buy it. Sell the company. Take whatever you can get. In another month you'll be broke anyway.

I'd sooner have cut off my arm. I didn't spend twenty years working up from delivering brochures to running a public company to give up now. Because a bunch of jerks on Wall Street were running scared? Why the hell had I ever gotten involved with Wall Street to begin with?

I had never run a business that consciously and willingly lost money before I met the Wall Street crowd. That was their stupid idea, grow and lose money and you'll be worth even more. Just come back to us for a money fix every now and then, and if we still find you attractive, we'll give it to you. This wasn't business, it was dependence. The same kind of dependence that a drug peddler or pimp feeds on.

Why didn't I just listen to my grandmother and stay away from these guys? They'd turned the whole world upside down. Being a public company was walking the high ground, being respectable. Earning a profit and growing rationally was like being in the gutter. But now where were we? We'd walked the high ground and we were about to go broke because we couldn't fund the losses the Wall Street business plans called for. Now it looked like we were going to wind up in the gutter anyway.

But you know, if it was gonna happen anyway, why wait? Why let the market kill you and drop you in the gutter? Why not escape like a resistance fighter and run there while you're still alive? Why not earn a profit? That would totally confound Wall Street. You can't go broke if you're earning a profit. Fact is, it makes your stock go up.

Sure, it's not pretty. It doesn't follow the business plan. You're not going to be able to go back to them for money if you don't follow the plan. Won't get to be dependent. But so what? If you're making money, you don't need them.

Wall Street, the establishment, thinks they own or control everything, but they don't control the gutter. In the gutter the invisible hand rules. Make a profit, grow. Lose money, die. No mercy. No Road Shows. No gatekeepers. The dreaded reality of the marketplace. The ultimate force, before which even governments and Wall Street must bend.

No favoritism, no prejudice—just prove yourself on merit. That seemed fair enough to me. If the gutter was the only choice, I wasn't going to walk there. I'd run. Investment banks, gatekeepers, lying rumors, falling stock prices—this stuff I'd never really understood. This was Harvard, the world I'd rejected. The gutter I understood just fine. Hot dogs, all-night brochure distribution, flying coach, selling the ads, and no matter what, balancing the checkbook. I could do the gutter as well as anyone. I was happy. I was gonna show them all, and succeed on my own terms. I was returning to the gutter. I was gonna make a profit. I was going home.

Sometimes, though, turning a profit means painful self-sacrifice. If you really want to earn your stripes in the American Mafia, you have to kill someone. Once you've rubbed someone out, then you're really accepted. You've proved yourself. You're a member of the club. A made man.

In Japan, things aren't as simple. There they realize it takes no great courage or commitment to wipe out someone else. In Japan, if you want to join the mob, all the senior guys get together at a table to listen as you swear your loyalty to the organization. Oh, and just one more thing: While they're at the table they also watch as you take out a knife and without complaint amputate half of your own finger to prove your commitment and courage. This, you can be sure, is a lot more serious than just pointing a gun at some stranger and firing.

The American Mafia is a sort of fringe organization. They engage in drug peddling, prostitution, gambling, hijacking, and the like. Everyone acts tough and lives well. Then, periodically, the government decides it has had enough. Soon everyone is arrested. People are falling over each other to be the first to violate the secret oath and turn state's evidence, and soon the whole leadership is locked away in the federal pen. Till it all starts up again.

The Japanese mob, on the other hand, is all-powerful. Their tentacles reach into the giant corporations and into almost every level of government. Reportedly, every big financial transaction has to include a share for them. Almost no one is prosecuted and no one ever seems to rat on anyone else. The American mob is strictly a bunch of amateurs compared to their Japanese counterparts. Considering the admissions procedure, is this really a surprise?

Recently, in America, a new kind of financial hero has been getting some good press: the turnaround artist. The hired gun goes into an older, faltering company and just starts firing. The marketing and advertising department, bang. Corporate jets and country clubs, bang, bang, bang. Middle management, bang. Senior management, bang.

By the time he's finished, nobody except a few Joes on the assembly line, wearing earplugs to block out the shooting, are left standing. The company is profitable. (Of course, it probably has no long-range viability other than to be merged into a real organization, but that's another story.) The stock price soars and the hero is interviewed for the cover of *Business Week*.

"Well," he says, "it was a hard job letting all those people go. Really hard, but someone had to do it. Someone had to save the jobs for everyone else. It was rough. It was horrible. I'm so emotionally drained, I need to take off six months [and write a book about it] before my next turnaround."

Then the hero gives his best General Grant ("Yeah, my heart is heavy for all the boys lost at Gettysburg, but at least their families know they didn't die in vain") pose for the camera and goes off to cash in his millions in options.

What a crock! He loves firing everyone. That's what he gets paid for. He doesn't even know the people he fired. He has no idea what went into building the divisions he just dismantled. He's shown no more courage or determination than the Mafia's made man. If he really wants to prove something, why not try it the Japanese way? Give up the options and quick-exit strategy. Make a long-term commitment to the company and then decide what or who to shoot. Not really interested in the job? I didn't think so!

With cash flow running millions of dollars negative and our nest egg rapidly shrinking to nothing, it was clear I was going to have no choice but to cut. There simply wasn't time to grow our way out of the problem. I was not a hired gun, though, brought in to start recklessly and heartlessly blasting away. This was my company. I built it. My soul was poured into it. These were my people. I had hired them. They had faith in me. Soon a lot of the company would be gone, and a lot of the people would feel abandoned and betrayed. I was going to have to go through a Japanese-style initiation, and I wasn't looking forward to it. This was a time for serious consideration and surgically precise moves. How did I get into this situation in the first place?

The answer to that question would be the key to extracting us from our current problems. Like Hansel and Gretel, the key to getting out of the forest was to retrace our steps going in.

Our telephony business had always been profitable. The close to 100 percent markup we were able to charge on callback virtually ensured that. True, in order to meet Wall Street's growth expectation we'd let the division grow fat, recently hiring too many salespeople and spending too much on direct consumer advertising, but this could be cut back. The installed customer base and strong worldwide rep network would then be generating good profitable cash flow again.

Our new carrier division also seemed okay. It was already the company's fastest-growing business. It was well position in the world's fastest-growing industry. It took very few people (read salaries) to run. And, most importantly, it played to our unique corporate strength. In the carrier business, the three most important talents you need are negotiation skills to drive down prices, analytical abilities to figure out the best place to put in the network and how to price the phone usage, and diplomatic ability to arrange favorable telephone tariffs with foreign governments.

Howie's unrivaled analytic abilities always put us two steps ahead of anyone else in the industry. Jim, along with Jack Lerer, was virtu- ally running his own state department, securing more favorable inter- national arrangements than any of our competitors. And when it came to negotiating, well, AT&T or MCI might be able to field a team that could beat us at tennis or squash, but at negotiating, they weren't even in our league. The carrier business wouldn't be touched.

Net2Phone—our unrivaled technology for placing telephone calls over the Internet—was the future. The division was small, cost little to run, and was leading the industry in developing real Internet tele- phony products. It would be nuts to get rid of this. Sure, it was losing money, but in a year or so it might be worth more than the whole company. For sure, a way had to be found to move the developments quickly to the marketplace. Maybe there was even some fat to trim. But this wasn't where the massacre was going to happen.

The big problem was with our consumer Internet business. This was the division that was pulling the company under. This was the part of the business that was losing more than all the others made. This is where the big cuts were going to come.

Ironically, it was the consumer Internet business that attracted Wall Street's attention and had given us such a high valuation. Cutting it would undoubtedly hammer our stock. On the other hand, going bankrupt would bury it. Better to be hammered than buried, I figured. Plenty of fighters with beat-in faces go on to be champions. Relatively few dead people, however, have gone on to receive much renown.

There was, in the beginning, nothing wrong with the Internet business. In fact, in the beginning, we even ran it profitably. Clients who knew what they were doing would be attracted to us by our low prices and good service. We'd charge them $15 or $20 per month for a service that only cost $8 to provide. We were making almost 100 percent profit and had a few thousand clients. Our advertising costs, mostly in trade journals with smaller classified ads, was minimal.

Then Wall Street said if you could just step up the growth, we could back you.

"Step it up how much?" we asked.

"Oh, not that much," they replied. "Maybe ten- or twentyfold."

Ten- or twentyfold? How were we going to do that? Where would we get the money?

"Borrow it," they replied. "Listen, if we do an IPO for you, this company will be worth five hundred dollars for every Internet client you have. Five hundred dollars! How much is it costing you to get an account now? Maybe ten in advertising. So just spend more. Even if your cost increases to twenty, that's still four hundred eighty dollars profit, plus your eight bucks a month. Don't be a jerk, go for it!"

That small voice inside me said be careful. But it was too late. I'd already been offered the keys to the vault.

Growing by a thousand accounts a day turned out to be quite a different thing than growing by a few dozen. A few dozen will find you. They'll comb the classifieds, talk to other techies, and discover you. A thousand, on the other hand, require you to find them.

You have to run large ads in the big papers. Large, expensive ads. And you need to run TV and radio commercials. Not the cheap ten P.M.–to–two A.M. spots you run on radio when you're happy if three or four clients call in, but expensive prime-time slots. Soon it's not costing you $10 to make a sale, but $40—as much as you'll make on the client the first six months. But wait, the best is yet to come.

Seems there's not enough people in New York, Los Angeles, and Washington—where your equipment is—to sign up a thousand new accounts a day. So soon you're installing equipment all over the country. Expensive equipment for which the clients aren't yet signed. You even contract with other local Internet providers to handle your accounts, but not all of them know what they're doing and soon accounts start to complain and even cancel.

Speaking of not knowing what they're doing, congratulations. You're selling to the general public now, not a bunch of techies. They don't even know how to install the software when it arrives. They just want to wave it in front of the computer, say "Internet, Internet, Internet" three times, spit over their shoulder, turn the computer on—and magic—there they are on the Internet checking out Madonna's Web site.

They can't connect. They still have only a 2400-band Atari modem. Well, that's not their fault. You never said the modem can't be ten years old. If you're lucky, you never said in the ad you needed a modem at all.

"Now you're telling me I need a modem. I'm calling the consumer authorities."

"But sir, how do you expect to connect without a modem? What are you going to plug the phone line into?"

"You mean I need a phone line too? Your ad didn't say anything about needing a phone line. I'm going to the district attorney. Don't even try to refund my money, you fraudulent bastard."

I kid you not. People even asked for refunds when, on reading our installation instructions, they realized they needed a computer!

Sure, sure, you can deal with one or two nontechnical people who need help. But what about when thousands start calling? More tech support. More money. Soon the good users can't get through and they're canceling too.

By now it's costing $80 to sign an account as opposed to the original $10. So many people are quitting up front that the average time you keep an account is down to eight or ten months as opposed to forever in the beginning. This means you're only making a $64 margin on the average signup it cost $80 to get. You're losing $15 for every account you sign. Insane. But the business is growing. Wall Street is happy. They think each account is worth $500 and they're paying. Until suddenly someone spreads a rumor about you or the romance for Internet stocks is over and the price collapses. Or both. Welcome to January 1997.

Not that there's anything wrong with the Internet business itself. The hundred thousand or so accounts you've successfully gotten on line are still paying you $20 a month. It still only costs $12 or so to service them, even with a now national network and tech support. In fact, once they're on, they don't even call tech support too much. You could actually make a lot of money servicing this base and just pushing for referrals and corporate business. You'd just have to disappoint Wall Street and stop growing. Or start growing more in the telecom area where you're really focused anyway. See, it's not all that complicated.

Before starting to rub out other people, though, you gotta set priorities. You gotta start with your own finger and take a 50 percent pay cut for the year. This makes it easier for all senior managers to accept a six-month pay freeze, and it makes everyone feel a little better before the real pain, when heads really start to roll. It doesn't do a whole lot for you, though. To you it feels like you're hacking off your arm.

Like a condemned prisoner who wants to enjoy his last meal before facing the agony of the chair, there was one firing I wanted to do first. One I sort of enjoyed. The pompous investor relations guy, the one who was always talking to Wall Street and telling us what they wanted us to do. At first I offered him another position. (He didn't take it. Who wants to deal with mere mortals once you've talked face-to-face with the Masters of the Universe?) But the important thing was the position was gone. From now on we'd answer to the bottom line, the invisible hand, not the Street.

Then the massacre began. Ironically, only a few weeks earlier I'd been hailed in the local paper as the "Maestro of Growth." My wife had just had twins, a boy and a girl, our seventh and eighth children, and the paper's photographer actually came to the hospital to photograph us with the babies. Employment had swelled past five hundred, and with the rumors finally behind us, we were told new financing would come shortly. Just as my family was growing, I told reporters, so would IDT's workforce. Now this. I was going to look like a worse liar than Nixon. I couldn't understand it. My grandmother always said, "Every baby brings its own luck." I had believed this. Having kids was not only the best part of my life, it always seemed to bring good luck. Not only the luck of having the kids themselves, but even unrelated, personal upswings as well.

Whenever I hear someone in the office is having a baby, I think, great, now we're really going to succeed. Even my management style is predicated on fatherhood. I try to give all my managers and employees, like my kids, as much freedom as possible to make it on their own. I try to "courage" them to act on their own, without me. In retrospect, it seems the twins really did bring luck; they saved us just at the brink. At the time, though, it seemed like Dad had gone nuts and was about to start randomly shooting the kids.

My whole management style is based on deferring to my managers' judgments and trying to come to consensus decisions. This is not just to give the managers independence by letting them think that their own judgment is usually right. The fact is, in most instances, I actually do value their judgment over my own. I deliberately set out to hire people who are smarter and more talented than I am, and in many cases I've succeeded. Howie Balter, our COO, is not only a better hands-on manager than I, but far smarter and more analytical. If I have a new idea and he shoots it down, the great odds are it deserved to be shot down. In a few minutes of conversation, he's usually able to persuade me I'm wrong. Only occasionally can I persuade him that I'm right or that the idea's at least worth trying. Over the years we've watched competitors lose millions trying out the very ideas we came to realize through debate and consensus weren't valuable. Paradoxically, we've also had the opportunity to be first with more new ideas than anyone else.

The same process that goes on between Howie, Jim, Hal, and I also goes on between us and our senior division managers, and between them and their managers. In most cases, the junior guy winds up winning. This isn't only because we try, as I stated, to hire brilliant junior guys, but because the junior guy is usually closer to the situation and is in a better position to see exactly what will happen in a given instance. He knows better than the "ivory tower" senior manager the current temper of the market and the employees. He knows the particular stresses and balances in the operation and what may have to be sacrificed in one place to succeed elsewhere. I've come to have almost total faith in our senior managers. If they say something absolutely won't work, I can be sure it won't.

The heart of our consensus management style is our Tuesday senior management meetings. Here the top twenty managers gather, report on their divisions' progress, and we all discuss what actions to take or how to make things better. Later, we're joined by the next twenty senior managers. We tell them the consensus we've come to and then get their input on situations before all coming to a final consensus.

In a typical Tuesday meeting, Howie and I would open up, set the agenda, and propose a few new approaches. Soon, though, someone in the group would usually take over and force us to see things another way until we all could work things out and come to a final resolution. I've often marveled how I came in the boss, but after a few minutes allowed myself to be reduced to a mere observer, listening to the fireworks, wondering which position was really correct, and enjoying the action, waiting to see how it would all work out.

Now, in February 1997, our financial position destroyed, Tuesday afternoons became the worst part of the week. Sure, we'd try to start the meetings upbeat with some new approach, but the financial guys would start to hammer us with the realities of our eroding cash position. Each manager would then amplify this with his own consensus.

Things were catastrophic, and we'd have to come up with a variety of
Band-Aids to stanch the bleeding.

No one suggested the really radical surgery I was contemplating,
however. Maybe this is what leadership is all about. To come to the
rescue and assert yourself in times of crisis. Perhaps this is why only
crisis produces history's great leaders. In the good times, your job is to
stand back and give general direction and guidance. Let the guys actually doing the job make the nitty-gritty decisions. Now was the time
to be assertive. The past few months of Tuesday meetings had set the
stage. The managers knew things were catastrophic. They were ready
for something radical. They were ready for someone to ride up on a
white horse, take charge, and break the siege. The time for listening to
debate had ended. The time for getting on the white horse had come.
The Tuesday management meeting that took place on February 11,
1997, would be different.

"Look," I told them, to start things off, "I'm tired of all this nega-
tivism and pessimism. We're running a very profitable business
here."

A profitable business? Had I lost my mind? they all wondered. But
I had their attention.

"Yes, a very profitable business. You guys should get an award, not
be downcast. You're doing way better than anyone in the industry."

Get an award? Oh, G-d, we're really in trouble, they all thought.
The boss has cracked completely. The pressure must've been too
much. Any minute we're going to have to call in the paddy wagons
and take this guy away.

"Yes," I continued, "the reason our business is so good is because
we always thought like a small business. We never sold any service we
couldn't make a profit on, and we built capacity only to meet our customers' needs. Remember, not that long ago, we were financing our
growth just out of operations and still making a profit? Our competitors, on the other hand, are the ones in real trouble. They're engaged
in an 'if you build it, they will come' type of mentality. They've built

networks they'll never fill and need to sign up more clients than they can ever manage. Look, every one of our competitors is losing five times what we do. Sure, we got nuts with the public money and everything, but all we have to do is cut back to our original plan and we'll be generating cash."

"Are you insane?" one of the managers called out. "Do you know the scale of the problem?"

"Forget the scale of the problem," I said. "And forget about Wall Street. Let's just look at each of the divisions, one by one, and see if we can make money. Let's start with the worst money bleeder, the Internet business.

"Fish," I said, "supposing we just cut the advertising to zero. You wouldn't need forty telemarketers then."

"True," our most senior manager, Michael Fischberger, replied.

"And how much tech support is going to support those new sales?"

"More than half," he responded. "We could probably eliminate sixty positions there without the new sign-up," he added, now clearly getting it.

"And how much more would we lose if we did it?"

"Very little. Most of the new sign-ups are quitting anyway because we can't service them properly. In fact, if we didn't have to worry about so much new business, we could probably take better care of our regular accounts, and they'd stay with us forever. Not only that, but we could cut hundreds of thousands in connectivity costs we're paying to hook up new cities where we have almost no clients now and just service our top twenty markets. This would cut our tech cost as well."

"It looks to me," I said, "like if we do this we could go from negative a million a month to positive a million in a month."

The finance guys had out their calculators now. "Well, positive half a million looks more like it," they said. "And with the severance cuts and such, you're looking at closer to two or three months."

"Let's not quibble over details," I said. "A million, half a million; one month, two months. The point is we'd be making money. Even our worst loser would be a cash cow.

"Now look at the telecom side. We're already making money, but there's surely plenty of fat."

"You said," Geoff Rochwarger, our second most senior manager, replied, "I could probably get rid of twenty-five percent of the expense just by cutting the deadweight if I had a free hand."

"Well, you've got it now, but I want you to cut the bad debt out of the carrier business as well."

"Are you sure?" he asked. "This is our quickest-growing business. If we cut service to any client we thought was risky, I don't know what would happen."

"We're not going to cut service," I replied. "We'll just make them pay up front."

"But no one demands up-front payment. They'll all quit."

"Look," I said, "if they quit, they quit. Bad debt's wiping all our profit out anyway. Even if only half stay, we'll be making hundreds of thousands more a month than now. And with the low price we'll be able to charge, maybe they won't quit. Maybe more will sign up."

"Here, here," Steve Brown, our chief financial officer, called out approvingly. "If this plan includes getting rid of the bad debt, you can count me in."

"And Net2Phone?" our controller asked. "I guess we leave that alone." He was referring to our ace-in-the-hole development project.

"Nothing's sacrosanct," I said with a wild look in my eye. "Everything has to make a profit. Forget about the market. Let's cut the fat out of Net2Phone first. Second, let's stop putting so much effort into pushing our phone-to-phone product to market. That's at least six months away. Everyone's working on it. Instead, let's really push our product for making real phone calls from computers on the Net. That's a real niche market we can dominate, and right now we have it all to ourselves. If we make a real profit there, and really perfect the service, we'll be the ones everybody goes to when they're ready to do it with just a phone instead of a computer."

By now Howie was into it and began to take over the meeting. As the various managers and financial people called out their estimates, he began to outline on the whiteboard the specific cuts and budget targets we had to achieve; and the timetable. It was a big job. Within three months, by the end of the quarter, we needed to achieve 20 percent growth and cut costs by 30 percent. Then we'd become profitable again. It was a big job, but these guys couldn't wait to get started.

The firings were scheduled for Monday. Word leaked out early, though, and everyone froze and went into a panic when they heard what was going to happen. Everyone. Both great employees and poor ones were worried that they'd soon be gone. The Internet division was in a particular panic. We were left with no choice but to move things up and do the whole job on Friday.

I was particularly disturbed that many of our best employees were worried about their jobs. A hired gun comes into a company and just eliminates whole divisions, firing the good with the bad—but that wasn't going to happen here. I insisted that all of our more than five hundred employees be evaluated by their own supervisors at every level. There was no quota for how many employees a given division could hold on to. If the best ones happened to be in an area that was going to have particularly severe cuts, we'd transfer them to a different group, where they'd replace a less-qualified or -motivated coworker. Sure, this would cost us time and money in order to get the transferee retrained and up to speed, but that was a small price to pay. Dedicated, loyal, unbelievably talented and hardworking employees were the heart of our business, the key to our success. We have always been like a family, and at least when this was over, I wanted the best and the brightest to remain.

Okay, it was a time of financial crisis. Maybe the long-lost, loafing uncle who just showed up recently and moved into a bedroom or the distant cousin who didn't contribute to the household but showed up at meals was going to have to be asked to leave, but were we going to start throwing members of the immediate family or close relatives into the street? No, the family was all going to pull together and make it as a unit.

Having worked for years as a brochure deliveryman and ad salesman for struggling publications, I am well aware that the lack of spectacular results in a particular business is no indication that the staff in that business is untalented. Some businesses are simply highly profitable or in areas of the economy experiencing high growth at a particular time and others aren't. It takes no greater talent to run a telecommunications company than to manufacture shoes, for instance. Telecom just happens to be a sexy, profitable, growth-oriented business and shoes aren't.

Of course, one can argue that the choice one makes about which business to go into is indicative of one's abilities in general. In some cases this is true, but in most cases (like ours, for instance) it is more happenstance than planning that usually determines where one winds up. In the case of the employees, this was particularly the case. The fact that one person might be in a profitable telecom division while another was in a money-losing group was only because, on the basis of their particular talents and our particular needs, we, the management, assigned them to one group or the other. For us to now penalize the workers for trusting our decision making and doing the best job wherever they were assigned would have been both foolish and wrong.

My priority, as the captain of a ship going through rough seas, was to calm and give confidence to the crew who was going to go through the journey with me. It was important, therefore, that all firing happen at once and not in waves, to avoid having everyone worrying, "What's next?" It was also important that everyone know exactly what we were doing and why. And what our game plan was for the future. People have often accused me of being too honest. Pathologically honest. I need to be literally kept incommunicado during the legal silent periods before our quarterly earnings are reported because of my tendency toward complete openness.

In this situation, however, honesty was definitely the best policy, and the fact that people knew I'd never lied to them before added credibility to my reassurances. While the personnel staff worked overtime firing and arranging generous severance packages for the roughly 125 workers being let go, Jim and I held two mass meetings for the roughly 400 workers we were planning to keep.

"Yes, it's terrible," we told them. "Yes, management is cutting their own salaries and sharing the pain. Yes, if Wall Street hadn't abandoned us we would surely have been able, over time, to grow our way to profitability."

But we had to face facts. The only way to save the company and everyone's jobs was to become profitable now. The cuts guaranteed this would happen. The next few months would be rough, but in the end we'd all be better and more secure for it. We weren't a dying company. We were a growing one—one of the fastest-growing in the world, in one of the fastest-growing industries in the world. The pains we were experiencing weren't the pain of death, they were growing pains. Achieving profitability would be like growing up. It would set us apart from everyone else and really open up every possibility for us.

Then watch out! The sky would be the limit and everyone would go further than they ever dreamed. If we met this challenge, we could do anything!

To my surprise, most people were ecstatic. They'd come here to share a dream, and our fiscal crisis had made everyone wary that the dream was going down the drain. No one really wanted to leave for an ordinary company and just give up, but no one saw how we were going to get out of this either. It turned out everyone had been depressed for months following our stock's seemingly moment-by-moment continual fall on their computers. Now suddenly there was hope. People were gung-ho like never before. They were going to show the market. Matters were in our hands now. We'd prove the market wrong.

Not before the market gave us one more good kick in the head, though. When, as required, we released the news of the layoffs and the cessation of Internet advertising, the stock collapsed entirely, settling at 4. At this price, all but the most contrarian were obviously just waiting for the bankruptcy. My paper wealth, once close to $200 million, had dropped below $50 million. I'd lost over $100 million in less than a year. I couldn't even protect my family by selling some stock to make a larger nest egg. If I'd sold, the stock would have collapsed entirely. Wow! Even more significant, new potential lenders who'd been attracted to us by the lure of undervalued warrants that might appreciate, thus giving them a windfall, now lost interest. This stock, they reasoned, was headed for the toilet bowl. Our last source of financing had dried up. Every financial maneuver I was able to pull off still wouldn't leave us enough cash for the turnaround. Investors who used to want to give me money now ran like I had the plague. It was as if someone had hung a big sign with the stock price and the word LOSER around my neck. Those who bought because they'd previously thought highly of me now had only losses to show for it. My staff also complained that whereas once friends treated them with awe as an IDT employee, they were now almost laughed at.

What a world! If Wall Street, the banks, investors, and even friends wanted nothing to do with us, where would the money come from? I had no place left to look but the mirror. It was time to put up or shut up. I put up.

When I was at Harvard, I did an extensive research project on the Mitsui Company, one of the seven giant firms that control the Japanese economy. What impressed me was not the billions in sales or their banks, shipping firms, or manufacturing operations, not their millions of dependents or hundreds of subsidiaries. What impressed me was their origins. Centuries ago, the original Mitsuis opened a small bar near Edo, now Tokyo. Travelers would stop there and not only drink sake but sometimes take a loan or change currency. Thanks to the profits from these transactions, the owners of the bar were able to put some money aside as savings, burying their silver coinage deep beneath the bar's earthen floor. In time, they expanded to banking, then other businesses. But still they ran the bar and still each generation continued to make some just-in-case deposits beneath the floor of the original bar.

In time they grew to be a gigantic firm. Then disaster struck as dictatorial regimes came to power and seized everyone's assets. The Mitsuis were finished. The dictatorial regimes soon fell and the new rulers put the assets back up for sale. There were no buyers, though, as everyone's assets had been seized and no one had money. Then one old Mitsui remembered about the bar and the floor. He dug down, recovered the coins, and reacquired the company. The giant Mitsui Zaibatsu, larger and more powerful than any Western company, was reborn—mainly from the bartenders' savings.

I didn't own a bar or have a dirt floor, but I'd spent twenty years distributing brochures, publishing trade journals, and doing small real estate transactions. It wasn't glamorous—no more than running a bar—but it was profitable. And the 25 percent of my annual income I'd squirreled away over the years was now a considerable sum. This money, however, I didn't want to touch. It was for a rainy day so my family would be okay if everything went wrong. It was not in stocks or speculative investments for my savings. Not even bank CDs. (Grandma said you never know when one of those banks will go under.) No 100 percent U.S. Treasuries for me. This was family money, not to be risked. If I was willing to use it for IDT, I'd never have had to take in early-stage investors.

Now, however, there was no choice. A decision had to be made. The money was family money, but IDT was my family's company. It was against all my principles to go for broke, but these were not ordinary times.

I mentioned that at this time we'd just had twins. Twins meant that our already tight house could no longer contain us without putting three kids in a bedroom. We had one kid living in the dingy basement, and we could barely fit around the dining room table, which doubles as homework command central during the year. We'd already begun looking for something larger and more expensive. But I was worried. The house we already lived in was all paid up. A new one would cost much more, and if the old one didn't sell, it would cost that much more again.

On paper I was still worth millions. I had savings, a profitable publishing business, real estate holdings, and ran a public company. But who knew once I had to start putting money into IDT how much it might take? Maybe the house money could be the difference for the company. Or maybe I'd be living in a big house, but my company would be broke and the house would just be a reminder of better days. My wife kept making excursions with the real estate brokers, but I told her I was having second thoughts.

At about this time I went to a wedding with Geoff Rochwarger, a friend, though a dozen years younger than me, and the head of our telecom division. Geoff is a really solid guy—hardworking, good morals, smart, trustworthy—the kind of guy I'd like to be when I grow up, or that I'd like my son to turn out like. I told him about my house worries—three kids in a bedroom, a house like a sardine can.

"Well," he said, "we grew up with four boys in a room."

"And how did you like it?"

"It was great," he said. "We're all still really close."

That was it. You could grow up four kids to a room and still turn out like Geoff. As my wife's friend Sandy says, geese grow fat in a small barn. But how would it be to grow up in a big house with a dad who'd lost everything because he didn't have the courage to stand behind his own life's great undertaking? What kind of father would set an example like that?

I told my wife to forget about moving, just as she found a house she was in love with. It had more bedrooms for the kids and a large dining room for company. It had a perfect yard for playing ball with the kids and a little terrace just off the master bedroom where we could sit and have coffee in the mornings. Frankly, I was in love with it too. But now wasn't the time for a dream house. Now was the time to prepare for the worst.

"I don't think we can afford it," I told Debbie.

Can't afford it? Was I kidding? She must have thought so. This was, after all, no mansion, just a nice house for a large family.

"Look," she said, "I'd gladly live in a one-bedroom apartment if we had to. But are you sure we can't afford it, or is your paranoid, worrying side just getting the better of you?"

"Debs," I told her, "if I don't put my own money into IDT, it's going under. I don't know what to do. Deep down inside, I'm not a hundred percent sure if I can turn this thing around or not."

"Of course you can," she told me. "Thank G-d we have money to put in. This old house has so many good memories, and the best neighbors in the world." So for the time being we stayed put.

So here we were, a multimillion-dollar company, trading on the NASDAQ big board, with agents in over a hundred countries, developers of the most advanced Internet telephony software in the world, with well over $100 million in annual sales. And we were being kept alive with money I'd earned delivering brochures to hotels in the middle of the night with an old Chevy station wagon. If I had a deep-seated psychological need to reject everything about Harvard, some deep craving to be independent and make it on my own, without any help from the normal institutional interests that companies depend on, that need was more than satisfied.

We were swimming across the ocean with the flimsiest of life preservers and the sharks were circling. Getting on some financial institution's boat seemed mighty attractive now that we were on our own. There was no boat in sight, though, and so our only option was to hope that our plan had pointed us in the right direction, and to stroke like mad.

Surprisingly, the plan worked, and land came into sight much sooner than I'd expected. In fact, we seemed to swim right into some sort of tropical paradise with gold in the streets, way ahead of schedule. The luck that the twins brought could finally be seen.

Chapter Fourteen
The Great Comeback

❖

Maybe an alarm clock went off in heaven and our oversleeping guardian angel suddenly awoke with a start, frantic to make up for lost time, much as unforeseen circumstances had seemed to conspire against us, driving us to the verge of insolvency, because suddenly all sorts of unexpected events started working for us.

Our first blessing was that soon, in the wake of the firings, another thirty or so relatively highly paid employees, many of them technical, jumped ship and resigned. At first, of course, this panicked us. People had lost faith in us and it was every man for himself. Morale was utterly collapsing, we thought. We worked valiantly, scheduling more meetings, sending out newsletters, opening more channels of communication with our staff to let them know things were basically okay. We shifted more and more responsibilities to the remaining staff. Still, it took weeks for the wave of resignations to abate.

When it finally did and the personnel situation stabilized, we braced ourselves for the obvious repercussions that were bound to follow. Would our service collapse with the missing programmers? Would the billing system go under? Would sales slow? Where would the cracks in the dam show up first?

We waited and waited. And nothing happened. Well, actually something did happen. The tech service cue dropped from ten minutes to thirty-seven seconds. Internet customers stopped getting busy signals and their connection speeds doubled. Our international phone networks started to go up at double their previous speed. Sales picked up. All over the company things started to go right. A large part of this was due to the new fighting spirit of the troops and their positive reaction to being given more responsibility. Things actually started to work better.

A large part, though, was also due to the departure of the grousers. After these people left it became clear that some of them, however talented, were doing nothing but taking up space, or worse. When the company was growing, funded by Wall Street money, it was easy for some to slip into the cracks, pretending to be busy but in fact doing nothing, dispiriting the honest, diligent personnel with their attitude. Under the new regime, though, I think it became clear to these loafers that they'd soon be found out and fired. Obviously, once fired they wouldn't any longer be so desirable in the employment market.

The game, it seemed, was to go to our large competitors and tell them, "You know that IDT magic? You know who did it? Me. I got the systems up. I thought up the new algorithms. I boosted sales. Yeah, and now they're going under. Fired over a hundred people. A real shame. If there was any hope, I'd stay with them. But you know how it is. Best if I just get out now. Why, if you hired me, I could probably bring that ol' entrepreneurial verve here. Maybe even get some co-workers to come along. It's like you'd be buying IDT and all you'll have to do is just pay little ol' me."

This must have been irresistible to the big companies they approached. Wow, just steal our staff and you could be a leader in callback, international telephone, Internet telephony, the Internet access business. Sure, it might seem a little dirty. But what the hell, business was business. IDT would probably soon be gone anyway, and what an opportunity to combat their own corporate incompetence. Of course, they'd be glad to raid our staff. They'd be instant winners.

It reminds me of a time when I was twelve and a half years old.

The phone rang, and when I answered it there was a sexy female disc jockey on the line.

"Congratulations," she told me. "You've been randomly selected to compete for our grand prize. Just identify these three tunes."

" 'Hey Jude,' " I screamed out as soon as the first one started to play.

"Right," she gushed. "Now this one."

"It's the Beach Boys' 'Surfin' USA.' "

"Incredible," she screamed. "You still have almost thirty seconds left to identify our third tune and win the grand prize."

The music started to play. I recognized it. But I just couldn't get it. I couldn't place it. What was it? I was in a panic. I could hear the sound effect *tick tock,* ticking my time away over the phone. I was in a panic.

I screamed out, "Mom, Mom! Quick, get on the extension. Ma, it's a radio contest. What's this song?"

" 'Raindrops Keep Falling on My Head,' " she yelled, just an instant before the disc jockey shouted, "Time's up." That was it! My mother had gotten it, under the buzzer.

"Correct," the disc jockey screamed. "You've won the Grand Prize."

"Ma, Ma, we did it! We won the Grand Prize!" I screamed jubilantly.

The Grand Prize! We were both going nuts over the phone, just like screwy game show contestants. We did it! Dad wasn't gonna believe this.

"Do you want to know what you won?" the sultry disc jockey now asked. "Yeah, yeah," we both gasped in unison.

"Well," she said, "for getting all three tunes, you, Howard Jonas, have won the Grand Prize." Pause . . . drumroll . . . "A bucket of shit!"

Then she clicked off. She'd hung up, completing her prank call, and now she must've been rolling around on the floor, laughing hysterically.

We were temporarily dumbstruck. Then we started laughing hysterically over the phone to each other too. A bucket of shit. A bucket of shit. We carried on hysterically. How could we have been so dumb? A normal contest I probably would have forgotten by now, but that bucket of shit has stayed with me always.

Even until now, apparently. In their anxiousness to cure their own corporate malaise, to win by stealing what they'd thought were our crown jewels, the big companies were stealing what they thought was the big prize while we were distracted with other problems. Unfortunately for them, all they got was my bucket.

I lay in bed laughing once again. The resignations had saved us millions more than we'd even hoped for, and made us much more efficient.

"Are you sure there's no one else waiting to resign?" I asked all the division managers. "Nobody else we could let AT&T steal from us?"

"Now, don't be a pig, Howard," they counseled.

The improvement in service on the Internet side was so dramatic that cancellations started to fall to levels undreamed of. From eight hundred a day, to six hundred, then soon under two hundred, then under a hundred. Soon more accounts were signing on by referral as a result of new large corporate accounts. The Internet business was not just turning a big profit, it was growing as well. Every other large Internet access company in the country was reporting multimillion-dollar monthly losses, and we were coining money. Wall Street, discouraged by the losses, was still valuing this segment of our business at almost nothing.

"Sell to a big phone company," the bankers advised. "We'll broker the deal."

Looking at the actual numbers, though, and at the organization we'd built, I was not too motivated by their advice.

"I'll listen to any absolutely unbelievable offer," I replied, "but, frankly, I'd much rather keep it."

And we did.

The crackdown on deadbeats in the carrier business produced even more dramatic results. A large number of smaller carriers and debit card companies had made it standard operating procedure to stiff the end providers of international telephone time. Their method was simple. They'd open an account with a large phone company and be given a small credit line. They quickly ran a lot of international calls, exhausting the line, and would promptly pay their bill and ask that the line be increased. The carriers, anxious to show Wall Street the increased revenue that selling expensive international time produces, would readily agree. The small company would now pay the bill again. This time, though, the payment would be slower and many of the individual charges would be protested. The customer by now, however, would be really important to the big carrier's total revenue projection, and so their continual request to have their credit lines increased would be granted again and again. Payments would continually come in slower and slower, and disputed items would increase. Eventually, the big carriers would find themselves millions or tens of millions behind. The little guys would then stiff them entirely and move their business to other carriers or force the big guys to compromise the bill by millions.

My decision to cut all credit off from these crooks and make them pay in advance would, six months earlier, have involved substantial cost. The little carriers would just have taken their business to another revenue-hungry sucker and Wall Street, noting a 50 percent decline in our carrier business, would have hammered the stock. Wall Street, however, no longer mattered to us.

Fortunately, however, Wall Street mattered to our competitors. Our competitors were forced to report the hundreds of millions in losses they'd had to take as a result of the little guys' scam.

When Wall Street saw this, they went nuts. Our competitors' stocks were hit worse than if they'd never shown the revenue in the first place. Many were forced to leave the business. All the others tightened their credit policy, selling only to reliable accounts.

Only we had developed a system to deal with bad debt, able to cut off a risky client the second his last dollar of deposit was used up. The would-be crooks had no choice but to pay up front. We had become their supplier of choice. We were after all still the least expensive supplier in the industry.

Many of these guys sold phone cards to immigrants for cash. Their business was so hand to mouth that they literally had to make deposits into our account daily, even on Sundays when the banks were closed. This meant having to meet messengers in parking lots who would deliver paper bags (sometimes greasy paper bags) with $50,000 or $80,000 in cash to hold their accounts open till Monday.

Our guys were nervous about going to make the pickups. "Why?" I asked. "They're bringing us the money. If you don't make it back, we'll just switch off their lines."

After opening my desk drawer, though, one Monday to get a pen and finding it filled with hundreds of thousands in weekend cash, I began to understand their concern and located a banker willing to open on Sundays and accept deposits on our behalf.

On the financial front, Steve Brown, our CFO, now largely freed of having to answer to Wall Street, was able to look for more traditional sources of capital. Steve had been my CPA almost from the beginning of the publishing business. His guidance had enabled us to grow. Like me, he was from the street—if anything, probably more so. His accounting background made him hyperaware of things like bad debt and negative cash flow. At our weekly management meetings, even when the stock was high and we were the darlings of Wall Street, it was Steve who would most carry on like an Old Testament prophet, warning against the evil path we were going down and railing for repentance. Like a prophet, powerless to stop his people's erring ways during our free spending, Steve seemed a lonely, tortured figure.

Now, with the business being run according to the fundamentals, his spirit lifted and he went to spread the word of our turnaround to the banks and leasing institutions. It was positive cash flow, not growth that mattered to these guys. And with our new business plan, Steve and Abe Farber, our in-house leasing expert, were able to persuade them that we met the criteria. By the end of the quarter, we were able to report that we had secured over $25 million in credit lines, relieving our financial worries and allowing us to grow unimpeded.

I'd always been an opponent of borrowing of any sort, paying cash even in large real estate transactions. Now, however, I began to see things differently. From a certain point of view, borrowing was actually the fiscally conservative thing to do. It encouraged living within your means. Take buying a large million-dollar piece of telecommunication equipment, for example. If you have millions of dollars of equity in the bank, you might decide, hey, that's a really cool new switch. Look at all the things it can do. My competitors are all buying switches like that. I don't want them to think I'm a wimp. I don't want everyone getting ahead of me. I'm gonna buy me a switch just like that. It's gotta be worth it.

This is the way aging yuppies think when they're about to get an expensive little sports car. It's not a way to decide on business purchases. But believe it or not, in my industry this is how it's usually done.

Borrowing for the switch puts a whole different spin on things. That million-dollar switch you now know is going to cost you twenty-five grand a month for five years. Is leasing this switch going to generate more than $25,000 a month in new profits? If yes, then it's a good move to get the switch. If no, then it's stupid. Forget about your ego and pass on it. It's that simple.

With our new credit lines we were able to lease some equipment we'd previously paid cash for, bringing much-needed liquidity into the business. Within a few months, this cash was being supplemented by the excess funds being generated by operations. Soon we were not only solvent, but we had extra capital.

One happy consequence for me was that the loan of my personal funds was repaid. I didn't run right out and buy a sports car, though.

That could wait. I'd suddenly become a much more conservative person.

As the time approached for us to report on our first quarterly results under the new plan, IDT's stock began to rise. This was not surprising. Our customers, suppliers, and lenders all knew how well we were doing from their dealing with us. Only the investment bankers were in the dark. The results, when reported, smashed all their forecasts. We reported our first quarterly profit as a public company. This, amazingly, even after absorbing the huge severance costs. It was the first profit ever reported for a public company so largely involved in the Internet industry. After the report was issued, investor enthusiasm drove our stock still higher, more than double its price just a few months earlier. I was worth over a hundred million dollars again. My phone started to ring. "Old friends" and fund-raisers suddenly wanted to renew acquaintances. Somehow, I was less than interested. My interest was engaged elsewhere. Running IDT had become fun again.

It turned out the bandwagon was only beginning to roll. Our small but extraordinarily talented Net2Phone development team, led by Jeff Goldberg, former chief technical officer of Charles River Engineering, free from having to continually take investor groups on lab tours, achieved a true breakthrough. Already we had the only technology enabling users to connect from multimedia PCs over the Internet to regular telephone users. The sound quality, though, like all "Internet telephony" products, was spotty at best. Conversations were always short, as the struggle to make out what was being said made anything more than a simple transmittal of the facts too painful to bother with. Sure, it was often 95 percent cheaper than a normal call, but if you can't hear, so what?

Jeff's new product, however, broke the sound barrier. It wasn't that the sound came somewhat closer to what normal telephone users had come to expect. It came the whole way. In fact, *PC* magazine not only bestowed its top award on the new product, it said that in test calls most users couldn't tell the difference between the Internet and the real call. Suddenly articles were appearing and software awards were coming in from all over the world.

Users were signing up so quickly that the personnel department could barely keep up with staffing needs. The average call time lengthened from two minutes to the normal call average of six minutes, indicating the quality was indeed comparable to that of an average call. Stunned by the new technologies, large foreign partners began to put up millions to procure national exclusives for the new phone-to-phone product, which was to be released imminently, or for traditional Net2Phone distributorship.

Foreign monopolies went into a panic over the new technology and started calling for international conferences to regulate this new threat. Senate and congressional committee chairpeople started calling for hearings to undermine any such anti-competitive legislation that foreign governments might impose. The White House called us to pledge support and was soon issuing statements warning against regulating us. By the time our computerless phone-to-phone product debuted in the summer, breaking the cost barrier for even domestic calls, we were riding a tiger and Net2Phone was way into the black.

Although we couldn't 100 percent keep up with demand, nobody complained. Instead, the press adulated us. What a change from just months earlier when we were being dragged through the mud. Things had gotten so bad my mother had turned off all the radios in her house for days, not being able to stand hearing all the bad reports, some of which seemed to attack me personally.

The difference in the reaction to the two events actually says more about the people of the press and the public than about us. The press and intelligentsia are generally quite negative and judgmental when it comes to business. All businessmen, they say, are greedy and crooked. They perform only because they have to in order to get ahead. Give them just one loophole and they'll take it. The little guy on the street is easily fed these lies. He doesn't know any corporate moguls personally. Of course, he's a little envious of their limousines and jets.

Maybe he even thinks it's unfair that he can't get ahead in the big company where he's employed because if he did, he'd run things a whole lot better and fairer than the current bosses.

The media, however, can't only have villains. There'd be no drama then. They need heroes, also. So they make the creative guys, whom they consider part of their groups, the heroes. Singers, athletes, models, designers—maybe even a crusading district attorney. These are the heroes. Want proof? When as the last time you saw a movie about a businessman? When was the last time he played the good guy? Almost never. In an Orwellian twist of the mind, the media would have you believe it's the businessmen who are the parasites of society, feeding off the little guys and creative stars who really make everything happen. (This, of course, is all upside down. We could easily live without Madonna, but who's ready to give up their car, food, indoor plumbing, telephone, or any of the other goodies the "evil" businessmen provide?)

In the competitive business landscape, where many businesses compete to supply the consumers' needs, none are seen as heroes. Any one could easily be done without. It's no problem, therefore, to selectively vilify one or another whenever news is slow or the regulators need some publicity. The inventor, however, is a whole 'nother ball of wax. He actually made something that no one had before. Everyone's life is improved because of the new product. You can't say someone else would have done it because if he would have, why didn't he?

The creative businessmen, like Steve Jobs of Apple Computer, who bring out a whole new product and improve everyone's lives, do far more than any actor or ballplayer. Steve is a real creative hero. He's a cowboy. He rode against the herd. In fact, his accomplishment almost seems to be in defiance of the established business culture than an affirmation of it. Everyone has to love this guy. He can do no wrong. Sure, he might be overwhelmed by demands (or, like Apple, overwhelmed by competitors), but everyone forgives him and roots for him, anyway.

This was the position we now found ourselves in. We were heroes again, just like with callback. After all the bad press, it was a welcome change. I didn't respond, though, this time to the flood of media requests for interviews and photos of the great inventor, as I had years previously with callback. First of all, I hadn't invented anything. I just thought it could be done and had been lucky enough to hire Jeff and his team to do it. More to the point, however, I had really been hurt by all the bad publicity. For years I was a hero, and suddenly I was a goat.

And what had I done? Only try my best to service our accounts. If the media was so fickle and fame was so transient, I thought I'd rather not be involved in that game at all. The media was, to me, a little like Wall Street. First they built you up, then they tore you down.

It wasn't the public, but the big players in the communications industry that really wound up driving our sales, though. Tightening credit on the bad risks along with more international deals and network build-out allowed us to really cut our prices. Suddenly no one could offer reliable international phone service with rates anywhere close to ours. We figured the big guys would never buy from us anyway and would keep directing their business to more established, "respectable" members of the club, not to street fighters like us. When we said good-bye to Wall Street and all the fancy trimmings, we figured we were saying good-bye to this end of the industry as well.

Boy, were we wrong. The big guys came running for our rate like bees to honey (or flies to you know what). Turns out they didn't give a damn about respectability. They could get all the respectability they wanted dealing with each other. What they wanted in a little company wasn't fancy offices. What they wanted was lean, mean, and competitive—some way to increase the bottom lines—new technology, different types of distribution, lower rates, especially lower rates.

Our giant former nemesis started buying time from us, the way a team of cowboys in from months on the cattle drive order beer. All the capacity in the world didn't seem like enough for them. Suddenly, we were ordering the million-dollar switches, not to ward off middle age but because we needed every ounce of horsepower. By the summer of '97, we, who had once only dreamed of handling a million minutes of international traffic a month, were handling far more than a million a day and scrambling to keep up with demand as more of the giants jumped on board. And best of all, we didn't have to deal with bags of cash anymore. These guys were all worth billions and they all paid their bills. That was a welcome change from the gutter.

Once we'd tasted doing business with the big guys, we couldn't get enough of it. I flew to Denver to meet with John Malone. Malone, I figured, was my kind of guy. He was nuts about his wife and kids, going away for at least a solid month with them, just like I did. He was a fanatic about running his company his way, single-handedly. He was determined to hold voting control of TCI, the nation's largest cable operator with over twenty million households, in his own hands, much as I did with IDT. Like me, he was a vocal libertarian. And he was also known as a visionary. I thought he'd probably click with me and I could sell him some small service and start a relationship.

Boy, was I wrong! He wound up wanting to buy everything IDT had to offer, including some services I hadn't even thought of myself. The guy was brilliant. He spent the whole day with me, called in all his top lieutenants, and told them he wanted to move on this now. I couldn't believe it. Here I was with the most powerful communications magnate in the world, the legendary John Malone, second as a businessman only to Bill Gates in power, and he was rushing to do business with me before he lost the opportunity. This had to be some kind of dream.

When I returned to work and told everybody what had happened, they thought I was kidding, hallucinating, or just exaggerating. Like the poor classmates of a character named Yankee Irving in a bedtime story for my kid, they thought I was nuts. In the story, Yankee Irving made a spectacular catch of a foul ball hit into the stands. Hours later, in the twentieth inning of an extra-inning game, one of the last nine

Yankee players eligible to play is hit by a pitch. Unfairly, the umpire tells the Yanks with only eight guys left they have to forfeit.

"What eight guys?" the manager responds. "We just hired a new player. He's our ninth."

"Who's that?" the ump asks.

"Him," the manager responds, pointing to the cheap grandstand seats.

Yankee Irving is rushed down, fitted in a pinstripe uniform, and inserted in the game. With his tiny strike zone (made smaller by crouching) he walks with the bases loaded, winning the game for the Yanks, who promise him lifetime free admission to the owner's box.

Naturally, the next day at school everyone thinks Yankee Irving has lost it entirely. Just like the guys in my office must've thought of me. The next day, though, when, during recess, the official team bus pulls up and Joe DiMaggio and all the Yankees disembark to thank their "ex-teammate" and distribute gloves, baseballs, bats, and tickets to all the students, his classmates' disbelief is shattered.

So too the next week when TCI's COO, president, and teams of top people arrived at our office, disbelief was shattered, and Yankee Howard's credibility was restored, and then some.

The TCI team, however, was only our first visit. Jonathan Reich, who formerly masterminded our consumer Internet customer acquisition program, had been freed by our new business plan to pursue strategic relationships. Now his and Jim's efforts began to bear fruit. The Roberts from Comcast, the Dolans from Cablevision, Cox Cable, Time Warner, all started meeting or negotiating deals with us at the high level.

The "Baby Bells" got into the act too. NYNEX, Bell Atlantic, Bell South, Pac Tel, Ameritech—the presidents were all in our office negotiating, or we were in theirs. Suddenly someone who wandered into our meeting room by mistake would've thought he'd discovered the private club of the movers and shakers in the telecom industry.

I began to start using the stairs to avoid having to meet and greet everyone visiting our offices coming up the elevator. It wasn't that I was unfriendly, it was just I knew the division leaders could handle these meetings better than me.

I was better at being the eccentric who casually dropped by. "You know, that guy in the jeans walking up is our chairman? Yeah, that's him, the famous Howard Jonas. He's a genius, he's a visionary. Why, here he is right now. Let me introduce him."

So we all shake hands and I make some modest small talk. And now they all stand around waiting for me to say something brilliant and memorable.

But guess what? I've got nothing brilliant to say. I can barely believe I'm standing here with these guys. They're really important. They run big companies. So I have to fake it.

"I'm so glad you're here," I tell them. "What an honor to meet you. I wish I could talk to you all day, but I've got an important call I've got to take from my investment banker."

"Oh, your investment banker. Better run and get it." This they understand.

A little white lie? Not at all. The bankers are on the phone all the time now. We've just passed a quarter billion in sales rates, with growth accelerating and profits up fivefold, and suddenly everyone wants to give us money again.

Howie says we should take it. We need it to keep growing, but this time it will be on our own terms. We'll grow because we need to, not because Wall Street tells us to keep up with the latest fashion. Howie's almost always right, so we'll probably take some of it. There is a fine line between being proud and lean, and being foolhardy. As I said before, modern businesses need to be capitalized on a scale unheard of in earlier generations. But I will never again be pushed into making business decisions that are unwise for the sake of the stock price or the market. I'll talk Howie into taking less than they're offering, and only what we can prudently use. I think it's better to run things lean. I've learned the hard way, and I'd much rather run a streetwise, profitable, growing operation than get spoiled by having too much money in the bank.

Today, however, I'm not going to take their calls. Our new investor relations person (okay, so I caved in, but we're a public company, after all) can handle their calls. It's been such a roller-coaster ride, I just need to get away and relax. To think. To plan the next move. Mostly to take a long vacation with my wife and kids, and spend time together. Think I'll be bored? Don't worry about it. Afternoons, I'll be by the water. Nights, the guys can reach me on the phone or fax. And how 'bout the mornings?

Oh, I don't know. I'd like to do something creative. Something stimulating. I think I'll just sit with Debbie and write. Not a novel. I don't have the imagination for that. I think I'll just write the IDT story. Yeah, that would be interesting.

No ghostwriter. No investment bankers. No computers. Just me, with a pen and pad and my wife. I bet people will really find it interesting. I mean, who could imagine that all this stuff really happened?

Epilogue
On a Roll

❖

So that's it. Do I think all the struggles and problems are behind me? That I'll just ride the IDT rocket into space? Gimme a break. The minute I come back, the problems'll start again. The Meligoth never goes away, you see. You just have to be ready to fight him every day. That's what business is all about, never giving up and always being ready to come back for more. It's never over. It's the same no matter what business you're in—hot dogs, brochures, publishing, or international telecommunications.

It reminds me of an old story. This guy brings his shoes in to the shoemaker to get fixed. The shoemaker gives him a little receipt tag, which the guy puts in his pocket. Then he goes home.

As soon as he gets home he turns on the radio, and what do you think? He hears the Japanese just attacked Pearl Harbor and America'll be going to war. My goodness, he doesn't know what to do. In a patriotic fervor, he rushes down to the draft booth and enlists, and almost right away they ship him off to basic training. From there, he's sent to the Pacific, where he spends four years under fire, fighting the Japanese every day. At one point he's even shot and gets a Purple Heart. But he keeps on fighting and even wins a Silver Star for bravery.

Finally, after four years, America wins and he can come home. He marches in the victory parade into Times Square and the crowd is going wild. Beautiful girls are all waving and cheering and kissing the new vets. He can barely wait to get home, take off his uniform, put on his civilian clothes, and go out to start living again.

As he puts on his clothes, though, he feels in his pocket the little tag from the shoes he'd brought in all those years ago.

Wow, he thinks, I wonder if that little shoe repair shop is still there. I'll walk over and see.

He walks over, and what do you know, it's still there. Wow, he thinks again, I wonder if the old Italian shoemaker is still alive, working in the shop. He opens the door, and what do you know? There old Geppetto is holding tacks in his mouth right in the middle of banging on a heel. Unbelievable. It's like a time warp.

"Listen," he interrupts when the heel is finished. "Well, I just found this tag, and I know this is a bit unusual, but I was wondering if it might be possible that you could check to see if you possibly have these shoes. If you don't mind, I'd really appreciate it."

The old shoemaker goes into the back and you hear tumbling and rumbling and boxes moving. Finally, the old man comes out with a smile on his face.

"Well," the guy asks, "do you have my shoes?"

"Yeah, we got 'em."

"And can I have them?" the guy asks.

"Sure you can," Geppetto replies. "But not right now. They'll be ready next week."

So you just gotta keep plugging. 'Cause it never ends.

And that's the fun of it. To never give up. To be Don Quixote. To wake up every day ready to take on that old Meligoth, even when it looks like everything's against you. If you reach way down inside, you can always come up with just that little extra you need. There may be almost no money in the bank. The market may have turned against you. You might not even have a job anymore. And then, just when everything seems hopeless, you roll out your newly refurbished hot dog stand, cook up a pot of onions, and suddenly the sun is shining and it's the best day of your life all over again.

And once again, you're on a roll.

Afterword

❖

When I finished this book in the summer of 1997, who could ever have imagined then that there'd be more? That instead of "high-tech millions," we'd be accurate in describing IDT as a Billion Dollar Company.

Well, that's just what's happened since then. Let me share a few highlights with you.

As our international phone traffic grew, we were able to start putting in our own international lines. This raised our profit margins and enabled us to lower our prices. Soon IDT was providing international service for most of the largest phone companies in the world. Ironically, AT&T and France Telecom, our former adversaries, were now among our most important relationships. Our formerly money-losing concern had, in fact, become a veritable profit machine. By early 1998, we were already earning millions of dollars a month for our shareholders on tens of millions of dollars in revenue. Even better, both revenue and profits growth not only are the fastest in the industry, they also show no sign of slowing.

Our Net2Phone service, which allows users to make phone calls over the Internet for a fraction of the price of a normal phone call, is not only a technical breakthrough but a business triumph as well. By early 1998 the new service, which pundits just a year ago said would never work, had already profitably done millions of dollars in business. IDT, the company that only a year earlier had teetered on the verge of bankruptcy, now virtually dominates this new field, which makes headlines daily. While larger competitors announced plans to experiment with this new technology, we've actually made it available to the general public at just 5¢ a minute for domestic long distance. That's less than half of our competitors' best prices. This guarantees IDT a position not only as a large international wholesale carrier but in the consumer market as well.

Naturally, all this good news on the business front couldn't help but have a big impact on our stock price. By early 1998 it had doubled. Suddenly, Wall Street loved us again. Underwriters began calling, imploring us to do a secondary stock offering. Just sell 4 million more shares of IDT stock and you'll have $80 million. Wow! With $80 million we'd be able to put our network all over the world. We said yes.

Out of loyalty, we wanted Cowen to participate in the offering, but they didn't want to share with our other underwriters. We were conflicted, but we had to do what was best for IDT, so we went with another firm. Soon after, Cowen and Co. was sold to a French banking conglomerate, and Maria Lewis, our guardian angel and confidante from the beginning, was terminated. Whatever lingering doubt I had about switching underwriters has been erased now that I've seen how my friend was treated.

The underwriters told us to expect that 4 million new shares on the market would push our stock price down. A funny thing happened, though. Once we got out on the road and were able to meet all the big institutional investors, they were so excited about IDT's prospects that the great majority put in big orders for our stock. Demand was so strong that the stock price climbed to 25 even before the shares were actually offered for sale. Then it wound up that even at the higher price there were enough institutional orders for over 20 million shares, even though we were offering only 4 million shares. To control demand we were compelled to sell an extra million shares, putting more than $120 million in IDT's bank account.

Bond investors then offered to lend us another $200 million. This money not only would further fuel our expansion, but virtually guaranteed we would never again be put in the position of having to sell equity to raise cash. Still, $200 million seemed a bit extreme to me. So I just took $100 million and turned down the rest.

I've already mentioned the old Yiddish saying that every baby brings its own luck, and that, on January 28, 1997, my wife gave birth to twins. When they were a few weeks old, our stock price had collapsed, the bottom fell out on our stock, and we fired closed to half our staff. Some luck, I thought to myself, as the babies cried and fussed into the night, and I put up my life's savings just to keep IDT afloat. Well, a year later, I see the luck. Twins didn't just double our good fortune, but in the year since their birth, IDT's value has risen 800 percent!

It's just unbelievable. A year ago we were on the skids, and today what a roll we're on! The company is worth a billion dollars. We've got over $225 million in the bank, and I just turned down $100 million more. What a country!

When money was really tight and hard to come by, a friend agreed to set up a meeting with a big-time financier, the kind of guy who could single-handedly change our destiny, or so I thought. A meeting was arranged between me and Mr. Big Bucks at the "21" Club. I put on my best Road Show suit and headed down there. An officious maître d' ushered me into a private dining room, where an elderly gentleman was sitting with a beautiful blonde, who appeared to be about nineteen. The gentleman shook my hand and invited me to make my presentation. While I went on and on about the virtues of IDT, its great promise and potential, the blond beauty kept stroking the leg of my financier. Well, he couldn't concentrate (on me, at least), and neither could I. IDT didn't make a penny that night—I can't speak for the blonde.

Last month I was once again invited to make a presentation at the "21" Club, this time in front of some of the industry's leading bankers and money managers. All eyes were on me as I walked to the podium. I told them about my previous experience at the "21" Club, and they all laughed nervously. I couldn't help but think of Tevye in *Fiddler on the Roof*, as he sings in "If I Were a Rich Man" that when you have money, people think you really know. Unlike my previous "21" experience, everyone was paying attention, focused on my presentation, my every word. The only thing that got stroked, though, was my ego, and IDT's valuation.

The funny thing is, I'm not any smarter than I ever was. I still know that it's just as hard to run a hot dog stand, and the real challenge in life is not to make money, but to run a business that even my grandmother would be proud of. Just because on paper your business is worth a billion dollars (a billion!) is no excuse to be stupid. You don't waste hot dog buns, or millions either.

In early 1998 IDT was named the seventh-fastest-growing high-tech company by the accounting firm Deloitte and Touche, and one of the one hundred most dynamic companies in America by *Forbes* magazine.

And yet, with all this success, there are days when I can't imagine anything sweeter than my hot dog stand. But do you know how many days it takes to make a billion dollars with a hot dog cart? Forty thousand, and that's only if you've got a really great spot.

Nonetheless, if you learn one thing from this book, I hope it's this: Never count the little guy out. One day he's cooking onions over propane in a converted baby buggy, and the next thing you know . . . he's on a roll!

Acknowledgments

❖

To my wife, Debbie . . . who I fall in love with a little more every day. You've always been there for me and I wouldn't be anywhere without you. Sitting across from you writing our books and drinking coffee every morning in the Hebrew University Cafeteria were the best moments I've ever lived. No matter how big a bestseller your novel becomes, no one will ever enjoy reading it as much as I enjoyed being there when you wrote it. Thanks also for the wealth of talent, insight, and effort you put into editing this book.

To my children—Shmuel, Mishi, Davidi, Liora, Yoni, Racheli, Tamar, and Yosef. You are the real meaning in my life. You're the proof that G-d is good, and also that He has a sense of humor.

To my beloved parents, sisters and their families, and mother-in-law . . . who have always loved, inspired, and supported me in even my most harebrained schemes.

To my other family at IDT; I wish I could mention each one of you by name. You are the best and the brightest. Let's continue to go from strength to strength together.

Special thanks to Simon Lermer, Howie Millendorf, Michael Horen, Sharon Bar David, and J. J. Gross, not only for your help putting this book together, but for your friendship that means so much to me.

A SPECIAL OFFER
FROM HOWARD JONAS

Now that you've read all about IDT, I'm willing to bet you the price of this book that you'll like my company as much as you've liked my story! Would you expect anything less from an old salesman like me? Here's my offer. You can get back the price of this book in the form of a $25 credit on your long-distance phone bill if you switch your carrier to IDT's low-cost long-distance service. You need to send the proof of purchase (your sales receipt) to the address below, along with your name and mailing address or fax number, and we'll mail or fax you a simple form to fill out that authorizes IDT to do a routine credit investigation and make the transfer. Once you become an IDT customer, you will receive your $25 credit. To get things moving more quickly, just call us toll free at 1-877-HOTDOG-1 (1-877-468-3641).

We must receive your proof of purchase by December 31, 1998. Please allow up to four weeks for the processing of your application. This offer is good only for phone calls originating in the continental United States. Void where prohibited.

Mail your name, address, and proof of purchase of *On a Roll* to:

Book Offer
IDT CORPORATION
190 Main Street
Hackensack, NJ 07601

or call 1-877-HOTDOG-1